MW01630420

The Founding Documents of Los Angeles

The Founding Documents of Los Angeles: A Bilingual Edition

Edited with an Introduction by

DOYCE B. NUNIS, JR.

HISTORICAL SOCIETY OF SOUTHERN CALIFORNIA
AND THE
ZAMORANO CLUB OF LOS ANGELES
2004

Library of Congress Catalogue Number: 2003113153

ISBN (Historical Society of Southern California edition): 091442131X
ISBN (Zamorano Club of Los Angeles edition): 097245340X

Historical Society of Southern California
200 East Avenue 43
Los Angeles, California 90031
Telephone (323) 222-0546

Zamorano Club of Los Angeles
Post Office Box 465
Pasadena, California 91102

PRINTED IN THE UNITED STATES OF AMERICA

In Memory of the Founders of the

HISTORICAL SOCIETY OF SOUTHERN CALIFORNIA

and the

ZAMORANO CLUB OF LOS ANGELES

Contents

Illustrations

Copublisher's Foreword

The distinguished George F. Kennan perhaps said it best when he wrote, "The very concept of history implies the scholar and the reader. Without a generation of civilized people to study history, to preserve its records, to absorb its lessons and relate them to its own problems, history too, would lose its meaning." *The Founding Documents of Los Angeles: A Bilingual Edition* is published with Professor Kennan's words in mind.

The "scholar" in this case is the volume's editor, Doyce B. Nunis, Jr., Distinguished Professor Emeritus of History at the University of Southern California and long-time editor of the *Southern California Quarterly*. The "reader" is you, and hundreds like you who will turn to the pages of this book for information and understanding. The "generation of civilized people" is the interested and informed citizens of our great metropolitan area.

For the past 120 years, one of the Historical Society of Southern California's guiding principles has been a commitment to the exacting scholarship of history as illustrated in this volume. A second principle is the Society's commitment to see that schools and libraries have adequate resources for the teaching and learning of history. Today we are finding new and exciting ways to express and share those principles with the community at large.

The Historical Society therefore is pleased to join with the Zamorano Club of Los Angeles, a distinguished group of bibliophiles, to place copies of this volume without charge in the schools and libraries of Los Angeles County. I believe this is an appropriate way to commemorate the noteworthy anniversaries of the Zamorano Club (seventy-fifth) and the Historical Society of Southern California (one hundred and twentieth).

It is my hope that you find this book to be a worthy keepsake of such milestones and a valuable addition to the growing list of works published about Los Angeles.

THOMAS F. ANDREWS, PH.D.
Executive Director, Historical Society of Southern California

Copublisher's Foreword

The Zamorano Club of Los Angeles, in 2003, celebrated its seventy-fifth year as an organization of bibliophiles – collectors, librarians, printers, sellers, and scholars – having an avowed mission of fostering interest in and education relating to the book arts.

The minutes of the founding meeting of the club on 25 January 1928, noted that the aims of the club included encouraging the arts of the book and occasional production of such books and pamphlets promoting such aims. The club continues to maintain that as our goal to this day.

When the opportunity presented itself for Zamorano and the Historical Society of Southern California jointly to republish *The Founding Documents of Los Angeles* with a contemporary commentary, we realized that this would be an excellent point on the continuum of Zamorano's historical role in supporting fine printing and scholarship. The collaboration with the Historical Society of Southern California and the placement of copies of the book, free of charge, in institutions of higher education, public and private secondary schools, and in public libraries, additionally demonstrates once again Zamorano's commitment to book- and printing-dependent education.

STEPHEN A. KANTER, M.D.
President, Zamorano Club of Los Angeles

Acknowledgments

The publication of this revised edition of *The Founding Documents of Los Angeles* was selected by the Zamorano Club of Los Angeles to honor the seventy-fifth anniversary of its founding in 1928. It was the first club of bibliophiles to be established in the city and still is very active. To insure that this work would reach a larger audience, the Club approached the Historical Society of Southern California to ascertain if they would be interested in becoming the copublisher. The response was affirmative.

Actually, there are two editions of this revised edition, one for the Zamorano Club, limited to 250 copies, and the second for the Historical Society, 1,600 copies. It is the intent of the Society to see that the book is placed in countywide education institutions – schools, colleges, and libraries. The Zamorano Club's edition will be for members with other copies being placed in major research depositories both in the state and nation.

To aid the educational outreach program of the Historical Society, support grants were received from The Ahmanson Foundation, The John Randolph Haynes and Dora Haynes Foundation, Dan Murphy Foundation, The Ann Peppers Foundation, Roth Family Foundation, Sidney Stern Memorial Trust, and The Zamorano Club. To each of these granting agencies, appreciation and gratitude is expressed for their financial assistance to the publication project.

The editor of this revised edition of *The Founding Documents* wishes to acknowledge his gratitude for assistance in the preparation of this volume by a number of individuals who graciously offered invaluable aid. First and foremost, Dana Church Cordrey, a Club member, has played a major role in the preparation and structure of this new addition. His selfless service has been constant and has greatly benefited the editor's discharge of his textual responsibilities. He was ably assisted by Martha Fares. She is a true treasure – an eagle-eyed, sharp, lady – a proof reader supreme. A great debt is owed to both of these wonderful colleagues and collaborators.

A dear friend and academic colleague, Rose Marie Beebe, Professor of Spanish, University of Santa Clara, willingly gave of her skills and talent to help define more precisely some of the Spanish text and graciously offered a number of corrections to the English translations. She is the current president of the California Mission Studies Association and coauthor with Robert Senkewicz, also of the University of Santa Clara, of three important recent books: *Lands of Promise and Despair: Chronicles of Early California, 1535–1846*; *The History of Alta California: Memoirs of Mexican California* by Antonio María Osio, and *Guide to the Manuscripts of Baja California* in the collections of The Bancroft Library.

Special research assistance has been provided by Robert V. Laburee, Social Science Librarian, Von Kleinsmid Library, University of Southern California. Carrie Marsh, Head, Special Collections, Honnold/Mudd Library, Claremont, and her assistant, Kelley Wolfe, provided invaluable information on Marion Parks whose papers are housed at the Honnold. Another dear friend, Cecilia Rasmussen, *Los Angeles Times*, provided copies of a number of newspaper clippings that were a gold mine of biographical information utilized in preparing the introduction. David Zeidberg, Avery Director of the Library, Huntington Library, and Nicholas A. Curry provided special help on two illusive biographical queries. Lastly, Susan Snyder, Bancroft Library, University of California, Berkeley, obtained copies of two important early maps of Los Angeles which are included as illustrations.

To one and all, collective thanks is extended.

– DOYCE B. NUNIS, JR., Editor
Distinguished Professor Emeritus of History
University of Southern California

Introduction

THE BACKGROUND AND ORIGIN OF THE 1931 EDITION

The genesis of the original publication of *The Founding Documents of Los Angeles* in 1931, printed in the *Annual Publications of the Historical Society of Southern California*, Volume XV, Part I, is obscured by the lack of detailed, firsthand information. It is obvious what the motive was: to commemorate September 4, 1931, the 150th anniversary of the founding of the city as a pueblo, the second planned, civilian settlement authorized by the Spanish government that then held sovereignty over the land. The first pueblo, San Jose de Guadalupe (the latter was the name of the nearby river), had been formally established on November 29, 1777.

From what records that do exist, it appears that the germinal idea for a gala celebration was launched in 1926 when the Historical Society joined with two other like minded groups, the Native Sons and Daughters of the Golden West and the City Planning Association, to approach the commercial community "with the suggestion that preliminary work be started so that the sesquicentennial might be observed on a monumental scale in 1931." The proposal was curtly dismissed. However, that negative response was dramatically altered on November 29, 1930 when Mayor John C. Porter, responding to a suggestion from the Downtown Business Men's Association, "called together a group of citizens to consider the advisability and prospects for a fitting observation of the historic founding of Los Angeles." To that end, representatives from the "historical, commercial, social, fraternal, [and] religious" communities convened in the mayor's office to pursue the prospects. From this gathering came the momentum for a spectacular "La Fiesta de Los Angeles" to be held during September 4–13, 1931. This ten-day birthday party was truly a broad-based, community endeavor – conceived, planned, and executed by an executive committee of leading community personalities, supported by thirty-five other committees.

Funding the event became a primary concern. With the Wall Street stock market crash in October 1929, the nation was being engulfed by a gradual wave of financial problems which eventually led to the Great Depression. Fortunately, that crisis had not yet peaked by 1930–31, so there was still a reasonable base and hope for monetary support from citizens and the community at large. That support proved crucial for when the final books were balanced by the La Fiesta de Los Angeles Association, all expenditures were paid in full: no debt was incurred. The prospect for that satisfactory financial result appeared dim at the outset because of the impact the Depression was already having on many of the common citizenry.

But that bleak outlook brightened as the time for the celebration neared, mainly due to the highly successful imaginative and innovative educational outreach programs launched by the sponsors. "Innumerable talks, illustrated and otherwise, were given from club to club, school to school, and from lodge and church to lodge and church. Circular and personal letters in untold numbers burdened the postmen." As a stimulus, the city and county governments provided $100,000 toward the estimated half million dollar price tag. As a result of these efforts, average citizens finally were swept up in a crescendo of growing public enthusiasm and burgeoning civic pride.

To stimulate public involvement in the planned La Fiesta Week events, a striking advertisement campaign was launched as the celebratory dates approached:

> ... gorgeous street decorations of Spanish shawls and finely designed historical banners began to go up in the last days of August.... Nobody had ever seen anything quite so unique and appropriate. Pendent at each downtown street intersection was a large painting, 20 by 30 feet ... of an event or person in early California history. From this time on people waxed enthusiastic and more and more of the gloomy doubts gave way to eager anticipation. Los Angeles became immensely proud of itself.

Even the weather was auspicious, much to the planners' relief, for on September 3 it was cloudy and rainy. But September 4 dawned "clear, bright and warm ... followed [by] ten glorious sunshiny days such as one reads in the most expansive California boost literature."

The principal account of La Fiesta events remarked:

> ... from the beginning the spirit of the people seemed attuned to the glory of the days. They forgot their troubles and entered into La Fiesta

> beyond the fondest hopes of the hard-working committeemen [planners]. Dispelling thoughts of economic stress from their minds and heedful of their debt to the city's founders and pioneers, they joined whole-heartedly and enthusiastically in what is conceded to have been the outstanding community birthday observance in America.

The citywide buildup to La Fiesta Week included a gigantic replica of a birthday cake placed on a high platform over the fountain in Pershing Square. The inaugural program was launched by an impressive gathering on Friday, September 4, held at the Main Street entrance to the new City Hall. President Herbert Hoover sent a congratulatory telegram that proclaimed Los Angeles "as old as the Republic – as young as Today." A host of dignitaries headed by Governor James Rolph, Jr., were in attendance. Mayor Porter and Isidore B. Dockweiler, president of La Fiesta Association, officially opened the ten-days of festivities, with an impressive ceremony and parade held in the newly built Olympic Stadium (today the Los Angeles Coliseum). An extensive Transportation Parade, honoring both historic and modern modes of conveyance, was held the following day, September 5. That evening in the harbor area, ten U.S. Navy "dreadnaughts" gave shore leave to their crews while fireworks blazed the sky above Terminal Island. In the city itself, "the Japanese held open house and celebrated with a parade, singing, dancing, speech making and a colorful reception at First and Weller Streets." Throughout La Fiesta, every night visitors thronged "the Japanese quarter where paper cherry blossoms and lanterns festooned the streets for many blocks and special entertainments were presented." Nearby in the Plaza and on Olvera Street, "where the fiesta spirit had its deepest roots," there was almost continuous "gay hours of music and dancing."

Sunday, September 6, was marked with two major religious events. A Solemn Pontifical Mass was held at noon in Olympic Stadium. The *Los Angeles Times* proclaimed: "One of the most magnificent religious dramas in the United States held 105,000 people spellbound in Olympic Stadium ... with many of the highest priests in the Catholic Church in America and John McCormack, beloved Irish tenor, playing important roles." The Pope sent the Vatican's Apostolic Delegate to the United States to represent him. That evening an Interdenominational Vesper Service was held in the Hollywood Bowl. Thronged with some 35,000 attendees, "other thousands [were] turned back" because there was no more seating or standing space available. A chorus of

1,000, drawn from various Protestant faiths, their voices swelled "up to the stars." "Divines of great repute took part ... no seat was vacated until the last word of benediction fell upon a hushed and reverent assembly."

With the new week, Monday's highlight was a Rodeo and Congress of Rough Riders, held again in Olympic Stadium, which paid tribute to the region's western heritage. The crowd was entertained by "the greatest aggregation of trick riders most of the audience had ever seen and 'they ate it alive.'" Tuesday was Mission Day with special programs at the city's nearby Franciscan missions, San Gabriel and San Fernando, which held open houses as did all the Franciscan missions from Santa Barbara to San Diego. That evening the Banda de Policia from Mexico City joined the Los Angeles Philharmonic Orchestra in concert at the Hollywood Bowl. Other local activities were also held throughout the day in various locales.

September 9, the day on which California was admitted to the Union as the thirty-fifth state, was heralded by a vast number of visitors from all over the state, especially from San Francisco, including that city's mayor. The highlight of the day was a parade dubbed California the Great, with representation from each of the state's fifty-eight counties. The primary hosts for this day's activities was the Native Sons and Daughters of the Golden State. The day's program concluded with an Admission Day formal dinner and historic entertainment for 5,000 at the Biltmore Hotel. It was described as the "most brilliant affair ever staged by the Native Sons and Daughters."

The following day's main event was the wedding of "a modern young couple of Spanish blood in the dear old Plaza Church by an *ancient* Spanish ceremony." It was all-in-all a picturesque affair. That evening, an opera based on life in early California, *La Rubinos*, was given its premier performance at the Greek Theatre in Griffith Park.

By far the most brilliant and imaginative event took place on Friday night, September 11, "Hollywood's ... 'splendiferous' fling ... 'The pageant of Jewels,'" sponsored and staged by the Association of Motion Picture Producers. It attracted the largest crowd during La Fiesta. The Olympic Stadium was filled to capacity – 110,000 in number. Outside milled thousands more to glimpse the parade entering the vast arena. What captivated the audience was the fact that all of the specially designed and built floats were decorated with electric lights, while open automobiles, carrying some of the luminaries of the silver screen, were bedecked with garlands of flowers. It was, indeed, "a unique and colorful affair, and the greatest procession – gloriously wrought and gloriously lighted – float after float stunned the audience into an almost inarticulate maze. Never was there a more splendid electrical spectacle anywhere at any time." At the conclusion of the program, around 11:30 P.M., the *Star Spangled Banner* was sung by Madame Ernestine Schumann-Heink, a much beloved and admired diva, accompanied by "ten massed bands of 1000 pieces." Overhead flew a "silvery-bodied blimp ... [which] made a circuit of the stadium, bearing a silken American flag" illuminated by huge searchlights.

The final planned event which capped La Fiesta spanned the last two days and was held at the Municipal Airport, September 12–13. On the first day, some 40,000 "enthusiastic celebrators roared, screamed, ducked and thrilled as Army and Navy planes, in the most amazing fashion, vied in hair-raising stunts." A host of "bombers and sparrow-like pursuit planes raced, wheeled, diving in unison and climbed again into the cerulean blue."

Not to be outdone, "Commercial planes then took the stage, pulling acrobatic stunts galore and indulging in unbelievable tests of speed." Among the 150 planes participating in the air show, one was flown by a woman who, "excelling in swiftness in the seven [competitive] events," won handily over her five male contestants. "On Sunday a similar program drew 50,000 on the last day of La Fiesta."

∞

In looking back at the programmed events, it becomes quite obvious, with some exceptions, that the main thematic element which dominated throughout was an emphasis on the historical. Although the events described above are remembered today mainly by photographs and film, perhaps the most enduring tribute to the city's one hundred and fiftieth founding anniversary was the publication of *The Founding Documents of Los Angeles* that are reproduced in this volume. However, the story of how that project came to fruition is somewhat murky because of the lack of precise documentation. It seems reasonable to assume that the publication proposal was initiated several years prior to 1931, most likely it was initiated by Miss Marion Parks and supported by several others. After the idea was conceived by Historical Society of Southern California members, the scheme had to be implemented. The primary step was the location and identification of the documents to be included – a very demanding research task in itself.

Once located and copies acquired, the next step was the translation of the Spanish language texts into English. Again, this was a time-consuming requirement and a demanding one. It is for this reason that the translations were undertaken by a group of dedicated, knowledgeable volunteers, all with solid credentials as historians. Their names are appended to the text(s) which each translated.

In the research effort, it became clear to the parties engaged in the project that there were no doubt important documents housed in the National Archives in Mexico City. To that end, the Automobile Club of Southern California sponsored a research trip to Mexico undertaken by Vernon D. Tate, a man who was obviously versed in the Spanish language and had the ability to read eighteenth-century Spanish calligraphy – no mean accomplishment. His successful effort enhanced the final work, for he discovered some very important texts which were not available in the documentary materials at the Bancroft Library, University of California, Berkeley, the principal source for the documents that were included in the 1931 edition.

For the first time, the 1931 *Annual Publications of the Historical Society of Southern California* listed a Publications Committee. It was chaired by Marion Parks. Members included Arthur M. Ellis, Laurance L. Hill, Lindley Bynum, all four being well versed in the history of Los Angeles and California. And two of that number, Bynum and Parks, contributed directly to *The Founding Documents* with translations, while Miss Parks served as the volume's editor.

Five members of the Historical Society played an active role in the initial publication. They were Lindley Bynum, Phil Townsend Hanna, Marion Parks, Thomas Workman Temple II, and Henry R. Wagner. An important posthumous contribution was included that was translated by Charles Fletcher Lummis (1859–1928). Their individual credentials bear witness to their respective historical skills. A tribute to each of these individuals follows.

THE CONTRIBUTORS TO THE 1931 EDITION

LINDLEY BYNUM, a second-generation Californian, was born in Los Angeles, 1898. Educated in the local public schools, he enrolled at Stanford University where he earned his undergraduate degree in history. On graduation, he launched his career as a newspaperman, but after a decade he abandoned journalism for the world of history. What prompted this dramatic decision remains unclear for it was a hundred and eighty degree turn professionally. Thus, in 1933 he joined the staff of the Henry E. Huntington Library, a public research institution formally opened in 1919 on what had been Huntington's estate in San Marino.

The shift to the world of books and libraries launched Bynum into what was to be the compelling professional activity that dominated the remainder of his active employment — he became a scout for precious historical materials relating to California and the America West. Later in life, he estimated that in pursuit of historical documents, letters, maps, photographs, diaries, and journals maintained by early pioneer settlers that detailed the events of their lives and times, he traveled over 100,000 miles. Much of his effort was literally to rescue valuable historical sources from an unintentional or intentional fate, meaning their destruction, whether accidental or deliberate. And what a success he was at his job!

In 1941, at the behest of his friend, Dr. Robert Gordon Sproul, president of the University of California, Bynum accepted an official appointment as special assistant to the president. This gave him free statewide range to forage for historic materials to be deposited either in the two existing UC campus libraries at Berkeley or Los Angeles. As one account recorded: "So intent has Bynum been on his pursuit of California historical lore that he has never been out of the country," nor farther east than Gallup, New Mexico!

Looking back on his twenty-five years of sleuthing and rescuing precious historical sources from oblivion, Bynum estimated he had gathered over a half million books, documents, maps, and photographs and placed them in safe and secure depositories for research purposes for generations to come, for such materials are the very heart of the historical process in trying to comprehend and understand the past. In addition, he salvaged at least 50,000 pamphlets, newspapers, and other printed matter relating to California history.

In mid-1958, when President Sproul retired from the UC presidency, Bynum also took early retirement. He could afford to do that since he had recently received a handsome inheritance from a distant relative living in France. With that substantial windfall, he and his wife bought land and built their dream house in the vicinity of St. Helena in Napa County. "The new house was everything the Bynums could desire, high set, with a view of Mount St. Helena through the pines," a friend observed.

During his active career, not content with collecting history, Bynum also enjoyed life fully. He was a marvelous story teller, holding his audience captive by his talent. "He loved the length and breadth of California, especially the mountain areas. He knew its flora and fauna and delighted in applying the scientific names to botanical specimens," so wrote his longtime friend, the noted historian of southern California local history, W.W. Robinson. But more. He was a wine connoisseur – after all he was of French descent – and wrote a short book on the subject, *California Wines and How to Enjoy Them* (1955). It was a pioneering publication, praising the state's vineyards and their bottled products. As Robinson recalled: "We see him at wine-tastings, north and south, his mouth and lips purple with the vintages he so expertly tasted and (usually) named." Moving to the wine country in retirement was a deliberate decision. He was in his avocational element.

With Idwal Jones, he co-authored in 1950 a biography of Eugene W. Biscailuz, the colorful and flamboyant career law-enforcement officer who served as sheriff of Los Angeles County, 1932–58. He also contributed articles, translations, and reviews to historical quarterlies and other scholarly journals.

His last months were plagued by recurring illness. After several weeks of hospitalization in Berkeley, he died on September 20, 1965. His career as a field historian or historical scout won him an international reputation. Few have served the cause of California history better than Lindley Bynum.

PHIL TOWNSEND HANNA, a native of Los Angeles, was born in 1897. Attending local school, he graduated from Polytechnic High and thereafter enrolled at the University of Southern California where he took his bachelor's degree. He started his career in journalism as automobile editor for the *Los Angeles Tribune* in 1915, joined the *Los Angeles Times* in 1917, and the Associated Press two years later. In 1922 he found his permanent niche when he became art director and, in December 1926, editor of the Automobile Club of Southern California's monthly magazine, *Touring Topics*, later renamed *Westways*. He became general manager of the magazine in 1941 with the dual post of public relations counsel for the Auto Club.

He was an ardent student of California history, a love reflected in the consistent historical themes of many *Touring Topics*/*Westways* articles during his editorship. He authored several books, among them: *California Through Four Centuries: A Handbook of Memorable Date ...* (c. 1935); *California Under Twelve Flags* (1937); *The Dictionary of California Land Names ...* (1946), and *Death Valley Tales* (1955). He also edited Geronimo Boscana's *Chingigchinich, A Historical Account of the Origin, Customs, and Traditions of the Indians of the Missionary Establishment of St. Juan Capistrano, Alta California ...* (1933). Needless to say, he wrote a host of historical articles for *Touring Topics*/*Westways*. The index to that publication lists two pages of his contributions. In addition, he wrote several books dealing with the American Southwest, Mexico, and Central America.

Death claimed him suddenly: he was felled by a heart attack on June 1, 1957 at his home at 1244 South Fourth Avenue. Burial followed at Forest Lawn, Glendale. He was greatly mourned by the historical community. The *Los Angeles Times*, June 6, published a memorial tribute from the past president of the California and History Landmarks Club of Los Angeles, writing that he was "one of the kindest of men, a very able man who sought to perpetuate the true history and beauty of California through a life spent studying them and publishing others' findings." The letter ended – "History and California have lost a very fine writer and friend!"

CHARLES FLETCHER LUMMIS was born in Lynn, Massachusetts, March 1, 1859. When only two years old, his young mother died. Later he moved to Bristol, New Hampshire, where he lived with his grandparents before returning to his father's home. A bright and sickly child, he was determined to overcome his physical frailty by embracing a life of exercise and self-discipline. He matriculated at Harvard University, but left without graduating in 1881.

He found his calling as a journalist and began that career as editor of the *Scioto Gazette* in Chillicothe, Ohio, in 1882. Two years later he decided to take Horace Greeley's advice and go west. In anticipation of that overland trip on foot, he struck a deal with Harrison Gray Otis, founding publisher of the *Los Angeles Times*, to send periodic communiqués of his trek experiences en route to the newspaper. It was a marvelous adventure which has been captured in his second book, based on his letters to the *Times*, *A Tramp Across the Continent*, published in 1892, wherein he details his 3,507 miles journey which took 143 days to cover.

Joining the staff at the *Times* in 1885, he soon became the paper's city editor, but shortly after, due in no small part to his workaholic habits, he suffered a severe stroke that paralyzed him on one side. Determined to regain his health, he moved to the small New Mexican Indian pueblo of Isleta. Over the ensuing five years he made a complete recovery from his affliction. At the same time, he became versed in Spanish as well as several Indian languages and found his true life's work, the study and defense of the native peoples and the Spanish heritage of the American Southwest.

To support himself during his New Mexican sojourn, he wrote a variety of articles detailing the native people and the Spanish heritage that marked the region he was championing. Joining a small, select band of like contemporaries, he became a self-taught ethnologist. He assiduously collected native folktales and legends and was among the earliest of his contemporaries to photograph Pueblo Indian life and customs, especially their native ceremonies. For the rest of his life, he was a devotee of the Indians and the lifestyle of the Spanish-speaking inhabitants of the Southwest. The essence of his New Mexican years was beautifully captured in one of his best books, *The Land of Poco Tiempo* (1893).

Returning to Los Angeles, Lummis edited a promotional magazine, *Land of Sunshine* (1894–1901), later retitled *Out West* (1902–09). The readership was treated to writings by a burgeoning group of highly talented Californian authors, among them Mary Austin, Edwin Markham, Joaquin Miller, and Charles Warren Stoddard. The magazines were also active boosters not only for the Golden State, but also the Southwest, a region popularized by Lummis in the magazines as well as his personal writings. He was a regular contributor to both publications. One of his contributions was the translation of Governor Felipe de Neve's *Reglamento* (Regulation), 1781, which has earned the sobriquet, "California's first constitution." This contribution is included in this new, revised edition, first published in the 1931 edition.

Lummis became a leader in the Indian rights movement, spearheaded by the establishment of the Sequoya League in 1901, which was the handiwork of Lummis himself. While living in New Mexico, he had his baptism in civil rights for the Indians in several head on clashes about the prevailing ill treatment afforded the native peoples. This cause, too, became an integral part of his life's work. As his prestige as an authority on the American Southwest grew, he became a formidable lobbyist for the Indians, even gaining the ear of his former Harvard classmate, President Theodore Roosevelt. Short of stature, he was a giant in the cause in behalf of Indian peoples' rights and received due recognition for his pioneering role in their behalf.

A man of multiple talents and interests, he was one of the founders and first president of The Landmarks Club in 1895, which became a premier lobbying agency for historic preservation of California's Hispanic past, with particular attention to salvaging the ruins of California's missions, beginning with San Juan Capistrano, San Gabriel, and San Fernando, as well as other historic buildings.

When he became city librarian of the Los Angeles Public Library in 1905, he dedicated himself to collecting materials relating to the Southwest and California. It was a major achievement during his five-year tenure in that post.

One of his enduring monuments was the founding and construction of the

Southwest Museum in the Mount Washington area in 1914. Its primary focus was to accumulate and preserve artifacts relating to the culture of American Indians, with particular attention to the native people of the Southwest and California. That museum, happily, has survived its recent vicissitudes and now appears to be on a firmer financial footing which will insure the continuation of its mission – a stellar institution for the presentation and study of American Indian culture.

In looking at Lummis' life, his epitaph is written large: anthropologist, antiquarian, author, booster, champion, collector, editor, ethnologist, explorer, historian, humanitarian, journalist, librarian, linguist, lobbyist, musicologist, philanthropist, photographer, preservationist, and propagandist. When he died in Los Angeles, November 25, 1928, Eugene Manlove Rhodes paid this "final tribute to his friend and patron: '...In twenty ways, Lummis was the most remarkable man I ever knew – his scholarly thoroughness, his appalling industry, his rapier-like wit, and the militant heart that never feared to make a foe in a good cause. He finished what he started and he paid for what he broke.'"

∞

MARION PARKS played a major role in the planning and publication of the 1931 edition of *The Founding Documents of Los Angeles*. She was fluent in Spanish and had mastered eighteenth-century Spanish calligraphy, both essential ingredients in the implementation of the overall project. But more. She also served as chair of the Historical Society of Southern California's Publication Committee, the committee charged with preparing *The Founding Documents* in honor of the 150th anniversary of the city's founding as a Spanish pueblo. Not content with this role, Miss Parks also helped design the historical elements which dominated La Fiesta Week. In that respect, she was the first woman to address the Los Angeles Realty Board since it's founding in 1906. In her talk to a board luncheon meeting, May 19, 1931, she spoke on the forthcoming celebration events planned for September 4–11.

> In La Fiesta we shall celebrate on September 4 the birthday of the city, the anniversary on that day when the ... settlers ... found[ed] the city. On September 5 we shall celebrate the fifty-fifth anniversary of the first transcontinental railroad to Los Angeles. September 6, the 101st anniversary of the old Spanish trail between Los Angeles and Santa Fe will be commemorated. [That same day, Sunday,] religious servic-

> es will be conducted ... and on the following day, Labor Day, there will be a rodeo. On September 8 the founding of the San Fernando and San Gabriel missions will be observed and on September 9 the admission of California to the Union will be celebrated. All of these events are landmarks in Los Angeles history.

Miss Parks' father, having "read a Tournament of Roses pamphlet while in chilly Vermont promptly transferr[ed] the family to Pasadena. However, some uncles and grandpa were good old forty-niners before that." Because of her parents move, Miss Parks – happily for her later career – was born in Pasadena in 1903. While attending Pasadena schools, "as a small girl with long curls, the boys in public school nicknamed her 'Smarty Parks.'" As a youngster "she liked playing cowboy and challenging dad to shooting matches, being exceptionally expert for a small girl."

On completing high school in 1920 she attended nearby Occidental College for one year, then transferred to the newly founded University of California at Los Angeles, from which she received her B.A. in 1925. She majored in history, art, and modern languages. On graduation she received honors in history and had continued her study of Spanish which she had begun in the seventh grade. She also gained a reading knowledge of French. She then proceeded to have a most unhappy year jobless, and "wondering if she was doomed to be a failure." Her collegiate studies, however, would eventually prove valuable assets.

In the interim, she was employed in a clerical position at Pasadena High School, where she had graduated five years before. The meager salary of $85 "finally saved her pride, but she wasn't a success at this job." At this juncture of her young adulthood, fate smiled.

One day in 1926, after she had given a talk to a girls' club on California history, by chance she "met an employee of the Museum at Exposition Park – and discovered there was a temporary opening for a Spanish-English correspondent at $4 a day." She leapt at the opportunity to utilize her basic linguistic skills at the institution which is now called the Natural History Museum of Los Angeles County. The job was only a prelude of what was to come. "This led to her being placed in charge of a priceless loan exhibition for which she handled the programs, she wrote publicity and covered herself with such distinction that 100,000 persons visited in two months. Among there [sic] were many who later proved valuable professional contacts."

Shortly after the exhibition closed, Miss Parks was employed as assistant secretary of the Southwest Museum in Highland Park "and editing 'The Masterkey' [the Museum's scholarly journal], submerged in her beloved California history." This was, indeed, a huge stepping stone which greatly benefited her subsequent career.

The prelude to her established career in history was her authorship of an extensively researched study published in two volumes in the *Annual Publications of the Historical Society of Southern California*, 14, Pts. 1–2 (1928–29), entitled *In Pursuit of Vanished Days: Visits to Extant Historic Adobe Houses of Los Angeles County*. This scholarly endeavor bore eloquent testimony to her skills as an historian, researcher, and writer. This impressive work also earned her the chairmanship of the Landmarks Committee for the 1932 Olympic Games held in Los Angeles. That event also led to the publication of a small pamphlet, "Door to Yesterday: A Guide to Old Los Angeles" (c. 1932).

In 1929 Laurance L. Hill, Director of the Publicity Department at Security-First National Bank, offered Miss Parks a staff position. As a member of the Historical Society, Hill was familiar with her recently published account on county historic adobes and recognized her abilities by offering an appointment in his department which prepared a variety of historical publications relating to California history, especially the Southland. As early as 1922 the bank sponsored *In the Valley of Cahuengas: The Story of Hollywood*, which was in its fifth edition by 1924. Notable was Hill's *La Reina, Los Angeles in Three Centuries* that appeared in 1929 – the first project Miss Parks worked on. In 1930 she coauthored with Hill *Santa Barbara, Tierra Adorada, A Community History*.

Another pamphlet endeavor was published possibly in 1935, "Historic La Purisima, Lompoc, Santa Barbara County, California." Miss Parks supplied the historical data for this National Park publication which was reprinted around 1950. Her last major book appeared in 1939, edited by Owen H. O'Neill, *History of Santa Barbara County, State of California*, a massive tome, wherein she provided the historical narrative while O'Neill wrote the biographical section.

Her crowning historical achievement, however, was her editorship of the original publication of *The Founding Documents* in 1931. That responsibility infers that she had a prominent role in the development and realization of that important project. Her mastery of Spanish also proved invaluable since the 1931 edition was bilingual: the full text of the Spanish documents were reprinted *verbatim*, and full English translations of them were the primary focus of that notable issue of the *Annual Publications of the Historical Society of Southern California*.

By 1934 Miss Parks had moved on, for by that year she was editor of the women's department of the Southern California Banker. She was also "... on the committee of the American Institute of Bankers, making speeches galore on California history, godmothering Los Fiesteros de la Calle Olvera [The Entertainers of Olvera Street] (which she helped found) and thoroughly involved everywhere with everything having to do with the history of her beloved State."

She was married in 1936 to Nelson H. Partridge, Jr., on July 16. Their nuptials were consummated in "the memorial pergola of the Thatcher School in Ojai." Her husband had attended Thatcher and was a graduate of Harvard and the University of California. After spending the remainder of the summer at Santa Monica, they made their home in Pasadena. At the time of her marriage, Miss Parks was "supervisor of the Index of American Design in [the] Federal Arts Project," sponsored by the Works Progress Administration of President Franklin Roosevelt's New Deal.

Miss Parks was appointed supervisor in charge of the Index of American Design project. It was established to undertake the identification and recording of all types of original design created by artists and craftsmen from the Spanish era to 1900. She initiated the Los Angeles office with a staff of twenty-five artists and research workers, charged with surveying the seven southern California counties. The completed survey was to be preserved in the Library of Congress for future scholarly reference use and research.

Parallel with this WPA appointment, Miss Parks originated and commenced the translating of the surviving original Spanish/Mexican archives held by Los Angeles County, principally under her guidance as secretary of the Historical Society of Southern California. "It involved not only advance in historical research but ... in supervision of a large staff of workers as well, many of whom had to be trained as well as supervised in the work." This effort, too, was sponsored by the WPA.

Her wedding did not impede nor interfere with her dedication to history as witness the publication of the massive tome on Santa Barbara published in 1939. While working on that impressive study, she made a number of startling new discoveries. The Los Angeles *Times*, January 13, 1938, informed its readership under the heading "NEW HISTORY FACTS DISCLOSED. Early Day California materials Dug Up at Santa Barbara." The heart of the column's story read:

> Miss Marion Parks, historian of Reina Del Mar Parlor, Native Daughters of the Golden West, recently has uncovered new historical source material that will change current history versions in several important particulars.
>
> One of the sources is an account of the discovery of California written by Juan Rodrigues Cabrillo never before recorded by historians. Miss Parks comments that its being overlooked may be considered a criticism of accepted historians for not delving deeper into source materials.
>
> She also has had access to a manuscript history of early California obtained by the Huntington Library. New materials regarding the Santa Barbara Indians and new items of military history have been found. The history curator of the Los Angeles Public Library brought to light an entirely new account of the lost Indian woman of San Nicholas, one of the channel islands.

These materials were incorporated in the 1939 *History of Santa Barbara*, a publication delayed by twenty lawsuits brought by the publisher, Harold Meir, "against subscribers whose pictures and biographies were made a part of the history." On April 6, 1940, Justice C.P. Moore dismissed the lawsuits in his Carpinteria court, ruling that "Meier had no right to sue them [the subscribers] since his name did not appear on the contracts which they signed." The *Los Angeles Times* article noted: "Owen O'Neill, county surveyor, edited the volume and Marion Parks Partridge, Southland historian, of Los Angeles, wrote the descriptive history after long regional research." This is the only time that her married name was used in newspaper accounts.

Mrs. Partridge's marriage appears to have dissolved either by divorce or death. When and how has not been determined. One slender undated newspaper clipping provides clues and is quoted in full:

> Marion Parks, who used to aid Laurence [*sic*] Hill in preparing historical booklets about Los Angeles which probably did more to acquaint our population with our history than anything else, and who was a valued aide at the Southwest Museum before that and a prime mover in that fine group, Los Fiesteros de Los Angeles, afterward, is in the American Republic Affairs section of the State Department now, and writes me that they certainly stay on the job in that department, starting to work early and working late. In the Aug. 13 number of the

Department of State Bulletin Miss Parks has an interesting article, "A New Pattern in International Wartime Collaboration," dealing with the importation of Mexican labor to rescue the harvests of California.

The title of her August 13, 1944 article indicates that the time frame was World War II. Her State Department service apparently continued, for the *Alumni Directory for Occidental College*, 1991, lists her under her maiden name, living at 3021 Cambridge Place NW, Washington, D.C. It indicates only that she attended Occidental in 1924 (actually 1920–21) and was a member of Alpha, a campus sorority. Her name vanishes from subsequent directories, indicating no doubt her demise, for she was quite advanced in age by 1991.

THOMAS WORKMAN TEMPLE II was born on January 4, 1905, at Mission Viejo, on the Rancho La Merced, located near present-day Montebello, the eldest of four children. He was the descendant of two illustrious American pioneers, William Workman, who came overland from Santa Fe in 1841, and John Temple, an 1827 arrival who became one of Los Angeles' first merchants. Both men left their heirs well off, one in land, the other in business interests primarily. Thomas' mother, Lorenz, was a descendant of Manuel Ygnacio de Lugo, one of the seventeen soldiers who acted as escorts to the forty-four settlers who founded the pueblo of Los Angeles in 1781. Perhaps because of his lineage, he was destined to become an outstanding genealogist, specializing in *Californio* family history as well as American pioneers.

Not far from Mission San Gabriel, he attended Temple Grammar School (named for his great grandfather), situated near the Rio Hondo. Completing his public school education, he graduated with his bachelor's degree from the University of Santa Clara, followed by acceptance in 1926 by Harvard University School of Law. On receiving his law degree, he was admitted to the California bar, although he never practiced that profession.

Two events helped to shape Temple's life. The first took place in 1914. At the age of nine he made an accidental discovery on his father's Rancho La Merced. "He saw a tiny pool of rain-water, bastioned in the rocks, its surface bubbling fumes of gas ... it was a jet of natural gas." Subsequently, his mother would "amuse friends by frying eggs over the natural gas." This phenomenon finally caught the attention of the Standard Oil Company. As a result, in 1917 the company acquired a lease and on drilling discovered a rich oil field. This discovery, the Montebello Field, made the Temple fortune; unhappily one that was utterly wiped out in the Depression of 1929.

The second event occurred after Temple completed law school. It appears that for some years – perhaps high school or certainly from his undergraduate days at Santa Clara – he had become fascinated with the study of family history. Shortly after completing his law studies, he received encouragement from San Francisco Archbishop Edward J. Hanna "to pursue his genealogical interests as a lifetime vocation." Turning from law, Temple immersed himself in family history research for the remainder of his life – it was both his avocation and gainful career. He thus "earned a modest livelihood by fulfilling [genealogical] commissions from families, foundations and historical societies."

With extraordinary patience, coupled with his mastery of Spanish and Spanish calligraphy, he spent the ensuing forty years avidly transcribing California Spanish era documents, concentrating not on the native peoples *per se*, but focused on the family histories of Spanish settlers and Mexican pioneers. Rev. Msgr. Francis J. Weber, founding and longtime archivist for the Archdiocese of Los Angeles, summed up much of Temple's life work: "In 1965, the Chancery Archives of the Archdiocese ... acquired the Thomas Workman Temple Collection of Historical Transcripts, part of an extensive survey made of California's missions, *padres* and people. The 2,000 typed pages also include data on the *gente de razón* from sixteen of the state's twenty-one missions, as well as several [mission] Foundations in Peninsular [Baja] California."

Because of his abiding interest in Alta California family history, Temple also became involved with two other elements that treaded his life: the history of California, especially the Southland, and the preservation of its Hispanic heritage, notably his long association with Mission San Gabriel where he established the mission's museum. He also edited the *Bulletin of the Old Mission Parish*, at San Gabriel, and was the mission's historian and consultant.

Although he published only about a dozen historical articles and translations during his lifetime, no one questioned his extensive knowledge of California's Hispanic era. Thus it was natural that Miss Marion Parks, editor of the 1931 edition of *The Founding Documents of Los Angeles*, would invite Temple to participate in that project, both as a contributor and translator. As a result, he authored the lengthy historical introduction to the 1931 endeavor, as well as providing several translations and important commentaries.

When he died in 1972, he was given the singular honor of burial in the priests' cemetery which is immediately adjacent to Mission San Gabriel on the north side. He was laid to rest practically next to the mission. Thus he is the only lay person to join the numerous Claretians buried in the same grave site, priests who have served the Archdiocese of Los Angeles, staffing the San Gabriel Parish, which includes the old mission.

Msgr. Weber probably has expressed best a suitable epitaph: "No living authority was better versed than [Thomas] Workman Temple III [*sic*] about the familiar relationships of California's Provincial era as recorded in the old mission registers, *presidio* muster rolls and early census reports."

HENRY RAUP WAGNER (1862–1957) was an extraordinary bibliographer and historian. His prodigious achievements have marked him as one of the great scholars of the first half of the twentieth century. He wrote more than 170 scholarly publications in the field of Latin American and Western American studies. Most of his prodigious output was produced after he retired from a profitable career in business in 1920. Secure with solid financial assets, he flung himself into the world of manuscripts and books, researching, and writing. Not content with his scholarly output, throughout his adult years he acquired over 100,000 books and pamphlets, forming all-in-all about a dozen collections, all of which were subsequently sold to major research depositories. (The sale of these collections also handsomely augmented Wagner's finances.)

He also was a prime mover in the founding of the Friends of the Bancroft Library, University of California, Berkeley; the Quivira Society, a scholarly organization interested in the history of the American Southwest and the Borderlands; helped revitalize the Cortés Society, dedicated to the history of early Mexico, and the California Historical Society. He served as president of the Historical Society of Southern California, 1932–34.

The latter association began when he relocated to San Marino in 1928, having retired first to Berkeley from his busy life in mining. It was a deliberate decision since he wanted to be near the Henry E. Huntington Library, a premier research center. His home was within easy walking distance. It was for the same reason he and his wife, Blanche, moved to Berkeley in 1920: he wanted to be near the Bancroft Library with its rich treasure trove of historical sources.

His published contributions, being too numerous to detail in this brief essay, included a narrative history of Sir Francis Drake's voyage around the world (1926), sixteenth-century Spanish voyages to the Pacific Northwest (1929), and posthumously *The Life and Writings of Bartolomé de las Casas* (1967), among others. He also authored a biography of Juan Rodríguez Cabrillo, the discoverer of California (1941).

He was born into an affluent Philadelphia family in 1862. On graduating from the Friends Central High School, he entered Yale College in 1880. Completing his undergraduate studies, he attended Yale School of Law, receiving his degree in 1886. His subsequent life is well recorded in his autobiography, *Bullion to Books*. Gradually he transitioned from the practice of law to mining. It proved the making of his fortune. It also provided him extensive travel in the Southwest, ranging as far north as Colorado and east to Texas. In 1898 he joined the American Smelting and Refining Company, working in the firm's business office for the two ensuing decades when he retired. During his tenure with the company, he traveled extensively – England, Mexico, and Chile. Wherever he went he purchased printed materials, for he was an avid collector who would later mine the acquired books and pamphlets to produce bibliographical and historical tomes. At the same time, he became well versed in Spanish which greatly aided his research interests.

His bibliographic contributions are legendary. Two themes will suffice: colonial Spanish sources and books relating to America's westward movement. The latter was an impressive contribution, *The Plains and the Rockies*, which appeared first in 1920. It was subsequently revised. Charles L. Camp joined in the preparation of the third edition in 1953, and Robert L. Becker undertook a major revision in 1982. Assuredly, it is one of Wagner's crowning achievements.

Wagner's contribution to the 1931 *Founding Documents* was a translation. He was certainly eminently qualified.

When Wagner died in 1957, his secular funeral was sponsored by the Zamorano Club of Los Angeles, of which he was a member. He was laid to rest next to his wife in Forest Lawn, Glendale.

CONTRIBUTORS TO THE 2003 EDITION

The prologue to this new edition of *The Founding Documents* was written by Harry E. Kelsey, a native of Alton, Illinois, born September 25, 1929. A product of parochial schools, he undertook his undergraduate education at Stanford University and received his Ph.D. in History from the University of Denver in 1965. He began his professional career as State Historian of Colorado, later serving as Historian and Director of the Michigan Historical Commission.

In 1971 he accepted appointment as Chief Curator of History at the Natural History Museum of Los Angeles County, retiring from that post in 1988 to devote himself to research and writing.

In 1969 the Colorado Historical Society published his biography of a former governor, *Frontier Capitalist: The Life of John Evans*, which was based on his doctoral dissertation. The Huntington Library, San Marino, published his meticulous and incisive biography of *Juan Rodríguez Cabrillo* (1986), which superceded Henry R. Wagner's 1941 treatment. The superb scholarship which distinguished Kelsey's publication was recognized by the Spanish government: he was awarded the Orden de Isabella la Católica. In addition, he has written numerous articles for scholarly journals.

With the permission of the California Historical Society, San Francisco, his splendid article, "A New Look at the Founding of Old Los Angeles," *California Historical Quarterly*, 55 (Winter 1976): 326–39, is by far the best current exposition detailing the founding of the Los Angeles pueblo by the Spanish government in 1781.

∞

The article which concludes Part I of *The Founding Documents* was authored by Theodore E. Treutlein, "Los Angeles, California: The Question of the City's Original Spanish Name," *Southern California Quarterly*, 55 (Spring 1973): 1–7, the publication of the Historical Society of Southern California and reprinted by permission. There has long existed confusion and controversy over what was the precise name given to the pueblo at its establishment in 1781. Treutlein provides a documented answer.

Treutlein (1906–86), a graduate of the University of California, Berkeley, where he received his Ph.D., spent his professional career as a member of the Department of History, California State University, San Francisco, retiring in 1971. He specialized in the history of the Borderlands and the Californias, both Baja and Alta. He translated and edited two studies relating to the Mexican province of Sonora, and published in 1968, *San Francisco Bay: Discovery and Colonization, 1769–1776*. A number of his articles and reviews appeared in numerous scholarly journals.

∞

Doyce B. Nunis, Jr. began his distinguished career with a Ph.D. at USC in 1958, and he taught at USC from 1965 until his retirement in 1989. His specialties were the history of the American West and California, and he has a most impressive list of publications in these fields. One of his signal contributions is as a respected editor of documents from the Spanish and Mexican periods. With coauthor Gloria R. Lothrop, he edited *A Guide to the History of California* (1989), a work expressing his career-long dedication to California history. His interest in Los Angeles history is evidenced in the monumental tome he helped to compile and edit, *Los Angeles and Its Environs in the Twentieth Century: A Bibliography of a Metropolis* (1975).

Professor Nunis has been the often-hailed editor of the *Southern California Quarterly* for forty-three years (1962–2004), an historical milestone few can claim. This leading scholarly journal of California history was improved and revamped during Nunis' years of brilliant editorship. As Thomas F. Andrews, executive director of the Historical Society of Southern California, commented on Nunis' contribution: "with uncommon skill, Doyce has combined his appreciation of fine printing, passion for research, dedication to fairness and social justice, and tireless energy to serve ... with distinction."

He has received numerous awards and honors. He is a Fellow of the California Historical Society and the Southern California Historical Society; the Henry R. Wagner Medal from the California Historical Society; three Awards of Merit from the American Association for State and Local History, among others. He has received research fellowships from the Guggenheim Foundation, the Huntington Library, the Haynes Foundation, and the American Philosophical Society. For his scholarly work and community service, Pope Paul VI conferred on him the Benemeriti Medal and Pope John Paul II made him a Knight Commander of St. Gregory. In recognition of his scholarly contributions to the history of Spanish California, King Juan Carlos of Spain decorated him with the Orden de Isabella la Católica in 1994. In appreciation for his stellar career as a teacher (he won all of his university's teaching awards — five in number) and scholar, USC awarded him the title of Distinguished Professor Emeritus.

EDITORIAL POLICY RESPECTING THE NEW EDITION

This 2003 edition of *The Founding Documents* is different from the 1931 original publication. First of all, two contributions to 1931 have been omitted, Lyndley Bynum's biographical sketch of "Governor Don Felipe de Neve" (7 pages) and Thomas Workman Temple II's "Se Fundaron un Pueblo de Espanoles ("A Village of Spaniards Was Founded," 29 pages) an historical overview leading up to the actual founding of the pueblo in 1781. The omissions of these two items was felt necessary, for both are historically out of date and contain misleading information. At the time they were written, however, Bynum and Temple relied on the available scholarship. In the seventy-two years that have lapsed between the original and present edition, there have been impressive advances made in discovering new documentary sources which have transformed our scholarly understanding of Los Angeles' early history. And discoveries no doubt will be made in the future that may well alter even the present high level of scholarship and require revision in light of new documentary evidence.

Such is the case with De Neve. In 1971, Edwin A. Beilharz published *Felipe de Neve, First Governor of California* which obviously supercedes Bynum's brief biographical essay in the 1931 edition. The same applies to Temple's historical overview as attested to in the new Prologue which replaces it in this new edition. As an illustration of his historical confusion, at the beginning of Temple's article he concluded a special introductory paragraph with this: "Mision de San Gabriel Arcangel, Día de la Indulgéncia de Nuestra Señora la Reyna de los Angeles de Porciúncula, Domingo, Agosto 2, 1931." (Translation: "Mission San Gabriel Archangel, Day of the Indulgence of Our Lady the Queen of Angels of the Porciuncula, Sunday, August 2, 1931.") He then begins to elaborate on this in the first paragraph of his essay. More confusion follows. There is some accuracy in what Temple writes, but it is flawed. August 2 is a day sacred to members of the Order of Friars Minor for it is a solemn feast day when an indulgence (forgiveness) may be obtained by observing it. The actual indulgence, however, is called "Our Lady of the Angels of Porciuncula." There is no use of "Queen" in the title. The Porciuncula – in Italian, Porziuncola – is a small chapel. It was a favorite place of St. Francis of Assisi who restored it, making it the center of the fledgling group of men he gathered around him that led to the establishment of the Order of Friars Minor (Franciscans). So in the vicinity of this chapel resided the first community of followers of St. Francis. In 1569, construction began on what is today called the Basicila of Santa Maria Delgi Angeli (translation: Basilica of Our Lady of the Angels). On August 2, 1769, the Spanish exploring party, led by Don Gaspar de Portolá, crossed a river into a verdant valley. Friar Juan Crespí, the diarist for the expedition, suggested that the river and valley be named in honor of Nuestra Señora de los Angeles de Porciúncula since it was the feast day of that indulgence. And so it was done. At the end of his essay, Temple concludes that the embryonic pueblo was placed "under the protection of Nuestra Señora la Reyna de los Angeles, Maria Santísimia de Porciúncula, September 4, 1781," by the settlers gathered "about ... the dusty plaza." The name is in error; there was no gathering – no formal establishment ceremony – no priest was present, and there was as yet no plaza. However, the misuse of the name for the feast day has continued to the present, for what Temple did was to combine the name given to the river in 1769 with the name given to the pueblo in Spanish documents when it was founded in 1781, El Pueblo de la Reyna de Los Angeles, the Pueblo of Queen of the Angels. Unhappily, Temple's title is engraved on the wooden cross erected at the south end of historic Olvera Street, a major tourist attraction. No doubt many read it and accept it as fact, mistaken though it is, and believe this is the Spanish name of Los Angeles.

When any essay begins and ends in an historical inaccuracy, though not deliberate, it is nevertheless misinformed: a flag of caution must be raised. For this reason and other like errors of fact, the dated version penned by Temple on Los Angeles' founding warrants that it be omitted in this new edition.

A second major alteration to the 1931 edition is the rearrangement of the documents, both the English translations and the Spanish text. In the 1931 edition the documents were not presented in an orderly and chronological fashion. This leads to confusion for those reading or trying to study the documents. Therefore, in this new edition the documents have been reordered both as to chronology and topic.

A third editorial problem was with the Spanish texts. In the eighteenth century, Spanish lexicography had not yet been formally stylized. Although there were primitive steps taken during that century to rectify the situation – as in England for the English language – common usage varied in respect to spelling and the use of accents. This was true for the 1931 edition, and it remains true in this new edition. There has been no effort to correct spelling (except where it might be confusing in translation) or to supply accents in light of present-day Spanish. Thus in some documents, accents are used, but these were used by the writer, while some are omitted or else are not consistent even in a given document. It was decided that in respect to the Spanish texts, to leave them as they appeared in the original documents as to spelling and accent usage.

A fourth editorial concern was with the English translations. Throughout there are occasional insertions of Spanish words in italics. (Italics are used in English to highlight foreign language words as they appear in the respective language, usually on first introduction of the foreign word, but thereafter the word is not italicized if used again. Some writers, on the other hand, are consistent. They supply italics when foreign words are repeated after their first use.) Unfortunately, an additional difficulty was that Spanish words used in the English texts were occasionally translated in footnotes, others were not. To be consistent, all Spanish words used in the translations have been translated either in notes or parenthetically in the text itself.

In editing both the translations and the original 1931 texts, it was discovered that there had been an occasional lapse in failing to translate some of the Spanish text. This oversight has been corrected in this new edition.

The original contributors to the 1931 edition are to be congratulated on the care they exercised in their respective translations. However, translations from another language are always tricky. One person may translate a text one way, another a different way. It is a matter of personal outlook and style. But in the final analysis, this becomes an academic question, and there are pros and cons galore. Suffice it to state that the 1931 translators did an excellent job. It may have some imperfections, but these are few and far between.

Other than the aforementioned editorial intrusions into the 1931 edition, this new edition still stands in the debt of the original six contributors. They deserve our appreciation and gratitude for a job well done in 1931, one that will now be made more available to a broader audience of readers and research users, thanks to the support of this new edition by foundations and individuals who are listed in the Acknowledgments, as well as those new contributors mentioned in the Introduction.

— DOYCE B. NUNIS, JR.

PART I

PROLOGUE

A New Look at the Founding of Old Los Angeles

BY HARRY KELSEY

In 1876, the United States Centennial Commission asked communities around the country to prepare and publish their own local histories. The studies were to cover "the earliest settlement to the present time." In Los Angeles three men – old timers, at least one of whom had lived in the city for nearly half a century – responded to the request with a slim volume entitled *An Historical Sketch of Los Angeles County, California*. Semi-centenarian author J.J. Warner included an account of the founding of Los Angeles based largely on a personal inspection of original sources in public archives. Warner's brief description of the event, phrasings which have appeared in many accounts since that day, has special interest, because his words are apparently accurate but subject to broad and varied interpretation: "The Town (Pueblo) of Nuestra Senora de Los Angeles [sic], under and in conformity to an order of the Governor of California, Phelipe de Neve, dated at the Mission of San Gabriel, August 26th, 1781, was founded in a formal manner on the fourth of September of the same year."[1]

Over the years Warner's account has become "fact," yet a new reading of more extensive records raises questions about the accepted whens, wheres, whos, and hows of the notable, if then inauspicious, events in 1781 on the banks of the River Porciúncula. Warner identified only one of his sources, a certified copy of Governor Neve's original order, which contained obvious and, as he said, inexcusable errors. He then concluded his account with the offhand remark that "other evidence before us fixed the date of the founding of Los Angeles in September, 1781." That other evidence was apparently a copy of the original *padron del vecindario* or poll of residents of November 19, 1781.[2]

Warner's account, dated 1876, is the earliest publication citing official records that documents the city's founding. While his choice of words is very much like that of another historical sketch published about 1872, the earlier account, also probably written by Warner, contained no documentation.[3] Contemporary accounts written by Father Francisco Palou during the 1770s and 1780s have been rejected by most historians.[4]

In 1886, Hubert Howe Bancroft published a detailed and carefully documented history of California which contained the first history of Los Angeles reflecting an extensive examination of archival materials. Bancroft's description of the actual founding, however, is a model of cautious understatement: "We only know that the pueblo was founded September 4th, with twelve settlers and their families, forty-six persons in all." Because one of the twelve was "at first absent at Loreto," as was the man's daughter, Bancroft concluded that the actual founding group contained eleven families with a total of forty-four persons.[5]

Later historians offered a few important details in variance with those put forth by Warner and Bancroft, particularly involving the number of people in the founding party, the existence of a military escort, previous military service or lack thereof on the part of the settlers, and the ceremony attending the foundation. But most historians have accepted that on September 4, 1781, about eleven families of settlers trekked from San Gabriel and took part in a ceremony establishing the city on the banks of the Río Porciúncula.[6]

If any doubt remained in the minds of researchers about the details surrounding the founding of Los Angeles, it seems to have been foreclosed in 1931. In that sesquicentennial year of the city's birth, Thomas Workman Temple published the results of his investigations, accompanied by lengthy translations of original documents. Temple concluded that eleven families of settlers – forty-four persons-settled Los Angeles on September 4, 1781.[7] However, a reevaluation of the sources, some of his own as well as other records now available, indicates that the city was founded in a somewhat different way than has been previously believed.

The story begins in April, 1781, when California Governor Felipe de Neve moved from Monterey to San Gabriel to await the arrival of the soldiers and settlers destined for the new pueblo of Los Angeles and the missions and presidio that he planned to establish in that Santa Barbara Channel region. Whether Neve took any steps to prepare the channel sites for settlement is unknown, but he did begin work immediately at the site selected for the new pueblo of Los Angeles.[8]

The site had been scheduled for a mission since 1769 when Franciscan Father Juan Crespí first saw it and named it *Nuestra Señora de Los Angeles de la Porciúncula* for the river on which it was located. An Indian town already occupied the spot, "a fine *ranchería*" where the Indians were "very docile and friendly," according to Crespí. They called the town Yabit, and, as the good fathers said, the people were "the cleanest we have seen." Most importantly, however, the Indians apparently liked the padres and wanted them to stay.[9]

The friendly disposition of the Indians at Yabit apparently did not change over the years, for in 1779 Teodoro de Croix, the frontier commandant general, remarked in a letter to Lieutenant Governor Fernando de Rivera y Moncada that the local natives were "docile and without malice." Taking advantage of this attitude, in the spring of 1781 Neve apparently traveled to the "fine *ranchería*" and selected three dozen boys and girls for conversion to Christianity. Neve himself acted as godfather at twelve of the baptisms. Just before the soldiers and settlers from Mexico began to arrive, Neve chose a young married couple, renamed them Felipe de Neve and Phelipa Theresa de Neve, and not only sponsored their baptism but remarried them "in the eyes of the Church."[10]

Neve's motivations for the unusual actions went unrecorded, but we do know that his new *Reglamento* or regulations for government and administration urged the founding of towns and missions. Effective on January 1, 1781, it was calculated in part to bring about a radical change in the mission system and, perhaps, a reduction in the temporal power of the padres. No longer were Christian Indians to reside at missions. Instead, they would live at their rancherías, practice a degree of self-government, and return to the missions from time to time for religious instruction.[11] The new group of youthful Indian converts at Yabit, headed by the young Indian couple renamed Neve, could well have been intended as the nucleus of a Christian Indian settlement adjoining the new pueblo of Los Angeles.

Title Fourteen of Neve's new Reglamento supports this interpretation. As put forth in the document, one major purpose of the new towns in California would be "to hasten the conversion ... of the countless pagans." Commandant General Croix's instructions to Rivera noted, moreover, that a prime duty of the Los Angeles settlers would be "to attract the Indians joyfully by the practice of true justice and good example to the knowledge of our Sacred Religion."[12]

Expecting opposition from the missionary priests, Neve remained silent while residing at San Gabriel in early 1781 about this aspect of his Reglamento. Instead, he told the fathers only that they lacked skill at proselytizing, an activity, he urged, at which he excelled.[13]

While the governor amused himself at San Gabriel and annoyed the missionaries with his conversion work, the settlers who had enlisted to establish the new town of Los Angeles were slowly making their way north to meet him at Mission San Gabriel. They were accompanied on their trek by a band of fresh recruits destined for the Upper California presidios.

The entire party had been recruited and organized with some difficulty by Captain Fernando de Rivera y Moncada in Sonora and Sinaloa. Rivera led the larger part of the group, including most of the soldiers, on a northerly overland trail through Sonora and Arizona. The Los Angeles settlers traveled with a smaller military escort by sea to Loreto and the northern end of the Baja California peninsula and then overland north to San Gabriel. (Fig. 1)

The original group of settlers destined for Los Angeles included about sixteen heads of families. Some fell by the wayside long before reaching San Gabriel, but all those who completed the sea and land journey traveled with their families and worldly possessions. So far as the financial records of the expedition now show,[14] those who enlisted were:

1. José de Lara, his wife María Antonia Campos, two sons, and a daughter;[15]
2. José Antonio Navarro, his wife María Regina Dorotea, two sons, and a daughter;[16]
3. Basilio Rosas, his wife María Manuela Calixtra, five sons, and one daughter;[17]
4. Antonio Mesa, his wife Ann Gertrudis López, a son, and a daughter;[18]
5. Antonio Villavicencio, his wife María de los Santos Severina, and one daughter;[19]
6. José Banegas, his wife María Máxima Aguilar, and one son;[20]
7. Alejandro Rosas, and his wife Juana Rodríguez;[21]
8. Pablo Rodríguez, his wife María Rosalía Noriega, and one daughter;[22]
9. Luis Quintero, his wife María Petra Ruvio, one son, and four daughters;[23]
10. Manuel Cameror, and his wife María Thomasa;[24]
11. José Moreno, and his wife María Guadalupe Gertrudis;[25]
12. Antonio Miranda Rodríguez, and one daughter;[26]
13. Pedro Pablo Rodríguez, one son, and two daughters;[27]

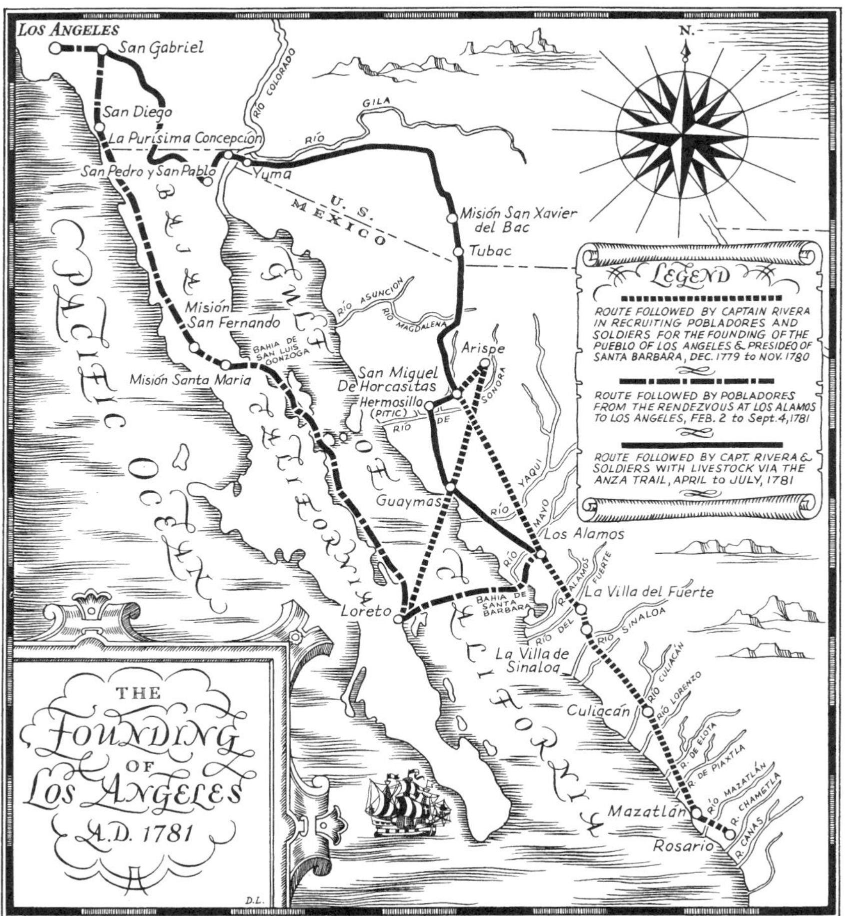

COURTESY PHIL TOWNSEND HANNA AND "TOURING TOPICS"

FIGURE 1. This map graphically details the routes used by the first recruited settlers and soldiers who would become the inhabitants of the new pueblo in 1781.

14. Nicolasa Ramírez, one son, and two daughters;[28]
15. Rafael Mesa and family;[29]
16. Miguel Villa, his wife, one son, and two daughters.[30]

Only the first eleven families, forty-four individuals in all, completed the journey to Los Angeles. Antonio Miranda Rodríguez remained in Loreto, Baja California, with his daughter who contracted smallpox.[31] Pedro Pablo Rodríguez died on August 28, 1780, in Real de Cosalá, where he had enlisted. His daughters Juana Simona and Lucinda, along with his son Vizente, traveled to California with the other settlers, and the girls almost immediately married soldiers at San Diego.[32]

Nicolasa Ramírez, a widow, had enlisted as a settler in October, 1780. Almost as soon as the party reached San Gabriel, she married Recruit Guillermo Soto, the only eligible bachelor among the enlisted men in the military escort, and thereby moved from the rank of settler to that of military personnel.[33] Although widows and widowers may have seemed dubious pioneer material, a precedent had been established in the founding of San José, and in any case the widow quickly found herself a husband.[34]

The settler Rafael Mesa deserted at Real de los Alamos about October 12, 1780. For a time the California officials debated whether Mesa was a soldier or a settler; however, a list prepared at Alamos on July 15, 1781, just a few days after his enlistment, specifically listed him as a settler.[35]

About the final family head, Miguel Villa, there was no question. He definitely enlisted as a settler, and he definitely deserted in Mexico about March 4, 1781.[36]

The military escort party consisted of the following fifteen soldiers, most married and with families:[37]

1. Lieutenant José de Zúñiga;[38]
2. Ensign Ramón Laso de la Vega;[39]
3. Recruit Julián Guerrero and his wife;[40]
4. Recruit Francisco Javier Sepúlveda, his wife, five sons, and one daughter;[41]
5. Recruit Augustín Leyva, his wife, and five sons;[42]
6. Recruit Victorino Féliz, his wife, and four children;[43]
7. Recruit Guillermo Soto, bachelor;[44]
8. Recruit Eugenio Valdéz and his new bride;[45]
9. Recruit Justo Hernández, his wife, one son, and two daughters;[46]
10. Recruit José Lovo, his wife, and four sons;[47]

11. Recruit Josef Antonio Cortéz and his new bride;[48]
12. Recruit Gaspar López, his wife, four sons, and a daughter;[49]
13. Recruit Joaquín Rodríguez and his new bride;[50]
14. Recruit Francisco Juárez, his wife, and one child;[51]
15. Recruit Fructuoso María Ruiz and his new wife.[52]

In addition, María Pasquala, wife of soldier Miguel Silva who was attached to the San Francisco presidio, traveled with the group to join her husband in California and brought along her daughters.[53]

While there may have been others, in September, 1781, Lieutenant Zúñiga claimed responsibility for only fifteen military families, eleven settler families, and two widows. Zúñiga's entire group had assembled in the inland town of Real de los Alamos following Commandant General Croix's detailed plan and Rivera's personal orders. They then departed for the Playa de Santa Bárbara at the mouth of the Río Mayo, here boats were to take them across the Gulf of California to Loreto.[54]

With so many civilian families in the party it was not easily organized. While most of the group departed Alamos for the coast on February 2, 1781, two sailors left earlier, perhaps to prepare a camp for the others, and settlers José Moreno and Antonio Miranda Rodríguez remained until February 16, perhaps in the company of another settler, Luis Quintero, who did not enlist until February 3, after most of the others had already departed.[55]

The settlers crossed the gulf and arrived in Loreto, Baja California, apparently bringing with them a smallpox epidemic which quickly spread throughout the entire peninsula. Most of the party seems to have stayed for some days in Loreto, perhaps in a quarantine camp. Then, on March 12, 1781, Ensign Laso took seventeen of the civilian and military families (probably the healthy ones) by ship up the gulf to the Bahía de San Luis. On April 24 they began the long march overland to San Gabriel.[56]

Lieutenant Zúñiga followed some days later with the remaining families. In the confusion Antonio Miranda Rodríguez and his daughter were left in Loreto. For a time it was thought that Rodriguez had deserted like Rafael Mesa and Miguel Villa, but word soon came that the poor fellow's daughter was recovering from smallpox and that he expected to continue the trip when she was well again.[57]

Considering the geographical isolation, communications between Upper and Lower California were surprisingly good. On April 16, 1781, Father Fermín Francisco Lasuén in San Diego reported that Zúñiga's party was on its way north with a total of 133 persons. His letter was written a full month before Governor Neve reported officially that Laso and part of the group was headed north from Bahía de San Luis, trailed by Zúñiga with the rest of the party. Before another month had passed, the first settlers arrived in San Gabriel.[58]

This June arrival date is definite from records dated March 22, 1782, that adjust the accounts of three settlers who were leaving Los Angeles. In words that speak of "this Mission" and "this destination," Lieutenant José Francisco Ortega, commandant of the proposed new presidio at Santa Barbara and the surrounding military district, reported that one Antonio Mesa had entered San Gabriel on "the ninth day of June, 1781."[59]

Apparently, at least three other settler families arrived with Mesa in June, and all settled quickly on their land. Father Francisco Palou, whose source was probably the priests at San Gabriel, relayed this information in much the same way as Lasuén reported on the progress of the settlers marching north from Bahía de San Luis. Very shortly after the information reached him, Palou probably sat down, as was his habit, and wrote the following account in his ongoing manuscript history of California: "There arrived first at San Gabriel the people who came by way of Old California, and as soon as part of them arrived he [Neve] gave them the order to found the projected town of Nuestra Señora de los Angeles with some four families [*unos cuatro familias*].... The rest of the troop was kept at San Gabriel Mission until the group arrived that came [overland] by way of the Colorado River."[60]

The exact date of Palou's entry has not been established, although historian Herbert E. Bolton has contended that each section of the manuscript was written soon after the event described.[61] Regardless, another of Palou's lengthy, undated entries about the presidios and missions of California must have been written soon after Los Angeles was founded and finished no later than the fall of 1782. In the manuscript Palou described the new pueblo: "*Town of Our Lady of the Angels*. About three leagues directly northwest [of San Gabriel] on the banks of the River named Porciúncula a town is started that had its beginning about June of 81. In it are established four families of people of reason and four soldiers of the escort."[62]

Some months later, in a similar but more extensive account of the missions and settlements of California, Palou repeated much the same information about the founding of Los Angeles. "This settlement," said Palou, "was started in June, 1781" He noted then, however, that there were eight families of settlers, rather than the original four who had come together on the site.[63]

These developments followed a certain logic, for Neve's own Reglamento provided that each settler be placed on the land just as soon as he arrived. According to this regulation each settler was entitled to 10 *pesos* a month in pay and 2 *reales* per day for rations, beginning at the time of his enlistment and ending when he was put in possession of his land. After that, salaries and rations were phased out by lowering the rates to 116 pesos 3½ reales per year for the first two years, then 60 pesos per year for the next three years, after which all payments ceased. Thus, as Neve explained, it was very much to the advantage of the government to put settlers on the land immediately so as to end the payment of salaries and rations at the high enlistment rate and start them on the five-year period of decreasing reimbursements.[64]

The names of the individuals and families who, with Antonio Mesa, established the settlement of Los Angeles on the banks of the River Porciúncula cannot be identified with certainty. Probably the widow Nicolasa Ramírez and soldier Guillermo Soto were in the first group, because they were known to have presented themselves at San Gabriel Mission on July 21 and asked to be married. They were accompanied by soldiers Augustín Leyba and Victorino Felix who testified that they were free to marry.[65]

On July 14, 1781, Lieutenant Diego Gonzales and Ensigns José Argüello and Cayetano Limón arrived at San Gabriel in command of the second party to arrive. This was the group that had trekked overland by way of the Colorado River with Rivera. (Rivera himself had remained in the Colorado River settlements with some of his soldiers and was murdered a few weeks later.) On July 22, 1781, more of the Los Angeles settlers arrived at San Gabriel, perhaps escorted by Ensign Josef Velásquez, sent from Monterey by Neve in March to help escort the Zúñiga party north.[66]

Included in the July 22 group were José Lara and Luis Quintero. Their exact arrival date in San Gabriel, like Antonio Mesa's, is established by the accounts prepared for them when they left the settlement of Los Angeles in March, 1782. For José Lara it was on "the 22nd of July 81 that he arrived at this destination." Similarly, for Luis Quintero it was "the 22nd of July of 81 that was his arrival date here."[67] (Fig. 2)

Did Lara and Quintero immediately move to the new townsite like the first families? The records are not clear. Palou implies that they did not, and their

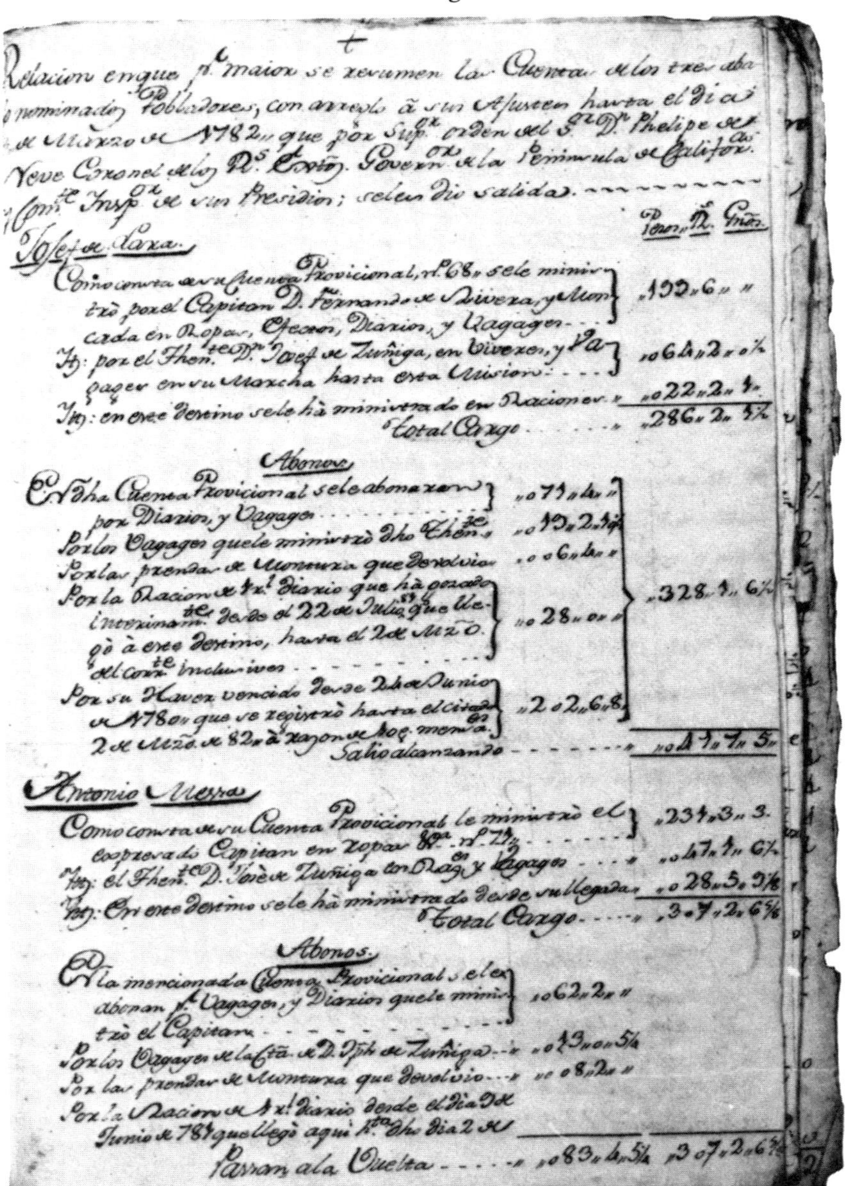

Relacion en que p.r maior se resumen las Cuentas de los tres abajo nominados Pobladores, con arreglo á sus Ajustes hasta el dia [illegible] de Marzo de 1782, que por Sup.or orden del S.or D.n Phelipe de Neve Coronel de los R.s Ex.tos Govern.or de la Peninsula de Californias y Com.te Insp.or de sus Presidios; se les dio salida.

Joseph de Lara — Pesos. R.s Gr.os

Como consta de su Cuenta Provicional, n.o 68, se le ministró por el Capitan D. Fernando de Rivera y Moncada en Ropas, Efectos, Diarios, y Bagages — 192, 6, "

Ytt: por el Then.te D.n Josef de Zuñiga, en Viveres, y Bagages en su Marcha hasta esta Mision — 064, 2, 0½

Ytt: en este destino se le hà ministrado en Raciones — 022, 2, 1

Total Cargo — 286, 2, 3½

Abonos

En d.ha Cuenta Provicional se le abonaron por Diarios, y Bagages — 077, 4, "

Por los Bagages que le ministró d.ho Then.te — 013, 2, 3½

Por las prendas de Montura que devolvió — 006, 4, "

Por la Racion de 4 r.s Diario que hà gozado interinam.te desde el 22 de Julio que llegó à este destino, hasta el 2 de Marzo del corr.te inclusives — 028, 0, "

Por su Haver vencido desde 2 de Junio de 1780, que se regisrtó hasta el citado 2 de Marzo de 82 à razon de 10 p.s mensuales — 202, 6, 8 — 328, 1, 6½

Salio alcanzando — 041, 7, 3

Antonio Mesa

Como consta de su Cuenta Provicional le ministró el expresado Capitan en Ropas [illegible] — 234, 3, 3

Ytt: el Then.te D. Josè de Zuñiga en Rac.s y Bagages — 047, 1, 6½

Ytt: En este destino se le hà ministrado desde su llegada — 028, 5, 9½

Total Cargo — 307, 2, 6½

Abonos.

En la mencionada Cuenta Provicional se le abonan p.r Bagages, y Diarios que le ministró el Capitan — 062, 2, "

Por los Bagages de la Cta. de D. Jph de Zuñiga — 043, 0, 5½

Por las prendas de Montura que devolvió — 008, 2, "

Por la Racion de 4 r.s Diario desde el Dia [illegible] Junio de 781 que llegó aqui h.ta d.ho dia 2 de [illegible]

Passan ala Buelta — 083, 4, 5½ — 307, 2, 6½

Figure 2. Lieutenant José Francisco Ortego adjured the accounts of departing settlers Mesa, Lara, and Quintero, and incidentally confirmed their arrival at Mission San Gabriel in June and July, 1871.

	Abonos	Cargo
Sumas dela Vuelta	083,,4,,5 1/6	307,,2,,[illegible]
Marzo que salio pagado	033,,3,,0	
Por su Haver vencido desde 4 de Junio de 1780 que se registrò hasta el citado 2 del corr.te Marzo à raz.n de 10 p.s mens.es	203,,3,,3 7/8	326,,2,,[illegible]
Salio alcanzando		042,,0,,2

Luis Quintero.

	Cargo
Por su Cuenta provicional n.o 76 consta le ministrò el Capitan D. Fernando de Rivera en ropas [illegible]	103,,7,,6
Ytt: el Ten.te D. Josè Zuñiga en Raziones, y Vagajes	034,,4,,3
Ytt: desde que llegò à este destino sele hà ministrado en Raciones	027,,2,,[illegible]
Total Cargo	191,,6,,[illegible]

Abona.

En su referida Cuenta provicional se le abonan p.s Diarios	002,,0,,	
Porlos Vagajes que le ministrò D. Josef de Zuñiga	013,,2,,4	
Por las prestas de moneda q. devolviò	007,,3,,	
Por 1 r.l Diario del goze (interino) de Raz.on desde el 22 de Julio de 81 que fue su llegada à esta, hasta el 2 del corr.te Marzo que lo es oy	028,,0,,	185,,7,,[illegible]
Por su Haver desde 3 de febrero de 781 q.e se registrò hasta el precitado 2 del Marzo del corr.te à razon de 10 p.s mensales	129,,1,,5 1/2	
Salio deviendo		005,,7,,[illegible]

Resumen Gral.

Cargos	785,,3,,1 7/8
Abonos	840,,3,,6 3/4
Total Alcanzes	055,,0,,4 7/8

Como manifiesta este Resumen asienden las Subministrac.s hechas à estos tres Individuos setecientos ochenta, y cinco p.s tres r.s Uno, y siete octavos granos, que deducidos de ochocientos quarenta p.s tres r.s seis, y tres quartos g.s resulta el Total Alcanze de Cinq.ta y cinco p.s q.tro. y siete octabos g.s San Gabriel 22 de Marzo de 1782.

Joseph Fran.co de Ortega

ARCHIVE GENERAL DE LA NACION [MEXICO CITY] PROVINCIAS

own accounts seem to support this interpretation.

A document prepared at Los Angeles on February 4, 1816, by Guillermo Soto offers evidence, however, that at least two other settlers received their allotments of planting fields in August, 1781, and had taken up residence at the new townsite. Titled "A list that shows the Settlers, Retired Soldiers, and Inhabitants with an Account of their entrance in this Pueblo," the document indicates that Manuel Camero and Basilio Rosas arrived in the new town in August, 1781, and received two *suertes* of land.[68]

In mid-August, the eighteenth to be exact, another party of straggling soldiers and settlers – the group led by Lieutenant Zúñiga – arrived at San Gabriel. Because some members of the party were still recovering from smallpox, Zúñiga had them temporarily quarantined a short distance away from the mission before sending them on to the site of the new town.[69]

A week or so later, Governor Neve, probably eager to make legal existing conditions, ordered that house lots in town and planting fields outside the town be marked off and distributed to the settlers. (San Gabriel Mission records noted that the town of Los Angeles "immediately adjoined" Yabit. But the area was not merely near Yabit; it was almost on top of it). Neve's original order is not extant, but copies and translations support the conclusion that settlers had been dispatched to build homes on the townsite even before Neve ordered the formal distribution of lots and fields.[70]

While Lieutenant José Darío Argüello some years later claimed that he had been "commissioned in the year 81 by Don Felipe de Neve, then governor California, to found the town with the title Queen of the Angels, and he founded it,"[71] no contemporary record supporting his statement has yet come to light. Argüello also maintained that he served for several months in the Colorado River settlements, an unlikely possibility. These statements are from his *hoja de servicio* or service record which was prepared in 1790 and signed by Pedro Fages, who a year later made some fanciful claims in his own hoya de servicio.[72]

Most accounts of the founding of Los Angeles argue for the presence of a military escort – a corporal and three private soldiers – as well as claiming that a formal founding ceremony occurred. The only basis for this assertion, however, is a heavily condensed version of the founding contained in Father Palou's biography of Junípero Serra. Interestingly, the same historians who accept Palou's story as proof of a foundation ceremony complete with military escort entirely reject the rest of Palou's account. In fact, it is not entirely clear from the passage that Palou meant to imply anything of the sort. The brevity of his reference to a corporal and three soldiers may merely indicate that a military escort of this composition lived in the town after its establishment.[73]

While some small ceremony may have marked the birth of Los Angeles, no definite archival record of it appears to exist. Nor is there a document suggesting that Zúñiga's eleven settler families gathered to participate in a formal distribution of land. In fact, the records seem to indicate that some settlers did not move to Los Angeles from San Gabriel for several weeks, while others moved to the land immediately after arriving.

Financial records drawn up by Zúñiga and his assistants at San Gabriel in September, 1781, supply the names of the residents in Los Angeles in that month. These records, the earliest original reports documenting the founding of the town, list six resident settlers and their families at Los Angeles at the date the statements of account were prepared: Basilio Rosas and family, Antonio Mesa and family, Antonio Villavicencio and family, José Banegas and family, Alejandro Rosas and wife, and Pablo Rodríguez and family. Each settler's account notes that "he is presently living as a citizen in the Town of the Queen of the Angels" (*queda avezindado en el Pueblo de la Reyna de los Angeles*).[74]

Probably at least one other individual was also in Los Angeles, though he was not counted as a citizen or a resident. José Lara, who had "fallen ill in the Town of the Queen of the Angeles,"[75] has found he was not cut out to be a farmer and badly wanted to leave the town.

Whether other settlers had arrived at Los Angeles in September is not clear. Historian Henry Raup Wagner, who reviewed most of the accounts that read *queda avezindado*, believed that the phrase implied citizenship but not necessarily residence.[76] A letter written by Commandant General Croix to José de Gálvez, which cites a communication from Neve dated November 19, 1781, may confirm Wagner's interpretation. In the letter Croix said that Neve "formally certified the establishment of the town" on September 4, 1781, with a portion of the settlers recruited by Rivera. He went on to say that the town had twelve *vecinos*, with a total of forty-six persons in all.[77] (Fig. 3)

The Croix letter seems to quote the *padron del vecindario* submitted by Neve on November 19 and apparently now extant only in the summary prepared by the copyist employed by historian Bancroft and in an 1872 newspaper reprint version. That summary stated that the town was founded on September 4, 1781, listed twelve householders, noted that one still remained in Loreto, and said that the lands and goods of the missing settler were being held for his arrival.[78]

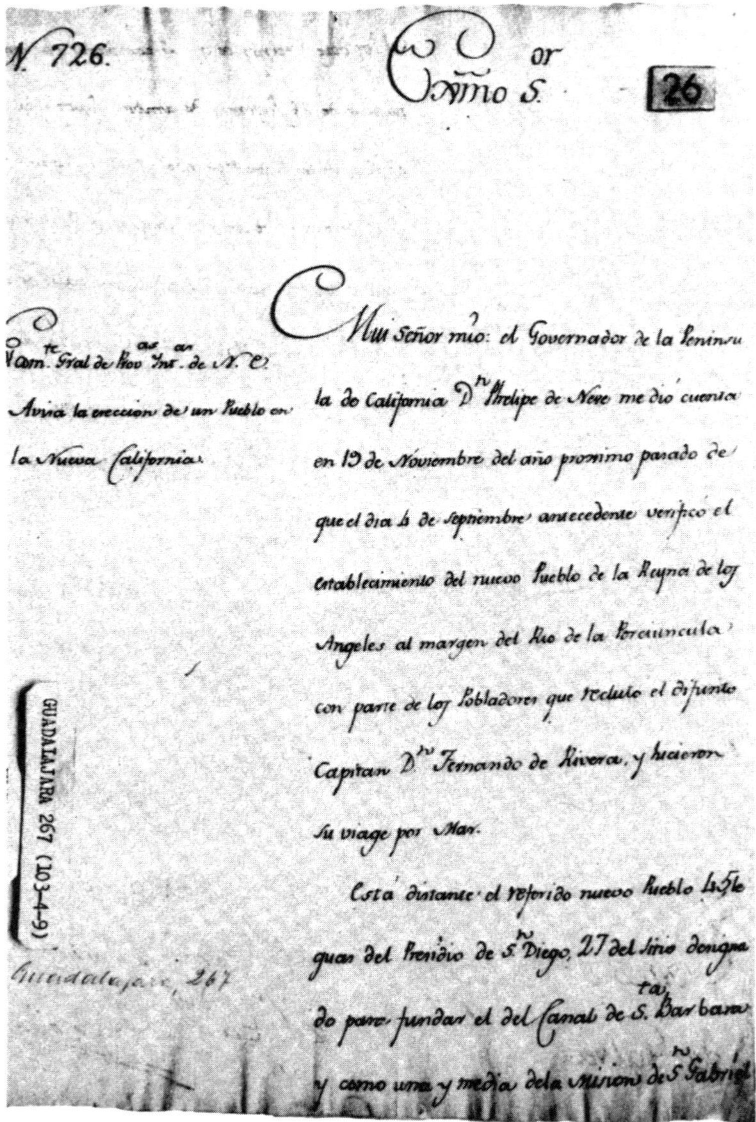

N. 726. Exmo S.or 26

El Com.te Gral de Prov.as Int.as de N. E.

Avisa la ereccion de un Pueblo en la Nueva California.

Mui Señor mio: el Governador de la Peninsula de California D.n Phelipe de Neve me dió cuenta en 19 de Noviembre del año proximo pasado de que el dia 4 de Septiembre antecedente verificó el establecimiento del nuevo Pueblo de la Reyna de los Angeles al margen del Rio de la Porciuncula con parte de los Pobladores que reclutó el difunto Capitan D.n Fernando de Rivera, y hicieron su viage por Mar.

Está distante el referido nuevo Pueblo 45 leguas del Presidio de S.n Diego, 27 del sitio designado para fundar el del Canal de S.ta Barbara y como una y media dela Mision de S.n Gabriel

FIGURE 3. Commandant-General Teodore de Croix wrote José de Gálvez, Viceroy of New Spain (Mexico), that Governor Felipe de Neve "formally certified the establishment of the town," meaning Los Angeles, on September 4, 1781, with a portion of the settlers that had been recruited by Fernando de Rivera y Moncada.

27

A los doze Vecinos de que se componen, y hacen el
numero de 46 Personas de ambos Sexos y de todas
edades se les han repartido Mulas, Yeguas, Ba
cas, Becerros, obejas, y Cabras. Suerte de tierra de
cultivo, y utensilios de labranza; con calidad de
reintegro á Real Hacienda estos y los Ganados:
cuyas noticias traslado á V.E. para que se sirva
hacerlas presentes á S.M. y prevenirme sus sobe
ranas resoluciones.

Nuestro S.or guarde á V.E. muchos
años Arispe 28 de Febrero de 1782.

Ex.mo Señor

B.l.M. de V.E. su mas
at.to seg.ro servidor
El Cav.ro De Croix

Ex.mo S.or D.n Joseph de Galvez

Thus, Croix counted one man as a resident who was still a thousand miles away from Los Angeles.

Regardless, all the settlers, except still-absent Miranda Rodríguez, seem to have been in Los Angeles by the end of October. A communication sent by Neve to Croix on October 29 stated that all eleven settlers and families were "in the process of founding the town" and had moved to the townsite, although only eight of the settlers were "useful." In this letter Neve spoke glowingly of the sturdy little huts the people were building for themselves, the irrigation ditch they had completed, and the fields they were planting.[79]

(The prospects of Los Angeles' survival did not look so good a year later when Neve readied to leave California to assume his promotion to inspector general of the Interior Provinces. On that occasion Neve warned the new governor, Pedro Pages, that these settlers needed firm supervision. The first wheat harvest had produced only two-thirds the amount expected, and the corn crop failed because the settlers neglected to irrigate the young plants.)[80]

The presence of the eleven settler families in Los Angeles was definitely confirmed by the padron del vecindario taken November 19, 1781. Another document drawn up by Lieutenant Ortega two weeks later stated that all eleven families were on the site and drawing pay and rations accordingly.[81]

And so, nearly two centuries ago and quite inauspiciously, began the new town of Los Angeles. Governor Neve had selected the site in the early spring of 1781 – a beautiful spot beside the Porciúncula River already inhabited by Indians of the ranchería called Yabit.

The first small settler parties from Mexico arrived in June, July, and August of 1781, although it was September 4, 1781, before the governor formally established the town. Within a few weeks all eleven families had taken up residence, but three of them departed again the following March, apparently without having contributed much toward civic betterment.

Similarly, San José was settled by small parties before formal recognition was accorded the founding of the town. Settlers moved to the site in early November, 1777, though a formal founding event did not take place until November 29. Other settlers apparently wandered in weeks after the original group had arrived and after the "foundation" had been accomplished.[82]

It is noteworthy that the ramifications of the revised analysis concerning the events surrounding the establishment of Los Angeles include restoration of the reputation of the almost universally discredited first historian of Upper

California, Francisco Palou. Palou's description of the founding of the town on the Río Porciúncula, written soon after the events themselves, reads: "The [governor] gathered all the settlers that had come as colonists, assigned them building sites and fields on the banks of the River about four leagues northwest of San Gabriel Mission, and there escorted by a corporal and three soldiers, they founded their town in the last months of the year [*a ultimos del año*] of 81 with the title Our Lady of the Angels of Porciúncula." [sic][83]

Condensing several months activity by numbers of people into one sentence, that is just about the way it happened.

NOTES

1. J.J. Warner, Benjamin Hayes, J.P. Widney, *An Historical Sketch of Los Angeles County, California* (Los Angeles, 1876), p. 11. See also Hubert Howe Bancroft, *History of California* (7 vols.; San Francisco, 1886–90); I:44; *An Illustrated History of Southern California* (Chicago, 1890), p. 730.

Although the sources quoted in this article employ a number of variations in the name of Los Angeles, only one official name was given to the town when it was established, *La Reyna de los Angeles*. See Theodore E. Treutlein, "Los Angeles, California: The Question of the City's Original Spanish Name," *Southern California Quarterly*, LV (Spring 1973): 1–7.

2. Warner, *Historical Sketch of Los Angeles*, 11; *La Cronica* (Los Angeles), May 18, 1872, p. 2.

3. *Los Angeles City and County Directory* 1872, pp. 19–20.

4. Some historians, mostly Franciscan scholars, accept Palou's account. See Zephyrin Engelhardt, *The Missions and Missionaries of California* (4 vols.; San Francisco, 1912), II:366–67. See also Maynard J. Geiger, *The Life and Times of Fray Junípero Serra, O.F.M.; or, The Man who Never Turned Back (1713–1784)* (2 vols.; Washington, D.C., 1959), II:270–71; and Geiger (trans. & ed.), *Palóu's Life of Fray Junípero Serra* (Washington, D.C., 1955), pp. 218, 459, n15. For a Franciscan scholar who does not agree with Palou, see Antonine Tibesar (ed.), *Writings of Junípero Serra* (4 vols.; Washington, D.C., 1966), IV:404, 446, n152.

5. Bancroft, *History of California*, I:345, n24.

6. See, for example, J.M. Gunn, *Historical and Biographical Record of Los Angeles and Vicinity* (Chicago, 1901), p. 34. See also *Illustrated History of Los Angeles*, 48. One of the most fanciful accounts was written by Helen Hunt Jackson, "Echoes in the City of the Angels," *Century Magazine*, XXVII (December 1883): 194–210.

7. Temple, "Se Fundaron un Pueblo de Espanoles," Historical Society of Southern California *Annual Publications*, XV, pt. I (1931): 69–98 (hereafter HSSC *Annual*).

8. Neve reached San Gabriel on April 11, according to a letter from Fermín Francisco de Lasuén to Francisco Pangua, April 16, 1781, in Finbar Kenneally (ed.), *Writings of Fermín Francisco de Lasuén* (2 vols.; Washington, D.C., 1965): I:79.

9. Juan Crespí, "*Diario y Caminata que hizo esta dha Expedicion de este Puerto y Nueva Mision del Sr San Diego de Alcala, en 14 Julio 1769 hacia Monte Rey*," Coleccion de Documentos para Historia de Mexico, Primera Serie, Tomo 2, Misiones de Alta California, fo. 65–66, Archivo General de la Nacion, Mexico City (hereafter, AGN). The name of the Indian town appears in numerous places in the San Gabriel baptismal register. In this article, quotations are spelled and accented as they appear in the original. Spanish names not in quotations are accented in their modern form.

10. Croix to Rivera, December 27, 1779, reprinted in HSSC *Annual*, XV, Pt. I (1931); 192, 257. San Gabriel Mission, baptismal register, vol. I, entries 583–86, 588–606, 615, 634–35, 641–48, 712, 732–33; San Gabriel marriage register, entry 135; microfilm at the Huntington Library, San Marino, California.

11. Engelhardt, *Missions and Missionaries*, II:350ff; Edwin A. Beilharz, *Felipe de Neve, First Governor of California* (San Francisco: California Historical Society, 1971), pp. 94–96; Bancroft, *History of California*, I:374–75, 379–81, 398–99; Tibesar, *Writings of Serra*, IV:440–41, n81; Serra to Pangua, July 17, 1782, ibid., pp. 153–55.

12. HSSC *Annual*, XV, Pt. I (1931):248, 257.

13. Serra to Pangua, July 17, 1782, in Tibesar, *Writings of Serra*, IV:153; Geiger, *Palóu's Life of Serra*, 229, 231–33; Francisco Palou, *Relacion Historica de la Vida y Apostolicas Tareas del Venerable Padre Fray Junípero Serra* (Mexico: Felipe de Zúñiga y Ontiveros, 1787), Huntington Library, rare book 57251 (cited hereafter as *Vida*).

14. The financial records of the expedition were reconstructed from notes and memory at San Gabriel following the destruction of the original records in the massacre of Rivera, his soldiers, and the Spanish inhabitants of the new missions and settlements along the Colorado River. These records, cited in footnotes 15–33, 35–38, and 40–53, are in *Provincias Internas*, Tomos 198 and 199, AGN.

15. *Cuenta* 68, *Provincias Internas*, Tomo 199, fo. 167–68.

16. *Cuenta* 69, Tomo 199, fo. 171–72.

17. *Cuenta* 70, Tomo 199, fo. 169–70.

18. *Cuenta* 71, Tomo 199, fo. 173–74.

19. *Cuenta* 72, Tomo 199, fo. 175–76. Their daughter, María Gerónima, was the first girl born after the settlers reached San Gabriel. See the San Gabriel baptismal register, vol. I, entry 749, October 3, 1781.

20. *Cuenta* 73, Tomo 199, fo. 177–78.

21. Ibid., fo. 179–80. Their son José Antonio was the first boy born after the settlers reached San Gabriel. See the San Gabriel baptismal register, vol. I, entry 793, November 18, 1781.

22. *Cuenta* 75, Tomo 199, fo. 181–82.

23. *Cuenta* 76, Tomo 199, fo. 183–84.

24. Cuenta 77, Tomo 199, fo. 185–86.

25. Cuenta 78, Tomo 199, fo. 187–88.

26. Cuenta 80, Tomo 199, fo. 189–90.

27. Cuenta 82, Tomo 198, fo. 170.

28. Cuenta 83, Tomo 198, fo. 165.

29. Cuenta 55, Tomo 199, fo. 28.

30. Cuenta 79, Tomo 199, fo. 34–35.

31. Cuenta 80, Tomo 199, fo. 189.

32. Cuenta 82, Tomo 198, fo. 170–172; San Diego Mission marriage register, entries 217 and 218, microfilm in the Huntington Library.

33. Cuenta 83, Tomo 199, fo. 165, AGN; San Gabriel marriage register, entry 139.

34. "Padron del Vecindario que Tiene el Pueblo de Sn. Joseph fundado el 29 de Noviembre de 1777," Provincias Internas, Tomo 121, fo. 19–20. Typed copy in the Huntington Library, MSS HM16781.

35. Cuenta 55, Tomo 199, fo. 28; Manuel Roiz, "Nota de los Soldados," July 15, 1780, Provincias Internas, Tomo 198, fo. 102.

36. Cuenta 79, Tomo 199, fo. 34–35.

37. Cuenta 81, Tomo 198, fo. 171.

38. Ibid.

39. Neve to Croix, May 16, 1781, California Archives, Provincial Records, State Papers, CA 22, Tomo II, 299, Bancroft Library (hereafter, CA).

40. Cuenta 23, Provincias Internas, Tomo 199, fo. 117–18.

41. Cuenta 35, Tomo 199, fo. 47–48.

42. Cuenta 36, Tomo 199, fo. 139–40.

44. Cuenta 38, Tomo 199, fo. 141–42.

45. Cuenta 40, Tomo 199, fo. 143–44.

46. Cuenta 41, Tomo 199, fo. 145–46.

47. Cuenta 42, Tomo 199, fo. 147–48.

48. Cuenta 44, Tomo 199, fo. 149–50.

49. Cuenta 45, Tomo 199, fo. 41–43.

50. Cuenta 46, Tomo 199, fo. 151–52.

51. Cuenta 49, Tomo 199, fo. 157–58.

52. Cuenta 50, Tomo 199, fo. 159–60.

53. Cuenta 85, Tomo 199, fo. 62.

54. José de Zúñiga, September 30, 1781, *Provincias Internas*, Tomo 198, fo. 171. In his report Zúñiga apparently counted only those individuals for whose pay and allowances he was responsible on that date. Thus, he omitted Antonio Miranda Rodríguez and his daughter, since they were the responsibility of officials at Loreto. The oldest daughter of Pedro Pablo Rodríguez was counted as a widow, since she was an unattached female with a dependent brother and sister, while Nicolasa Ramírez, a genuine widow, was not counted because her expenses were assumed by the soldier she married. María Pasquala Silva appeared as a widow for somewhat the same reason as the Rodríguez women. While confusing today, this enumeration proved equally confusing to the officers who had to reconstruct these records after the originals were destroyed in the Yuma massacre. Croix to Rivera, December 27, 1799, HSSC *Annual*, XV, Pt. I (1931): 260; Beilharz, *Felipe de Neve*, 106–07. The *cuentas* or accounts of the various soldiers and settlers name these major stopping places.

55. See the *cuentas* of the members of the party, especially the following: *Provincias Internas, cuentas* no. 23, fo. 117–18; no. 35, fo. 47–48; no. 76, fo. 183–84; no. 78, fo. 187–88; and no. 80, fo. 189–90, AGN.

56. Luis Sales, *Noticias de la Provincia de Californias* (Valencia, 1794), Carta I: p. 94–95 (Copy in the Huntington Library, rare book 9292). Neve to Croix, May 16, 1781, CA 22, Tomo II, 299, see note 39).

57. Neve to Croix, May 16, 1781, CA 22, Tomo II, 299; "*Padron del vecindario, el qe. tiene el pueblo de la Reyna de los Angeles*," November 19, 1781, CA 52, Tomo I, 102.

58. Lasuén to Pangua, April, 6, 1781, in *Writings of Lasuén*, 79; Neve to Croix, May 16, 1781, CA 22, Tomo II, 299.

59. Ortega, "*Relacion en que pa. maior se resumen las Cuentas de los tres abajo nominados Pobladores*," March 22, 1782, *Provincias Internas*, Tomo 198, fo. 207, AGN. See also the San Gabriel marriage register, entry 140, which lists Mesa as one of the *testigos* for a young couple who appeared at San Gabriel Mission on August 8 to be married. I am indebted to William M. Mason for directing me to this entry.

60. Palou, *Noticias de la California* (San Francisco: California Historical Society, 1874), IV:237, Huntington Library, rare book 500. The location of Palou's original manuscript is unknown. A copy prepared about 1790 is in AGN; a microfilm of this copy is in the Bancroft Library. Palou had probably never seen any of the official documents founding the town and therefore assumed it was named as Crespí had written.

61. Bolton, *Historical Memoirs of New California* (4 vols.; Berkeley; 1926), I:lxx. Interestingly, Bolton translates a key phrase in Palou's account, *unos quatro familias*, as "a few families." See vol. IV:209.

62. Palou, "*Noticia succinta de las 9. Miss., i 3 Presids. de la Nueva California*," *Documentos para Historia de Mexico*, Ser. II, Tomo XV, fo. 261–62, AGN. Father Serra thought the phrase *gente de razón*, or people of reason, ridiculous, complaining that the soldiers and settlers used the phrase "just as if the Indians did not have the use of reason too." Serra

to Pangua, December 8, 1782, in Tibesar, *Writings of Serra*, IV:169.

63. Palou, "*Remark's on a New Custody in California*," in Tibesar, *Writings of Serra*, IV:404.

64. Beilharz, *Felipe de Neve*, 88; HSSC *Annual*, XV, Pt. I (1931): 181, 249.

65. San Gabriel marriage register, entry 139.

66. Neve to Croix, July 14, 1781, CA 22, Tomo II, 304–05; Provincial State Papers, Benicia Military, II:142, Bancroft Library, cited in Temple, HSSC *Annual*, XV, pt. I (1931):84.

67. Ortega, "*Relacion... de los tres... Pobladores*," March 22, 1782, *Provincias Internas*, Tomo 198, fo. 207, AGN.

68. I am indebted to William M. Mason for directing me to this document, a copy of which is at the Huntington Library, fac 667 (603). The original is in the De la Guerra Collection of the Santa Barbara Mission Archive – Library. A *suerte* is a farm lot within the bounds of a pueblo.

69. Neve to Croix, October 29, 1781, CA 22, Tomo II, 306–07. Another document indicates that at least part of the group may have arrived August 16. See the *cuenta* of José Antonio Cortés, November 18, 1781, *Provincias Internas*, Tomo 198, fo. 363. AGN.

70. Bancroft, *History of California*, I:344–45 notes. San Gabriel baptismal register, entry 969, describes Yabit as "*immediata al Pueblo*."

71. Quoted in Martin de Landaeta, *Noticias acerca del Puerto de San Francisco* (*Alta California*), notes by Jose C. Valades (Mexico, 1949), p. 23, n17.

72. Fages' service record appears in *Californias*, Tomo XLVI, fo. 192, AGN, accompanied by a signed résumé by Fages dated February 4, 1792.

73. Palou, *Vida*, 243. Most historians accept the account of the founding of the city given by Thomas Workman Temple II in HSSC *Annual*, XV, Pt. I (1931):90, 96–98.

74. *Cuentas* no. 70, fo. 169–71; no. 71, fo. 173–74; no. 72, fo. 175–76; no. 73, fo. 177–78; no. 74, fo. 179–80; no. 75, fo. 181–82, *Provincias Internas*, Tomo, 199, AGN.

75. *Cuenta* 68, Tomo 199, fo. 167–68.

76. Henry R. Wagner, *The Earliest Documents of El Pueblo de Nuestra Señora de Los Angeles* (Los Angeles, 1931), pp. 3–4.

77. Croix to Gálvez, February 28, 1782, *Audiencia de Guadalajara*, legajo 103–4–9, *Archivo General de Indias*, microfilm Roll IV, reel 899, Bancroft Library. The letter is number 4518 in Charles E. Chapman, *Catalogue of Materials in the Archivo General de Indias* (Berkeley: University of California Press, 1919), p. 551. *Vecinos* are inhabitants or neighbors.

78. CA 52, Tomo I, fo. 101–02. J.J. Warner's slightly variant copy of this document is reprinted in *La Cronica* (Los Angeles), May 18, 1872, p. 2. I am indebted to Donald Chaput for calling my attention to this newspaper article. *Padron del vecindario* is a census or number of inhabitants in a given place.

79. CA 22, Tomo, II, fo. 306–07.

80. Neve to Fages, "*Ynstruccion reservada que dejó el Brigador Don Felipe de Neve a su subsesor en el Govierno de Californias Dn Pedro de Fages*," September 7, 1782; a copy. The *Provincinas Internas* was established by the Spanish government as a defensive measure against foreign encroachment or Indian depredations on the northern most frontier of New Spain (Mexico). Formally established on August 22, 1776, the first commandant general was Teodore de Croix who served from 1777 to 1784. Later the jurisdiction was divided into two commands, East and West. The *Provincias Occidente* (West) included Sinaloa, Sonora, California, North Viscaya, and New Mexico, with headquarters at Arispe, Sonora.

81. José Francisco de Ortega, "*Extracto de la Revista*," CA 52, Tomo I, fo. 104–05.

82. Bancroft, *History of California*, I:312, 348–49; Palou, *Vida*, 225; Palou, *Noticias*, IV:204.

83. Palou, *Vida*, p. 243. Maynard Geiger offers a concise and reasoned explanation of the meaning of the phrase "*a ultimos del año*" in *Palóu's Life of Fray Junípero Serra*, 459, n15.

Soldiers and Settlers of the Expedition of 1781

BY THOMAS WORKMAN TEMPLE II

As some of the members of this famous expedition were the founders and first settlers of the City of los Angeles, it becomes a matter of historical importance to know who and what they were, whence they came, and the imprint they left upon the land of their adoption. They were a diverse ethnic group — a mixture of Spanish, African, and Indian heritage. They founded the pueblo in 1781, today one of the great metropolises of the world. The complete list of these pioneers follows. The particulars concerning the families were taken from the mission registers at San Gabriel, San Buenaventura, and Santa Barbara, and from the manuscript copies in the Bancroft Library of the Spanish Archives of California, destroyed by the San Francisco fire of 1906, an end result of the earthquake that struck the city on April 18. In giving the members of the families, we enumerate only the children accompanying the expedition. Many more were born later.

During the rather uneventful early history of the pueblo, Vicente Felix, corporal of the guard, was the outstanding personality and guiding spirit. Lara, Mesa (Antonio), and Quintero had been declared unfit on their arrival with the rest of the settlers, but not until March 21, 1782, were they officially expelled from the young settlement, forfeiting their lands, stock, and other government aid. When the expedition to found the Presidio de Santa Bárbara left San Gabriel on the following day, Lara and Quintero joined the party and settled at the presidio. Of Mesa no other trace has been found in the mission records.

When Ortega reported on conditions to the governor in December of that year, there were but eight *pobladores*[1] living in the infant pueblo. Antonio Miranda Rodríguez was still absent in Loreto. Another poblador, Rafael Mesa,

1. Settler

seems to have been apprehended after deserting in Sonora and brought to California. Ortega, having received papers of his enlistment as a settler, December 2, 1782, forbade his joining the Santa Barbara Company, then still in the process of being formed.

In 1783, Governor Pedro Fages had to exclude the poblador Antonio Miranda Rodríguez since he was still in Baja California. The Presidio de Santa Bárbara furnished two of the pueblo guards, San Diego furnishing the other two members. Ygnácio Rochin was the new guard in 1784, Francisco Lugo, also of the Presidio de Santa Bárbara, still being on duty. That same year, Josef Francisco Sinoba, a soldier of the first expedition who had joined the San Francisco Company in 1776, asked to be brought into the pueblo as a settler. March 12, 1785, he was taken in, being granted lots, implements, and stock without, however, enjoying rations and pay. Juan Josef Domínguez, also a veteran of 1769, was a neighbor of the pueblo in 1785, having been granted the Rancho San Pedro by Fages. Other neighbors who figure prominently in the records were Manuel Pérez Nieto and Josef María Verdugo, also veterans of the 1769 expedition.

When it came time to confirm title to the settlers in September of 1786, only eight remained of the original group of fourteen listed below.

POBLADORES DE EL PUEBLO DE LOS ANGELES

1 ANTONIO CLEMENTE FÉLIZ VILLAVICENCIO, 30, native of Chiguagua [Chihuahua], was the first poblador to answer the call. He enlisted at la Villa Sinaloa, Sonora, May 30, 1780. His wife was MARÍA DE LOS SANTOS SEFERINA, 26, a native of el Real de Batopila, in the Archbishopric of Durango. They brought an adopted daughter.

MARÍA ANTONIA JOSEFA PIÑUELAS, 8, native of la Villa de Sinaloa, child of Francisco Piñuelas, deceased, and María Alcaraz, of said villa. She married Vicente Quijada, a soldier of the expedition and widower of Juana Mendoza, on January 20, 1785, at Misión San Gabriel. In the census of the pueblo for 1785, he is designated as a laborer and five years later as a *vaquero*.[2]

2 ANTONIO MESA, 38, a native of los Alamos, Sonora, enlisted at la Villa Sinaloa June 4, 1780. His wife, MARÍA ANA GERTRUDIS LÓPEZ, 27, was born at the same place. They brought two children.

2. Herdsman or cowboy

ANTONIO MARÍA, 8.

MARÍA PAULA, 10.

This was one of the families expelled from the pueblo March 21, 1782, some six months after its founding, and I find no further trace of them thereafter.

3 RAFAEL MESA, a native of los Alamos, enlisted June 12, 1780, but deserted on October 10 of the same year. He did not come with the expedition but seems to have been apprehended and brought to California later. He claimed to have enlisted as a soldier, but Lieutenant Ortega excluded him from the Santa Barbara Company on the grounds of his having deserted as a poblador (on December 2, 1781). There is no evidence that he remained in California nor that he was a brother of Antonio Mesa, above.

4 JOSEF FERNANDO DE VELASCO Y LARA, 50, was a native of the port of Cadiz, Spain; his wife, MARÍA ANTONIA CAMPOS, 23, a native of la Villa de Sinaloa. He served as a *padrino*[3] for the Indian neophytes confirmed by Fray Junípero Serra at San Gabriel, on March 22 and 25, 1782. This was, incidentally, Serra's first visit to the young pueblo. He spent the night of March 18 at the village, which he endearingly called la Porciúncula. Lara enlisted at la Villa de Sinaloa June 24, 1780. On March 21, 1782, he was expelled from the pueblo and joined the expedition to establish the Presidio de Santa Bárbara on March 26, 1782. He died there shortly afterwards, and his widow then married Luis Gonzaga Lugo, a soldier of the presidio and a veteran of 1769. Three children came with them.

JOSEF JULIÁN, 4, married María Antonia Moreno, daughter of the pobladores Josef Moreno and Guadalupe Pérez, at Santa Barbara.

MARÍA JUANA DE JESÚS, 6, married Nicolás Felipe, son of Josef Xavier Cortes, deceased, and María Nicolasa Ramírez, of the same expedition, at Santa Barbara.

MARÍA FAUSTINA, 2, was born at Cozala. She was married at Santa Barbara to Josef Francisco Solórzano, a native of Acapulco and a soldier at the presidio.

Their only child born in California, JOSEF YGNÁCIO MATEO, was baptized October 30, 1782, at the Presidio de Santa Bárbara, the second white child to be so honored.

3. Godfather

5 JOSEF VANEGAS, 28, was a native of el Real de Bolaños, Durango. His wife, MARÍA BONIFACIA MÁXIMA AGUILAR, 20, was a native of el Real del Rosario, Sinaloa, where Vanegas enlisted on August 11, 1780. One child accompanied them.

COSME DAMIEN, was but a year old. He married María Bernarda Alvarez y Marquez, widow of Josef Máximo Rosas, at San Gabriel on July 8, 1798.

Vanegas was the first alcalde of the new Pueblo de los Angeles, serving in 1786–88 and 1796. His wife was buried at San Gabriel on January 4, 1801.

6 PABLO RODRÍGUEZ, 25, was a native of el Real de Santa Rosa, Sinaloa, and his wife, MARÍA ROSALÍA NORIEGA, 26, a native of el Real del Rosario, where he enlisted August 13, 1780. There was one child.

MARÍA ANTONIA, one year old, later married Juan Patricio Ontiveros, son of Josef Ontiveros and Ana María Carrasco, natives of Chametla, Sinaloa, and members of the same expedition, on June 1, 1794, at Misión San Gabriel.

Rodríguez was *mayordomo*[4] of the Misión San Diego in 1807, after retiring from the pueblo. His wife died May 8, 1824 and was buried at San Gabriel.

7 MANUEL CAMERO, 30, was a native of el Real del Rosario, Sinaloa. His wife, MARÍA THOMASA GARCÍA, 24, was born at the same place, where he enlisted August 19, 1780. They brought no children with them and none seem to have been born to them in California. Camero was a *regidor*[5] of the pueblo in 1789, along with Felipe Santiago García, a veteran of 1774. Josef Francisco Sinoba, who became a settler in 1784, was the alcalde. Camero was buried at San Gabriel, May 31, 1819.

8 JOSEF ANTONIO NAVARRO, 42, a native of el Real del Rosario, enlisted August 21, 1780. His wife, also born at Rosario, was MARÍA REGINA DOROTEA GLORIA DE SOTO Y RODRÍGUEZ, 47. There were three children.

JOSEF MARÍA EDUARDO, 10, died single.

JOSEF CLEMENTE, 9, married María del Carmen Rochín May 15, 1791, at San Gabriel. She was a daughter of Ygnácio Rochín and Ana María Bojorquez, members of the same expedition and natives of los Alamos, Sonora. Clemente

4. Majordomo or steward
5. Councilman

was a soldier of the Presidio de Santa Bárbara, where most of his children were born.

MARÍANA JOSEFA, 4, accompanied her father to the Presidio de San Francisco before 1790. She was married at the Misión Santa Clara on October 30, 1791, to Juan Josef Higuera, son of Manuel Higuera and Antonia Redondo, pobladores of the Pueblo de San Josef de Guadalupe. Navarro, who was a tailor by trade, died at San Francisco September 3, 1793.

MARÍA REGINA SOTO, Spanish, died February 17, 1785, at San Gabriel.[6] She doubtless was the wife of Navarro, above.

9 JOSEF MORENO, 22, was a native of Rosario, Sinaloa, where he enlisted September 2, 1780, and where his wife, MARÍA GUADALUPE GERTRUDIS PÉREZ, 19, also was born. No children accompanied them, but eight children were baptized later at Misión San Gabriel. Moreno died May 10, 1806, and was buried at Misión San Gabriel.

10 JOSEF ANTONIO BASILIO ROSAS, 67, was a native of Fresnillo, in the Archbishopric of Durango. His wife, MARÍA MANUELA CALISTRA HERNÁNDEZ, 43, was a native of Rosario, where he enlisted September 6, 1780. Rosas died November 15, 1809, and his wife, May 18, 1823. They brought seven children with them.

ALEJANDRO ROSAS, 19, himself a poblador.

JOSEF MÁXIMO, 15, a native of Rosario, married María Antonia of the Jajamobit *ranchería*,[7] on January 7, 1785, at San Gabriel. He later married Ma. Bernarda Alvarez y Marquez, February 11, 1794, San Diego.

JOSEF CARLOS, 12, married María Dolores of the Yabit ranchería, adjacent to the pueblo, on July 4, 1784, at San Gabriel.

ANTONIO ROSALINO, 7, married María Petra Máxima Lugo, daughter of Luis Gonzaga Lugo and María Antonia Campos, on May 23, 1802, at Misión Santa Bárbara.

JOSEF MARCELINO, 4, married María Vejar of the Cahuepet ranchería, on January 14, 1796, at San Gabriel.

JUAN ESTEBAN, 2, married María Josefa Alvarez, daughter of Pedro Alvarez and María Teresa Marquez, on February 22, 1797, at Misión San Diego.

6. The mission record reads "Ma. Regina Soto española, d 17 Feb. 1785. S.G."

7. Indian village

MARÍA JOSEFA, 8, who died May 11, 1784, was buried at San Gabriel.

11 ALEJANDRO ROSAS, 19, who enlisted November 4, 1780, was a native of Rosario. His wife, JUANA MARÍA RODRÍGUEZ, 20, was the sister of the poblador Pablo Rodríguez. No children came with them, but two were born here. He died a widower on January 14, 1789.

12 ANTONIO MIRANDA RODRÍGUEZ, 50, a native of Sonora, enlisted at Rosario November 17, 1780. He accompanied the expedition as far as Loreto and never came to California, although his building lots, implements, and wages were ready for him should he appear. He is designated as absent on the first padron of the pueblo, November 19, 1781, also on the padron of December 2, 1781, and in those of 1785 and 1790. He was a widower with one child, JUANA MARÍA, 11 years old. He was excluded from the pueblo on December 5, 1783.

13 LUIS QUINTERO, 55, was a native of los Alamos, Sonora, where he enlisted February 3, 1781, on Rivera's return to Alamos from the south. He was evidently the last poblador to sign on the dotted line. His wife was MARÍA PETRA RUBIO, 40, also from los Alamos. Quintero also served as a padrino for the Indians confirmed by Junípero Serra at San Gabriel on March 22 and 25, 1782. He was the third poblador to be expelled from the pueblo and, like Lara, joined the Santa Barbara expedition that left San Gabriel on March 26, 1782. A tailor by trade, he lived at the Presidio de Santa Bárbara, where many of his children were married. Five children, including an adopted daughter, came with him and his wife.

MARÍA GERTRUDIS CASTELO, 16, daughter of Nicolás Castelo and Rita Gertrudis Valenzuela, natives of los Alamos, came as an adopted daughter and married Domingo Aruz, a Catalan volunteer, on November 12, 1782, at Misión San Buenaventura.

MARÍA CONCEPCIÓN, 9, married Josef Miguel Flores y Sandoval, a soldier of Presidio de Santa Bárbara, on December 26, 1782, at San Buenaventura.

MARÍA TOMASA, 7, married Rafael Gonzáles de la Cruz, soldier of Santa Barbara, on December 21, 1785, at Misión San Buenaventura.

MARÍA RAFAELA, 6, died at the Presidio de Santa Bárbara on July 5, 1783.

JOSEF CLEMENTE, 3, married María Josepha Rodríguez y Parra November 30, 1799, at Santa Barbara.

Three other daughters were MARÍA CATHARINA, 16, who was married to Joaquín Rodríguez, a soldier of the same expedition;

MARÍA JOSEFA QUINTERO, 18, who was married to Josef Rosalino Fernández of the expedition; and

FABIANA SEBASTIANA, 15, who was married to Eugenío Valdéz, soldier of the expedition.

14 MIGUEL VILLA, of whom nothing is known except that he enlisted in Sonora, deserted before the expedition got to Loreto. He never came to California, although a soldier with the same surname, Juan Josef Villa, native of San Miguel de Horcasitas, was among the soldiers destined for the Presidio de Santa Bárbara. Of the above-mentioned pobladores, all but Miguel Villa, Rafael Mesa, and Antonio Miranda Rodríguez arrived at San Gabriel August 18, 1781, and became the founders of el Pueblo de Nuestra Senora de los Angeles del Río Porciúncula [*sic*]. All began to draw rations and receive pay on their arrival at San Gabriel.

SOLDIERS WHO ACCOMPANIED POBLADORES ARRIVING AT MISIÓN SAN GABRIEL, AUGUST 18, 1781

1 JOSEF ANTONIO ONTIVEROS, 37, was a native of Chametla in the jurisdiction of Rosario, Sinaloa. His wife, ANA MARÍA BIRVIESCAS Y CARRASCO, 34, was a native of Rosario, where he enlisted. They had two children.

JUANA DE DIÓS, 13, was married to Josef Miguel Olivares, native of Guadalajara, Jalisco, on September 9, 1784, at Misión San Buenaventura. Later becoming a widow, she married Juan Matías Olivas, widower and soldier of the 1781 expedition, on June 24, 1793, at Misión San Gabriel.

JUAN PATRICIO, 9, was born at Chametla, like his sister, and married María Antonia Rodríguez y Noriega, daughter of the pobladores Pablo Rodríguez and María Rosalia Noriega, on June 1, 1794, at Misión San Gabriel.

2 MÁXIMO ALANIS Y CASILLAS, 21, was a native of Chametla, Sinaloa, where he enlisted. His wife was JUANA MARÍA MIRANDA, 20, a native of los Alamos, where they were married. No children came with them. He served at the Presidio de San Diego.

3 JUSTO LORENZO HERNÁNDEZ and his wife, ZIRIACA TRINIDAD DE

LEON, both were natives of Culiacán, where he enlisted. Three children came with them.

JUAN MARÍA JORGE, 5, who was born at Culiacán, married Francisca Lorenzana, who was living at San Jose in 1841. They had two children.

JUANA NEPOMUCENO.

MÁXIMA MARÍA TRINIDAD.

4 JUAN MATIAS OLIVAS, 22, and his wife, MARÍA DOROTEA ESPINOSA, 23, were natives of Rosario, Sinaloa, where he enlisted. She died at Santa Barbara, where her husband was a soldier in the presidio, on September 9, 1789. He later married Juana de Diós Ontiveros, supra, on June 1, 1794, at Misión San Gabriel. They brought two children.

MARÍA NICOLASA, 2, a native of Rosario, was married at Santa Barbara November 11, 1793, to Macedonio Barreras, a soldier of the Presidio de San Diego.

JOSEF PABLO, 1, married María Luciana Fernández y Quintero January 7, 1800, at Santa Barbara.

5 JUAN ANTONIO IBARRA, 21, and his wife, MARÍA DE LOS ANGELES VELÁSQUEZ, 21, both were natives of Mazatlán de los Mulatos, where he enlisted. There was one child.

JOSEF ALVINO, 2, married María Manuela Valenzuela, daughter of Pedro Valenzuela y María Dolores Parra, of the said expedition, on September 8, 1805, at San Gabriel.

6 JOAQUIN RODRÍGUEZ, 21, was a native of los Alamos. His wife, MARÍA CATARINA QUINTERO Y RUBIO, 16, also of los Alamos, was the daughter of the pobladores Luis Quintero and María Petra Rúbio. She died at Santa Barbara on October 28, 1798. No children came with them. Their first child, JOSEPH LEON, was born at el Parage de Agua Mansa on the way to found Misión San Buenaventura and was the first child buried at San Buenaventura.

7 JOSEF POLANCO, 28, was a native of Cocula, near Guadalajara, Jalisco. His wife, MARÍA MORBERTA DE LEON, 28, was a native of Rosario, where he enlisted. They had no children. He became alcalde of los Angeles in 1812 and was grantee of Rancho el Conejo in 1803.

8 JOSEF JULIÁN GUERRERO was a native of el Pueblo del Nombre de Díos,

and his wife, RITA GERTRUDIS SÁNCHEZ, a native of Rosario, where he enlisted. He died at San Gabriel May 9, 1784. There were no children. His wife died at San Diego November 22, 1785.

9 EUGENIO VALDÉZ, 26, was a native of los Alamos, where he enlisted. His wife, FABIANA SEBASTIANA QUINTERO Y RUBIO, 15, also of los Alamos, was the daughter of the pobladores Luis Quintero and María Petra Rubio. No children came with them.

10 MANUEL YGNÁCIO LUGO, 20, and his wife, GERTRUDIS LIMÓN Y SÁNCHEZ, 30, were natives of la Villa de Sinaloa, where he enlisted. Manuel was a younger brother of Francisco Salvador Lugo, who came with his family to California in 1774 and was founder of the older branch of that name. They brought one child.

JOSEF MIGUEL, 2, married María Isabel Fernández, daughter of Rosalino Fernández and María Josefa Quintero, of the same expedition, on February 4, 1799, at Misión Santa Bárbara.

11 ILDEFONSO DOMÍNGUEZ, a native of la Villa de Sinaloa, was the widower of María Ygnácia German, of the same place. He brought two children.

JOSEF MARÍA, 16, born at Sinaloa, married María Marcelina Féliz, daughter of Victorino Féliz y María Micaela Landera, at Santa Barbara.

MARÍA LUISA DEL CARMEN, 14, of Sinaloa, married Juan Francisco Reyes y Díaz, *soldado de cuera*[8] of Monterey and soldier of the Portolá Expedition of 1769, on January 1, 1782, at Misión San Gabriel.

12 FELIPE GONZÁLES, 48, was a native of la Villa de Sinaloa, and his wife, MARÍA FELIPA DE LA CRUZ, 38, a native of Nayarit. He enlisted at Sinaloa, and they brought one child.

TOMÁS, 15, married María Perseverancia Cortes y Ramírez, daughter of Josef Xavier Cortes and María Nicolasa Ramírez of the expedition, on October 13, 1787, at Misión Santa Bárbara.

13 JOSEF MANUEL VALENZUELA, 36, and his wife, MARÍA CONCEPCIÓN HIGUERA Y ARMENTA, 20, were natives of la Villa de Sinaloa, where he en-

8. Leather jacketed soldier

listed. She died at Santa Barbara July 14, 1799. There were no children. He later married María Josefa Alvarez, widow of Juan Esteban Rosas, on April 27, 1801, at Misión San Gabriel.

14 ISIDRO GERMAN, 26, and his wife, MARÍA MANUELA DE OCHOA, 17, were natives of la Villa de Sinaloa, where he enlisted. They had no children.

15 JUAN JOSEF VILLALOBO, 40, was a native of la Villa de Sinaloa, and his wife, MARÍA NICOLASA BELTRAN, 35, was a native of San Miguel de Orcasitas, Sonora. There were five children.

MARÍA FRANCISCO MAURICIA, 9, a native of Sinaloa, married Josef Bartolo Tapia y Hernández, son of Felipe Santiago Tapia and María Filomena Hernández of the Anza Expedition of 1776, on November 24, 1785, at Misión San Buenaventura.

JUANA JOSEFA, 7, married Doroteo Féliz y Pinuelas, of the Anza Expedition.

MARÍA RITA, 5, married Josef María Monroy y García, on March 7, 1791, at Misión San Gabriel.

MARÍA ANTONIA, 3, married Josef Jacobo Velarde y Contreras, on May 20, 1792, at Misión San Diego.

JOSEF PEDRO, 1.

16 FRANCISCO XAVIER SEPÚLVEDA, 39, and his wife, MARÍA CANDELARIA DE REDONDO, 35, were natives of la Villa de Sinaloa, where he enlisted. They had six children.

JUAN JOSEF, 17, a native of Sinaloa, married Tomasa Gutierrez y Arballo, on January 10, 1786, at Misión San Juan Capistrano. Tomasa came in the Anza Expedition with her widowed mother, María Feliciana Arballo, and died soon after 1800. Juan Josef then married Mariana Díaz Lorenzana, on May 20, 1804, at Misión San Diego. He was the ancestor of the older or Palos Verdes branch of that family. He died at San Gabriel October 16, 1808.

THERESA, 9, married Juan de Díos Ballesteros y Cosio, on February 10, 1787, at Misión San Juan Capistrano. They were the founders of the Ballesteros family.

RAFAEL, 15, was a settler of los Angeles in 1789.

SEBASTIÁN, 13, married María Luisa Botiller y Cota on January 31, 1799, at Misión San Gabriel. They moved to San José de Guadalupe, where most of their children were born. As a widow, she later married Josef Cornélio Rosales at Misión Santa Clara, July 27, 1814.

MANUEL, 11, married María Apolónia Cota y Lugo at Misión Santa Bárbara, January 17, 1796.

FRANCISCO, 6, married María Ramona Serrano y Silvas, on October 19, 1802, at Misión San Diego. They founded the San Vicente y Santa Monica branch of the Sepúlveda family.

17 JUAN MARÍA ROMERO, 30, was a native of Loreto, as was his wife, MARÍA LUGARDA SALGADO, 20. They had two children.

MARÍA JOSEFA, 4.

JOSEF ANTONIO, a child in arms, was born at the Presidio de Loreto while the expedition was on its way to California. He married María Dorotea Alanís y Miranda, daughter of Máximo Alanís y Juana Miranda of the expedition, on August 4, 1801, San Gabriel.

SOLDIERS WHO ACCOMPANIED RIVERA ARRIVING AT MISIÓN SAN GABRIEL, JULY 14, 1781

1 JOSEF DARÍO ARGÜELLO, 28, was a native of Querétaro, and his wife, MARÍA YGNÁCIA MORAGA, a native of the Presidio de Altar, Sonora. She was a niece of Lieutenant Josef Joaquín Moraga, the founder of San Francisco, who came with Anza in 1776.

Don Josef enlisted in the Mexico regiment of dragoons in 1773. He joined the presidial company of Altar, where he served as a private for six years and a sergeant for two and a half years, until he was commissioned alferez of the company just organized by Rivera for the proposed Presidio de Santa Bárbara in 1781. He accompanied Rivera on the march overland, left him on the Colorado, and with Lieutenant Diego Gonzáles and the company of soldiers and families, arrived at San Gabriel on July 14, 1781. He remained at San Gabriel until the expedition left to found the Presidio de Santa Bárbara on March 26, 1782. He went south to San Diego with the soldiers of the new company destined for the presidio there, where he witnessed their enlistment. His first public task of importance was as *comisionado*[9] appointed by Govenor Fages to confirm title to and distribute pueblo lands to the settlers of los Angeles in August of 1786. The following year he was promoted to lieutenant of the San Francisco Com-

9. Commissioner

pany in February and took that office in June. He served as comandante of San Francisco until 1791, and again from April 1796 until July 1806, having occupied that same post at Monterey from 1791 to 1796. In October of 1791 he was present at the dedication of Misión Soledad. He was promoted brevet captain in October of 1797, receiving his commission in February of the following year. He was made captain of the Santa Barbara Company on March 22, 1807, by the king, in consideration of his merits and services.

Argüello was as prominent and important a man as California could boast of in the years of his busy life. On the death of Governor Arrillaga in July 1814, he became acting governor, being the ranking officer in California. He remained at Santa Barbara, however, as comandante and did not move to Monterey. It was no doubt a matter of great disappointment to Argüello and his friends that he was not made governor. Instead he was commissioned on December 31, 1814, to govern the barren peninsula of Lower California. Don Josef Argüello passed the last years of his eventful life at Guadalajara, where he resided with his wife, and died early in 1828. His wife was also buried there.

Argüello's children were born in California. The oldest, JOSEF YGNÁCIO MÁXIMO, baptized at San Gabriel June 8, 1782, became the first native Californian to enter the priesthood. He was educated in Mexico and visited California in 1809 when he participated at the dedication of the Misión San Buenaventura on September 9, also saying a mass at San Gabriel.

LUIS ANTONIO, the second son, became governor of California. He was born at San Francisco June 21, 1784.

SANTIAGO and GERVASIO became equally prominent and left many children to carry on the glorious name, allied with many others of prominence, both native Californian and American.

MARÍA DE LA CONCEPCIÓN MARCELA is widely known for her romance with the Russian Rezanof.

MARÍA ISABEL married Josef Maríano Estrada.

2 DIEGO GONZÁLES, lieutenant of the expedition, was a native of Spain. He was in command of the Presidio de Monterey from 1781 to 1785, when he was transferred to the San Francisco Company. He brought no family with him and was sent to the frontier late in 1787. After 1793 he disappears from the rolls, with a record hardly equal to the rank he held.

3 JUAN YGNÁCIO VALENCIA, 46, was a native of el Real Presidio de Santa

Rosa de Corodeguachí, alias Fronteras, Sonora. His wife, MARÍA RITA ZAMORA Y GONZÁLES, 32, a native of la Villa de Sinaloa, was the widow of Andrés Bermudez, native of the Presidio de Santa Cruz de Sonora, situated between the presidios of Tubac and Terrenate, on the frontier. Three children came with them.

JOSEF DE LA CRUZ BERMUDEZ, 13, a native of the Presidio de Santa Cruz, married María Estéfana Villa y Martínez on February 5, 1796, at Misión San Gabriel. Later a widower, he married María Armenta, daughter of Joaquín Armenta and Hilária Avila y Urquidez, on August 12, 1823, also at San Gabriel.

JUAN HILARIO BERMUDEZ, 11, a native of the Presidio de Santa Cruz, married Ana María Lugo, daughter of Manuel Ygnácio Lugo and Gertrudis Sánchez, of the same expedition, on January 27, 1799, at Santa Barbara.

MARÍA FRANCISCA VALENCIA, 7, a native of Sinaloa, married Miguel Leyba y Salazar April 30, 1797, at Santa Barbara.

4 JOSEF MANUEL ORCHAGA Y MACHADO, 25, was a native of el Real de los Alamos, Sonora, where he enlisted. His wife, MARÍA DEL CARMEN VALENZUELA, 17, also was from los Alamos. She was a sister of Pedro Gabriel and Josef Segundo Valenzuela, soldiers of the same expedition. No children came with them, but eight were born in California. All reached majority age and married into the following families: Valdéz, Poyorena, Aguilar, Reyes, Buelna, Sepúlveda, Palomares, Cota, and Avila. The name, as it appears in the early presidio rosters and even down to 1850 when the first government census was taken, was Orchaga. Later it appears exclusively as Machado. This family was grantee of the Ranchos la Ballona and Aguaje del Centinela.

5 JUAN JOSEF VILLA, 38, was a native of the Presidio de San Miguel de Orcasitas, whence started Anza and his followers in 1775. His wife, MARÍA PAULA MARTÍNEZ, 30, was born at el Real de Santa Ana, Sonora. Two children came with them.

VICENTE FERRER was born at the Presidio de Tubac in 1775. On February 5, 1796, at San Gabriel, he married María Josefa Sinoba y Bojorquez, daughter of the retired soldier of 1769 and poblador of los Angeles, Josef Francisco Sinoba. As a widower, he later married María Rita Valdéz, daughter of Eugénio Valdéz and Sebastiana Quintero of said expedition, on February 16, 1808, also at San Gabriel. María Rita Valdéz de Villa was claimant of Rancho Rodeo de las Aguas, site of present Beverly Hills.

JOSEF MARÍA VILLA, adopted son (?).

Eight other children were born in California, marrying into the Bermudez, Aguilar, Cota, Domínguez, Soto, and García families.

6 JUAN ANDRES HILARIO MONTIEL, 35, and his wife, MARÍA ROSA RODRÍGUEZ, 38, were natives of los Alamos, Sonora, where he enlisted. Their daughter, MARÍA PETRA, 17, was already married to Josef Tadeo Sánchez, a soldier of the same expedition.

Their other child was MARÍA CONCEPCIÓN, 14, born at the Presidio de Buenavista, Sonora. She married Corporal Alejo de la Cruz Sotomayor, of the Santa Barbara Company, on August 30, 1782, at Misión San Buenaventura. This was the first marriage of gente de razon at said place.

7 JOSEF TADEO SÁNCHEZ, 25, a native of los Alamos, was accompanied by his young wife, MARÍA PETRA MONTIEL Y RODRÍGUEZ, 17, supra. They brought no children with them, but eight were born here. This generation married into the Higuera, Guevara, Arrellanes, Ortega, and López families.

8 JOSEF ANTONIO BASILIO PARRA, 25, was a native of Amatlán de las Canas, Sinaloa, and his wife, MARÍA ISABEL TALAMANTES, 21, a native of Rosario, where he enlisted. Parra joined the Santa Barbara Company and died soon afterward. His widow married Toríbio Martínez y Guzman, a soldier of Monterey, at San Buenaventura on September 8, 1784. There were no children.

9 JOSEF XAVIER CORTES was a native of Culiacán, where he evidently died. Although his name appears on the list of recruits made by Ortega at San Gabriel October 24, 1781, his widow, MARÍA NICOLASA RAMÍREZ, a native of el Real de Palo Blanco, near Culiacán, married Guillermo Soto, a soldier of the same expedition, at San Gabriel on July 21, 1781. He does not appear on the list of soldiers killed with Rivera on the Colorado, under the above date, and disappears from the Presidio de Santa Bárbara rolls after July 1, 1782. There were four children.

MARÍA PERSEVERANCIA first married Tomás Gonzáles y Leon at Santa Barbara October 13, 1787, and second, Luis Gonzaga Lugo, a veteran of 1769, on May 27, 1792, at the same place.

MARÍA ISABEL RAMONA, 6, married Josef Antonio Vásquez, soldado de cuera of Santa Barbara, May 25, 1789.

NICOLAS FELIPE, 14, a native of Culiacán, married María de Jesús Lara, daughter of the pobladores Josef Lara and María Antonia Campos, at Santa Barbara May 19, 1792.

MARÍA PAULA SEGUNDA, 12, married Luis Pena, soldado de cuera of Santa Barbara, on February 3, 1785, at San Buenaventura.

10 GUILLERMO SOTO Y LEON, 30 and single, was a native of el Real de Cozala, Sonora. He married, at San Gabriel, María Nicolasa Ramírez, widow of Josef Jávier Cortes, supra, on July 27, 1781. She died at San Buenaventura, where her husband was soldier of the guard, on January 26, 1786. Soto later married Juana María Pérez Nieto y Armenta, on November 17, 1787, at San Gabriel. Soto joined the Presidio de Santa Bárbara, being a guard at Misión San Buenaventura, then a settler of los Angeles in 1789, where he became alcalde in 1798 and 1809. One of his daughters, Casilda, was grantee of la Merced Rancho in 1844, and another, María Trinidad, married Ricardo Vejar. His son, Josef María, became a settler of los Angeles in 1815.

11 AGUSTÍN DE LEYBA, 41, was a native of el Pueblo de Tepic, and his wife, MARÍA GUADALUPE SALAZAR Y VELARDE, 38, a native of San Xavier de Cabazán, Sinaloa. He enlisted at Cozala, where their four children were born.

ROQUE ANASTACIO, 7, married María de la Ascención Rosas, daughter of the pobladores Alejandro Rosas and Rosa Rodríguez, on January 28, 1799, at San Gabriel.

JOSEF MIGUEL, 5, married María Francisco Valencia April 30, 1797, at Santa Barbara.

JOSEF RUFINO, 2, married María Francisca García February 19, 1796, at Santa Barbara.

JUAN JOSEPH, 9, married Juana Simona Rodríguez May 3, 1791, at Santa Barbara.

12 JUAN VICTORINO FÉLIZ and his wife, MARÍA MICAELA LANDERA, were natives of el Real de Cozala, Sinaloa. He died at Santa Barbara, where he was a soldier, on July 4, 1783. They had four children.

JUANA MARÍA, 9, married Josef Calixto Ayala, a native of Cozala, on December 3, 1786. This was the first marriage of gente de razon to take place in the newly established Misión Santa Bárbara.

JUAN MANUEL SALVADOR, 6.

MARÍA MARCELA, 10, married Josef María Domínguez, at Santa Barbara.

JOSEF YGNÁCIO, 1, married María Antonia Villa y Martínez August 27, 1798, at Santa Barbara.

13 JOSEF MIGUEL ESPINOSA, single, was a native of Rosario, where he enlisted. He married, at Misión Santa Clara, Gabriela María Higuera, May 20, 1795. He joined the Monterey Company.

14 GASPAR LÓPEZ was a native of el Pueblo de Zabala in the Archbishopric of Durango, and his wife, MARÍA GERTRUDIS GARCÍA, a native of la Villa de San Sebastián, in the same archbishopric. López joined the San Diego Company and died there March 2, 1782. A son, JOSEF MARÍA RAMON, was baptized at San Gabriel September 8, 1781, and became a settler of los Angeles in 1815. He was the first child of the soldiers of the 1781 expedition to be baptized at San Gabriel.

15 JOSEF ESTEBAN ROMERO, 30, was a native of el Real de San Antonio de la Huerta, Sonora, as was his wife, JUANA GERTRUDIS DELGADO, 23. Romero joined the Santa Barbara Company. Their child was JOSEF GERARDO.

MARÍA JOSEFA RODRÍGUEZ, daughter of Juan Rodríguez and María Antonia Delgado, deceased, came with them.

16 JOSEF DEL CARMEN ARAÑA, 23, and his wife, MARÍA MANUELA GUEVARA, 23, were natives of Cozala. No children came with them, and there is no record of any born in California.

17 FRANCISCO XAVIER CALBO, 27, was a native of Cozala, and his wife, MARÍA INEZ CAMPOS, 20, was also of Cozala. She died at Santa Barbara where her husband was a soldier, August 1, 1783. There were no children.

18 FRANCISCO JUÁREZ and his wife, TRINIDAD VICENTA DE LEON, were natives of Cozala. He died at San Gabriel March 1, 1782, where their only child, Josef Joaquín, was baptized on July 28, 1782. His widow then married Josef Antonio Rodríguez, soldado de cuera, at San Gabriel on August 11, 1782, and moved to Monterey.

19 FRANCISCO XAVIER MEJIAS and his wife, FRANCISCA XAVIER DE ORTEGA, were natives of la Villa de Sinaloa. To him was entrusted the Indian girl of four, native of the Gila River, as the expedition was leaving the Colorado foundations for California. Her pagan parents probably feared the Yuma massacre, which took place four days before she was baptized at San Gabriel on July 21, 1781. Two adult sons were members of the expedition and came as soldiers; a daughter accompanied her soldier-husband also.

MARÍA PETRA, 20, married Ramón Buelna, soldado de cuera of San Diego, on May 11, 1783, at San Diego.

20 PEDRO JOSEF MEJIAS, 22, and his wife, ANA MARÍA ORTEGA, were natives of la Villa de Sinaloa, where he enlisted. No children came with them. He joined the San Diego Company.

21 JUAN NORBERTO MEJIAS, 17, single, a native of la Villa de Sinaloa, joined the Monterey Company and was married at Misión San Antonio to Vividiana Sobredia, widow of Francisco Villagomez, in September of 1784.

JUAN URBANO, 4, was confirmed at Santa Barbara November 23, 1783.

22 JOSEF MARÍA MARTÍNEZ, single, a native of Topago, joined the Monterey Company. He married María Josefa García at Misión Santa Clara on February 7, 1785.

23 RAMON YBARRA, 18, a native of San Antonio Guernay, joined the Monterey Company and left no family.

24 JOSEF MARÍA GIL SAMANIEGO, 41, and his wife, JUANA MARÍA DE SOTOMAYOR, 25, were natives of los Alamos, where he enlisted. There were no children.

25 JOSEF YGNÁCIO RODRÍGUEZ, 21, was a native of Matape, Sonora, and his wife, JUANA PAULA PARRA, 16, a native of los Alamos, where he enlisted. One child came with them.

FRANCISCO XAVIER was born at los Alamos. There were twelve other children born at Santa Barbara, where their father was a soldier. They married into the Domínguez, Arrellanes, Ruiz, Leyba, Ortega, and Rosas families.

26 VICENTE QUIJADA, 26, and his wife, JUANA MARÍA ARMENTA Y LANDERA, 26, both were natives of los Alamos. She died at Santa Barbara July 27, 1783. They brought two children.

MARÍA ROSA married Bernardo Ramírez, a native of Tepic, at Santa Barbara.

MARÍA GERTRUDIS VALENZUELA, daughter of Francisco and María Rita Quijada of los Alamos, came with them. She married Anastácio Féliz y Castro, soldado de cuera, Santa Bárbara, at San Gabriel on August 28, 1781.

27 JOSEF ROSALINO FERNÁNDEZ, 24, and his wife, MARÍA JOSEFA QUINTERO, 18, were natives of el Fuerte, Sinaloa. Fernández joined the Santa Barbara Company. Only one child came with them.

MARÍA LUCIA, 1, married Joseph Pablo Olivas January 7, 1800, at Santa Barbara.

There were eight other children born in California.

28 EFIGENIO RUIZ, 36, and his wife, MARÍA ROSA LOPEZ Y SÁNCHEZ, 28, were natives of el Fuerte. He died at Santa Barbara June 13, 1795. They had three children.

MARÍA URSULA, 10, married Eugénio Rosalio Villavicencio, soldado de cuera of Monterey at Misión San Buenaventura, July 19, 1786.

JOSEF PEDRO, 7, married María Ygnácia Lugo y Vianazul at Santa Barbara on October 7, 1798.

JOSEF HILARIO, 1, married Júlia Sinoba y Bojorquez.

29 JOSEF ANTONIO MARÍA VEILARDE, 40, was born on the Piaxtla River, Sinaloa. His wife, MARÍA JULIANA QUIJADA, 45, was a native of los Alamos and sister of Vicente Quijada, supra. They had no children.

30 JUAN YGNÁCIO MARTÍNEZ and his wife, MARÍA JACINTA MORENO, were natives of los Alamos. He joined the Santa Barbara Company. There were three children.

JUAN JOSEF.

FRANCISCO DIEGO VICENTE.

JUAN JOSEF.

31 FRUCTUOSO MARÍA RUIZ, 21, and his wife, MARÍA ISABEL ARMEN-

TA Y ACOSTA, 14, both were natives of el Fuerte, where he enlisted. There were no children. She died June 25, 1792, at Santa Barbara, where her husband was a soldado de cuera. Ruiz later married María Dolores Lugo y Sánchez at Santa Barbara on October 9, 1795.

32 JOSEF MELESIO VALDEZ, 21, was accompanied by his wife, ANA MARÍA ALCALA, 18, of el Fuerte. They had no children.

33 JOSEF PEDRO LORETO SALAZAR, 45, and his wife, MARÍA LORETA GREGORIA ESPINOSA, 24, were natives of los Alamos. There were no children. Salazar died at San Gabriel on July 6, 1788, and his widow then married Sargento Maríano de la Luz Verdugo on November 26 of the same year. Verdugo had been a soldier of the Portolá Expedition of 1769 and a sergeant at Monterey, 1781–87. He settled at los Angeles in 1787, serving as alcalde in 1790–93 and 1802. He was grantee of the Portezuelo Rancho in 1795.

34 JOSEF VICTOR PATIÑO, 31, and his wife, MARÍA VICTORIA MARTÍNEZ, 24, were both of los Alamos, where he enlisted. They had no children. He died at Santa Barbara May 22, 1789.

35 FRANCISCO ONTIVEROS was a native of Chametla, in the jurisdiction of Rosario, where he enlisted. He appears on the list of the garrison for the Presidio de Santa Bárbara for October 30, 1781, but does not appear on the list for July 1, 1782. His name then disappears entirely from the records. He was single and left no family.

36 SEGUNDO VALENZUELA and his wife, MARÍA AGUSTINA ALCANTARA, were natives of el Real de los Alamos. Valenzuela was a soldier at San Diego. Three children came to California with them.

JOAQUÍN, 10, died at San Diego on October 5, 1782.

JOSEF MARÍA, 5, also died at San Diego, November 10, 1782.

MARÍA ANTONIA, 2, married Juan Josef Alvarado y Castro, a soldier of the Presidio de San Diego, on May 13, 1792.

Six other children were born in California and married into the García, Soto, and Rodríguez families.

37 PEDRO GABRIEL VALENZUELA, 23, and his wife, MARÍA DOLORES

PARRA, 20, were natives of los Alamos. They brought no children, but twelve were born here, uniting by marriage with the Varelas, Féliz, Rodríguez, and Ybarra families.

38 YGNÁCIO ROCHIN, 28, and his wife, ANA BOJORQUEZ, 30, were native of los Alamos. He joined the Santa Barbara Company and in 1790 was mayordomo of the Misión San Juan Capistrano. They had one child.

MARÍA DEL CARMEN, 2, married Josef Clemente Navarro, son of the pobladores Josef Antonio Navarro y María Regina de Soto, on May 15, 1791, at San Gabriel.

39 JOSEF PRUDENCIO ARANGURE is named as a recruit and is on the Presidio de Santa Bárbara rolls for October 24 and 30, 1781. But his name, as well as those of Francisco Ontiveros, Francisco Juárez, and Josef Jávier Cortes, disappears from the rolls by July 1, 1782. I have no further record of Arangure and Ontiveros. Cortes and Juárez were deceased.

From a list of recruits drawn up by Lieutenant Ortega at San Gabriel on October 24, 1781, we find the names of five soldiers of the expedition who were killed on the Colorado with Rivera: Francisco Castro, Antonio Pardo, Manuel Díaz, Josef Quijas, and Ascencio Alvarez. Alvarez, whose wife was Micaéla Uribes, and whose son, Buenaventura, seems to have come with the expedition, joined the Santa Barbara Company. He later married Juana Valenzuela at San Gabriel on September 6, 1807.

On the same list, we find that on that date Prudéncio López, Ygnácio Rochin, and Isidro German had deserted after reaching California. They returned, however, and we find them at Presidio de Santa Bárbara by the following year.

Los Angeles, California: The Question of the City's Original Spanish Name

BY THEODORE E. TREUTLEIN

On a Tuesday, the fourth of September 1781, Lieutenant Josef Darío Argüello, on the orders of Felipe de Neve, governor of Californias [sic], led a party of settlers to a site on the banks of the Porciúncula River, and founded a *pueblo* with the title, *La Reyna de los Angeles* (*The Queen of the Angels*).[1]

The background to the pueblo's founding had been Governor Neve's careful examination, a physical survey, from San Diego to San Francisco, early in the year 1777 to determine the water capability and soil conditions in upper California. In the Los Angeles region Neve wrote approvingly of the Santa Ana, San Gabriel, and Porciúncula rivers, and north, of the Guadalupe. His conclusion was to recommend the founding of two pueblos, one on the Guadalupe, which became San Joseph (San José), the other on the Porciúncula, which became Los Angeles.

When Neve's plans ultimately reached Don Teodoro de Croix, the governor and commandant general of the Interior Provinces, the latter gave his approval in a dispatch dated September 3, 1778. By that date San José had already been founded, and Croix gave specific permission for the establishment of the pueblo "en el Río de la Porciúncula."[2]

Although Governor Neve had initiated the idea of founding the pueblos (as well as other establishments), Commandant Croix's position required him to write of the projects as his own.[3] Croix now instructed Captain Fernando de Rivera y Moncada to recruit colonists for the Río Porciúncula pueblo. In his order to Rivera, dated at Arispe, Sonora, December 27, 1779, we find the first use of the original Spanish name for Los Angeles.

Croix's words are of historic importance because they do define the city's title and also make clear his primary role in the higher echelon of Spanish administration. Croix wrote: "With the due aims of defense, conservation and development of the Province of Californias [sic], toward which the service of God and King is especially directed, I have resolved upon occupation of the Channel of Santa Barbara with a Presidio of this name, and three Missions; the erection of a Pueblo with the title of *la Reyna de los Angeles* on the River of *la Porciúncula*, and His Majesty has approved the [pueblo] named San Joseph which I ordered founded on the margins of the river of Guadalupe...."[4]

In almost the same language Commandant Croix then informed Viceroy Martín de Mayorga (the successor to Viceroy Antonio Bucareli who had died in April 1779) of his decision about the Channel establishments and of his order to found a pueblo with the title of *la Reyna de los Angeles* on the river Porciúncula.[5]

On the 10th of February 1780 Commandant Croix also wrote to Governor Neve, stating in part, "... I have ordered the founding of a pueblo with the título de la Reyna de los Angeles sobre el Río de la Porciúncula."[6]

After the pueblo had been founded, Commandant Croix wrote to Minister of the Indies, Joseph de Gálvez, February 28, 1782: "The Governor of the Peninsula of California [sic] Don Phelipe de Neve informed me on November 19, of last year verifying that on the preceding September 4 there was founded 'el nuevo Pueblo de la Reyna de los Angeles al margen del Río de la Porciúncula' with some of the settlers recruited by the deceased Captain Don Fernando de Rivera...."[7]

Minister Gálvez then wrote to Commandant Croix on October 29, 1782 telling him that the King had been informed of the establishment of the "nuevo Pueblo de la Reyna de los Angeles al margen del Río de la Porciúncula en la Peninsula de Californias."[8]

The fact that The Queen of the Angels title was provided the King of Spain by the Minister of the Indies, Gálvez, would seem to confirm that this name for the pueblo was the accepted one. It should also be noted that when Croix referred to the Río Porciúncula he was indicating the site of the pueblo; the river's name is not a part of the pueblo's title.

Later in the year 1782 Governor Neve was named inspector general of the Interior Provinces (September 4, 1782). In his instructions to his successor, Don Pedro Fages, in article 9, Neve expressed the view that very special attention be given to support the new pueblos, and he referred to "the pueblo of Nuestra Señora de los Angeles."[9] This may be the only usage in the founding days of the form, *Nuestra Señora de los Angeles*, but the official form, as noted, had already been established.[10]

However, generations of writers on California history have apparently disregarded the documentation and have compounded the name for the pueblo or have modified its name. The examples of misuse are very numerous and very easy to come by. Some special examples have been selected for this paper.

In the *Annual Publication* of Historical Society of Southern California, 1931, one finds a feature article by Thomas W. Temple II, "Se Fundaron un Pueblo de Españoles." In this article there is reference to the city's Spanish name, as follows: "Governor Neve's Reglamento of 1 June, 1779 approved the founding of two pueblos, one provisionally established [i.e., San Joseph, or San José], the other to be known as Nuestra Señora de los Angeles, on the Porciúncula River."

Actually, the Reglamento states in the Fourteenth Title, "Political Government and Instructions for Settlement", Paragraph 1, "… the Pueblo of S. Joseph is already founded and settled, and the building of another is determined upon, for which settlers and their families must come from the Province of Sonora and Sinaloa…."

In other words, unless the reader is very careful in interpreting Mr. Temple's wording he would form the impression that the famous Neve *Reglamento* provided the name of the new pueblo, which it definitely does not do.[11] What makes the wording in the Temple article especially ironic and curious is that many of the documents reproduced in the extremely useful commemorative edition use the form, *La Reina de los Angeles*. Space will not permit citing all of these documents. However, it is worthy of special note that settlers were recruited in Sonora with the designation that they would be settled in the Pueblo de la Reina de los Angeles.[12]

Also in the review of settlers to determine those "who enjoy wages and draw rations," made by Lieutenant Josef Francisco de Ortega (December 2, 1781), the title of the piece is Pueblo de la Reyna de los Angeles.[13]

The census made on November 19, 1781, reads: "Padron del vecindario, el qe. tiene el pueblo de la Reyna de los Angeles fundado el 4 de Ste. del 1781, al margen del Río de Porciúncula…."[14]

The confirmation of titles to pueblo lands ordered in August 1786 by Governor Pedro Fages refers to the Pueblo de la Reyna de los Angeles, as does the Act of Obedience, September 1786 by José Argüello.[15]

There is also reference in the commemorative volume to a *Plano de el Pueblo de la Reyna de los Angeles, y tierras de Labor* [undated].[16]

Considerably later, in another era, there is record of a litigation: "Transcript of the Proceedings in case No. 422. City of Los Angeles Claimants vs. The United States, Defendant, for the Place named 'Pueblo Sands'." In the first paragraph there is stated: "For the foundation of the Pueblo of la Reina de los Angeles in the neighborhood of the River of Porciuncula, and upon the land selected for this purpose;... Samuel D. King, Surveyor Genl. Cal. His seal affixed April 20, 1852. Filed in his office, October 26, 1852. Geo. Fisher, Secty."[17]

Returning to the theme of the apparent disregard of the documentary evidence by writers on the history of the beginnings of Los Angeles, one notes that Henry Raup Wagner in an early publication used the title: "The Earliest Documents of El Pueblo de Nuestra Señora La Reina de los Angeles" (1931).

Zoeth Skinner Eldredge, *The Beginnings of San Francisco* (2 vols.; San Francisco, 1912), I, 91, third footnote, goes a step farther than Wagner and asserts: "Portolá crossed the Los Angeles river on the 2d of August, 1769, the day of the Feast of Porciúncula and named it in honor of the day Río de Nuestra Señora de los Angeles de Porciúncula. It is to this incident the city of Los Angeles owes its name which is in full Nuestra Señora La Reina de los Angeles de Porciúncula – Our Lady the Queen of the Angels of Porciúncula."

In writing this, Eldredge provided a clue to the cause for confusion which has surrounded the original Spanish name of the city; namely, he confused the official title (of which he was perhaps not aware), La Reina de los Angeles, with a religious festival which was celebrated by members of the Portolá expedition. It is very important to recognize that a pueblo was a civil, not a religious or a military community. No evidence exists that a priest was even present when the pueblo was founded.[18]

The most recent example of this confusion, in this writer's knowledge and estimation, is found in the otherwise excellent article entitled "The Man Who Named Los Angeles," by Raymund F. Wood wherein is quoted from Father Juan Crespí's diary (1769): "This river [the Porciúncula] can be seen flowing down, its bed not deeply sunken below the surrounding ground, through a very green, lush, wide-spreading valley – an extent, north and south, of some leagues of level soil ... so that it can truly be said to a most handsome garden [sic] ... and in time to come there may be a very large and rich mission of Our Lady of the Angels of the Porciúncula, this being the day upon which we came to it, when this well-known Indulgence is gained [*i.e.*, noon of August 1 to midnight of August 2] in our Seraphic order; and so we have proclaimed it El Río y Valle de Nuestra Señora de los Angeles de la Porciúncula."[19]

In note 13 of the Wood article we find: "The addition of the words 'la Reina' into the title of the city, even though these words are not to be found in the original name given by Crespí to the river, has aroused considerable argument." Mr. Wood then goes on to cite the use of the words, La Reina, in the instructions to Rivera, December 27, 1779.[20]

There truly should be no argument, and the discrepancy noted by Mr. Wood has an obvious reason. The religious festival of August 2, 1769, provided the historical background for the name selected by Commandant Croix, *La Reina de los Angeles* (The Queen of the Angels), which is the original Spanish title for the pueblo, but the religious festival did not establish the title for the pueblo itself.[21]

NOTES

1. The most recent and in this writer's estimation the best account of the founding of Los Angeles may be read in Edwin A. Beilharz. *Felipe de Neve, First Governor of California* (San Francisco: California Historical Society, 1971), Chapter 7, "San José and Los Angeles." A description of Argüello's work is found on p. 108 where that individual is referred to as a "Sub-lieutenant." The day of the week, Tuesday, was derived by this writer from the *Cronologia, Cronografia e Calendario Perpetuo* of A. Cappelli (Milano: Manuali Hoepli, 1930), p. 85. The service record of El teniente Josef Darío Argüello may be found in Fray Martín de Landaeta, *Noticias acerca del Puerto de San Francisco* (Mexico: Antigua Librería Robredo, 1949), p. 23, note 17. Excerpted here is the Spanish section on the charge given to and carried out by Argüello: "... *fue comisionado el año de* 81 por el Sor. Dn. Felipe de Neve Governador entonces de Californias para fundar el Pueblo con el título de la Reyna de los Angeles, y lo fundo con las ventajas y proporciones que manifiesta su situacion;..."

2. AGI, Aud. de Guad. No. 271, Roll I, microfilm, Bancroft Library, Chapman *Catalogue* No. 4104 (hereinafter cited AGI, Guad. numbers of roll, C- with number).

3. On the subject of the responsibilities of high-ranking officials, see Alfred Barnaby Thomas, *Teodoro de Croix and the Northern Frontier of New Spain, 1776–1783. From the Original Document in the Archives of the Indies, Seville* (Norman: University of Oklahoma, 1941); and Bernard E. Bobb, *The Viceregency of Antonio María Bucareli in New Spain, 1771–1779* (Austin: University of Texas, 1962). Professor Bobb, discussing Croix's role states, among other matters, that "Croix ... became the virtually independent chief of a vast area [which included the Californias], but in possession of a cushion on which to rely if necessary – help from the Viceroy of New Spain," p. 146. (See dispatch of Croix to Mayorga, this paper, note 5, post.)

4. AGI, Guad. No. 271, I, C-4058. The Spanish form: "Con los Justos fines de defensa conservacion y fomento de la Provincia de Californias, en que particularmente se interesan el servicio de Dios y del Rey, he resuelto la ocupacion del Canal de Sta Barbara con un Presidio de este Nombre, y tres Misiones, la ereccion de un Pueblo con el título de la Reyna de los Angeles sobre el Río de la Porciuncula, y S.M. ha aprovado el que

mande fundan á las margenes del de Guadalupe titulado S[n] Joseph." (Italics supplied in translation.)

This document in Spanish and translation can conveniently be read also in *Annual Publications of Historical Society of Southern California*, XV, Part I (1931), 140–142 and 212 (hereinafter cited HSSC, 1931).

5. This document is dated February 9, 1780. AGI, Guad. No. 271, I, C-4095. The document, inadequately identified, may be found in the English and Spanish forms in hssc, 1931, pp. 202–203 and 262 respectively.

6. This document is quoted (in the excerpt provided here) in a letter from Professor Beilharz to the writer; Croix to Neve, Arispe, Febr. 10, 1780. AGI, Guad., No. 271 "... he dispuesto ... la erección de un pueblo con el título ..." etc. The writer has not seen this document, but the quoted portion is almost identical in form and in information to that sent by Croix to Mayorga.

7. AGI, Guad. No. 267, IV, C-4518.

8. Ibid., C-4711.

9. Beilharz, *Neve*, p. 165, and p. 172, notes 1 and 2. The *Instrucción* is dated September 7, 1782, AGI, Guad. No. 283, C-4672.

10. Herbert E. Bolton, trans. and ed., *Palou's New California* (5 vols.; Berkeley: University of California Press, 1926–1930), IV, 209, for Father Palou's use of the *Nuestra Señora* form.

11. AGI, Guad. No. 277, C-3997.

12. HSSC, 1931, p. 221 ff.

13. Ibid., pp. 149 and 218.

14. Ibid., pp. 148–149 and 216.

15. Ibid., pp. 150–151 and 220.

16. Ibid., p. 217.

17. CA 178, Part II, Transcript of the Proceedings..., Bancroft Library.

18. Maynard Geiger, *The Life and Times of Fray Junípero Serra, O.F.M.* (2 vols., Washington, D.C.: Academy of American Franciscan History, 1959), II, Ch. LXXVII, "St. Francis Also Came to Los Angeles," states, p. 270: "There is no eye-witness account of the actual founding of Los Angeles." [A slight modification of this statement may be derived from note 1, *ante*, in this article.] In this beautifully written chapter, Father Geiger, this writer respectfully suggests, makes the same error as do others; namely, confusing the religious ceremony which marked and named the site for the future city with the actual establishment of the city's title as outlined in this paper.

19. *Southern California Quarterly*, LIII (September 1971), 212.

20. See note 4, *ante*.

21. See also Rev. Francis J. Weber, *El Pueblo de Nuestra Señora de Los Angeles. An Inquiry into early appellations* (Los Angeles, 1968). This little booklet has to be cited because the title relates to the subject under discussion in this paper. However, a lack of basic documentation allows the author to come to the conclusion that the appellation "la reina" is spurious. (p. 6)

PART II

THE FOUNDING DOCUMENTS IN ENGLISH

Introduction to the Documents

Dedicating this volume to Los Angeles's 150th anniversary [in 1931], its editors have endeavored to bring together herein all documents at present available pertaining to the founding of that city.

To justly evaluate them, one should bear in mind something of the picturesque history of Spanish-Californian documents in general. A vast amount of records had accumulated in the province during Spanish and Mexican rule. Following secularization of the missions and then the American occupation, many of them were lost, destroyed, or scattered; some were returned to Mexico, but even so, a large quantity remained.

In 1851, territorial records of the pre-American period were collected from all municipal governments and assembled in the office of the United States surveyor-general at San Francisco. Thus were brought together original documents of every description dating from before the establishment of the first mission down to 1847.

> All these ... were bound by the American authorities, but with almost no attempt at chronological or other arrangement ... [into] between four and five hundred bulky volumes averaging more than 1,000 pages each.... Stacked in a dim room in the Surveyor-General's office,... they remained for a quarter of a century without any serious attempt being made to reduce the chaotic mass to order.
>
> Then, in 1876, Hubert Howe Bancroft rented a room adjacent to the Surveyor-General's office, installed desks, etc., hired fifteen Spanish translators and, after a solid year of work and the expenditure of $18,000 succeeded in making an orderly transcript of the records.... The importance of Bancroft's abridgement of the archives was not fully recognized until a generation later when the fire of 1906 destroyed the original collection.

The Bancroft transcriptions referring to the founding of Los Angeles, printed herein, are from photostats supplied by the Bancroft Library at Berkeley. Apparently lost from that collection is the transcript of Felipe de Neve's order for the founding of the Pueblo de los Angeles, written at Misión San Gabriel August 26, 1781, and which definitely assigned the date September 4 for the founding. The original of this document was among those held in the surveyor-general's office. A certified traced copy of it was secured by the writers of the *Centennial History of Los Angeles*[1] in 1876, but has disappeared long since. Before that, a similar copy of a portion of the document was introduced as evidence in Los Angeles District Court Case No. 1344, filed March 11, 1869.

As the first collection of decrees and ordinances prepared for the government of Alta California, the *Reglamento para el Gobierno de la Provincia de Californias*, drafted by Felipe de Neve June 1, 1779, at the Presidio de San Carlos de Monterey, is among the most important of California documents. When completed by Neve it was forwarded to Madrid, received the king's approval in 1781, and was returned to Mexico where it was printed in 1784. Less than half a dozen copies are known to be extant in California.

Without doubt, future researches in the archives of Mexico and Spain will throw further light on the founding of Los Angeles. Last year [1931] Vernon D. Tate was commissioned jointly by the Historical Society of Southern California and the Automobile Club of Southern California to secure transcripts of documents bearing on this subject in the Archivo General de Mexico. As a result of this effort, the original Instrucción to Rivera for the recruitment of pobladores and soldiers of the Expedition of 1781, correspondence pertaining to this document and to the Reglamento, and the manuscript accounts of supplies issued to the pobladores were brought to light and are here printed for the first time. – EDITORS

1. This is a reference to *An Historical Sketch of Los Angeles County California*, written by J. J. Warner, Benjamin Hayes, and Dr. J. P. Whitney, published in Los Angeles by John Lewin & Co. in 1876 to honor the centennial of American independence.

Four Reports by Governor Neve[1]

No. 82 // 78

CONSTRUCTION

A report to His Excellency regarding the completion of the reconstruction of Mission San Diego as well as the completion of construction of Mission San Juan Capistrano. The fort of San Francisco has been completed; the mission closest to it bears the same name. Mission Santa Clara has been established. Since the fort finds itself unprotected, materials are being transported from Monterey so that it can be enclosed and protected as stipulated in the Royal Regulations regarding the construction of presidios.

Most Excellent Señor [Viceroy Bucareli]:

Señor. I account to you that on my Arrival at these new establishments, I found the Misión San Diego already rebuilt and the foundation of San Juan Capistrano concluded in the same place in which it was started, in both having guarded the implements of the censor; covering them with earth. Also I found built the fort of San Francisco and adjacent the Mission of the same Name, the former immediately at the entrance of the Port, and the second at a distance from the fort of five quarters of a league next to the lagoon of Our Lady of the Sorrows, one and another sites were occupied the 27 of June, and convenient to the Mission there is plenty of Water, firewood and Stone for building with lands proportionable for Cornfields, and with the advantage of a spring situated near at hand with water not difficult to draw out, which acquired, can succeed in benefiting with irrigation a large sown field.

The second Mission, which was called Our Lady of Santa Clara, was locat-

1. Provincias Internas Tom. 121, Archivo General de Mexico. Translated by Lindley Bynum from transcripts loaned by Henry R. Wagner. The original Spanish-language version of these documents can be found on pages 173–78.

ed the 4th day of last January, at 15 leagues distance to the southwestward from the fort on the Bank of the River of Our Lady of Guadalupe. It has, according to my information, much land for sowing on both sides of the River irrigated and moist, and very easy to bring the Water, although the mission and the tilled lands are exposed ... to the inundations which may be occasioned of which they have no experience following the year with the greatest scarcity of Water which may be experienced, the Gentiles who inhabit this Land are very numerous; as soon as I am free, and as soon as the scouting parties of this Presidio return, I leave to Examine those Missions and fort, of which I will inform you with more Particularity: moreover I have instructed the Lieutenant Don Joseph Joáquin de Moraga to arrange what is convenient to wall in the fort, to conform to the provisions of the Royal Reglamento of Presidios; which already is partially started and will continue until finished, in this one, because like the other it is composed of Barracks or huts without protection except the small house of the Commander and the Store House which are of adobe otherwise they should have already collapsed had they not been propped up during the past year as previously happened before to the Chapel, for which a small hut serves during the day, and to expedite the whole work it is necessary to employ the Troop with the few servants of the Presidio, which fact I make known to you hoping your benevolence may grant to these Companies the remuneration which is of your Superior pleasure.

Our Lord protect your excellent person many years. Monterey, February 25, 1777.

Excellent Señor
PHELIPE DE NEVE [rubric]

Most Excellent Señor Bailio Don Antonio Bucareli y Ursua.

No. 83 // 59

TROOPS

In which account is given to His Excellency of the state in which are found the Companies of the three presidios of California Septentrional as to Animals, Riding Equipment, Armaments and Mounted Troops, with statement of the number of mules and Horses which are deemed requisite, and a Relation of the supplies of Clothing, Accoutrements and Arms which are needed.

Most Excellent Señor [Viceroy Bucareli].

Señor: The third of the present month I arrived at this Presidio, not having been able to accomplish this with greater promptitude because of the great distance, and the preservation of the horses which transported me.

At my passing by the Presidio de San Diego I examined the condition of the Troops of the garrison, as they exercised at my passage, of the Horses and Soldiers employed as the guard of the Mission, as well as the Company of this Presidio, with one thing and another were found in a most deplorable state, the Clothes, as well as the Armament and Horses; first because they were seen not to conform to uniformity, indiscriminately short over-jackets [and] waist-coats of calico of varied colors were used, rarely are those who have a hat and sleeves remaining and [the clothes of] many have so greatly deteriorated that they are almost indecent.

The Armament besides being of unequal caliber from that prescribed is too disordered for safety. The Swords (with the exception of those which in the last year were sent to San Diego) are completely useless, because of their poor quality short or dull, there being various men who have none likewise the lances, almost all the Soldiers being found stripped of the necessities for their Mounts which in addition are very old, few of which do not lack some of the parts of this equipment.

The Cavalry which the Troop of these presidios has consists of 70 Mules and 37 Horses, that of San Diego distributed in 43 stalls of their own Garrison (excluding the 25 Recruits of Reserve who are mounted) 86 Mules and 41 Horses, that of Monterey. Divided into 45 Stalls of those composing the garrison, including 20 who protect the escorts of the three missions of San Luis, San Antonio, and Carmel. 31 Mules and 57 horses, that of San Francisco divided into thirty-four Stalls of those who make up their Company exclusive of the Lieutenant in which number of horsemen might be considered a fifth part that are useless.

In this Relation I would call to your attention the accompanying two Reports, one concerning the Clothing and Articles of Equipment which are necessary for the companies of each Presidio according to the state in which they now are, and the other of the Armament, Powder, and Balls corresponding to each one in this manner for their respective Armament as for that which should exist for future needs, so that being worthy of approval of yourself you may order to remit on the first occasion the articles of Clothing, Equipment, Armament and Munitions which will be sent to each one of the Referred Presidios.

Likewise I ought to state to you that notwithstanding how many Arms these Companies actually possess (excepting the twenty Soldiers of that of San Francisco), they are the property of the troop having been charged their value, it is convenient that they be gathered together and deposited in the Warehouses in order by this method to avoid the great inconvenience at which they are sold to the Pagans, who anxiously ask especially for Sword blades, fragments of these, points of sharp Lances and every kind of cutting Instrument. Cutters with which I saw many natives in the Santa Barbara Channel Armed, being worthy of notice the nicety with which they burnish, polish, and make a sharp thrust of a piece of sword. And if this should be to your satisfaction, the new Equipment could be distributed without charging it to the Soldier who alone would remain responsible for its repair and who is required to return it when he is either on Leave or Dead.

Regarding the Horses which at this time the three companies have, (excluding officers) 147, and the riding Animals and Mules that exist, 322 altogether, the approximately eighty Mules and 26 Horses which should come from Loreto makes 438 which is equal to three horses for a Stall, lacking three animals, without counting those which of this number are understood to be depreciated on account of Age and incapacity with which it is not possible that service can be done without considerable delay as one who experiences to suffer fatigue, those Soldiers who find themselves in better state for their journeys with borrowing from one another, leave those who remain in the Presidio almost unmounted; with which consideration and that of the Herds of this Presidio and that of San Diego, they find themselves so deteriorated that in order to help them, with 52 loads of corn from the frontier of Velicatá, and Misión San Luis it has been forced upon me to avail myself of 12 mules from the Misión San Diego and 23 from the Herd of the Presidio de San Francisco, not having been able to take in such emergency more than 17 Animals from the two remaining; on account of which in order to put the troops of these Presidios in a state of service, counting on the shipment of these beasts being late and a diminution of those on hand which might occur, I rule there are needed two hundred Mules and three hundred Horses, whose transport only could be accomplished by land following the route of Don Juan Bautista de Anza, without the loss of Horses and the increased delay of years which their shipping would cause, and the prolonged march coming from Loreto. All of this I represent to you in fulfillment of my obligation.

Our Father Guard your Excellent Person happy years. Monterey, 26 of February 1777.

Most Excellent Señor,
PHELIPE DE NEVE [rubric]

Most Excellent Generous Señor Don Antonio Bucareli y Ursua.

No. 71.

REGLAMENTO

In which Account is given of the urgency there will be of naming an Aide who will exercise in the 5 presidios of Californias the same functions as those of the Inspector in the presidios of the frontier, in the event that the provisions proposed for the new Reglamento are approved.

My Good Señor [Comandante-General de Croix], I proceed to inform you that thus in order to carry out the establishment of the Presidio and the Missions which are to be situated on the channel of Santa Barbara and the Pueblo which is to be founded bordering the River of Porsincula [sic] as you have decided, as likewise now to establish the new rule and reglamento which I have proposed, for the Presidios of this Peninsula, standardizing in all its adaptable parts its government to that specified in the Royal Reglamento of Presidios, being indispensable (for this plan to be approved) or that the governor be Named inspector for these, or that these functions be exercised by the Governor, given the great extension of the Province in which are his Presidios, it is impossible that anyone would be able to accomplish this without the Aid of an Assistant, and least [of all] I who have to formulate and Establish these new plans, called from these attentions, when my weakened head causes me to suffer these partial application and material work with which I was able to carry out those matters which were entrusted to me at another time, and finding myself at present in a place where I have no one whom I could entrust with the copying of a letter.

In attention to this matter I have addressed you entreating that should the proposed rules be approved for the change of Reglamento in this Peninsula, that you deign to name an Assistant who will exercise in these Presidios the functions which are those of Inspector in [the presidios] on the frontier, this post should be conferred on a Lieutenant of acknowledged intelligence and good conduct with the Salary which your grace may be pleased to grant him.

Our Father guard you many years. Monterrey and April 3, 1779.

I kiss the hand of your excellency.

Your attentive and trusted servant,
PHELIPE DE NEVE [rubric]

Señor Comandante General Cavallero de Croix.

No. 92 // 48

TROOPS AND FOOTING

Account is given of the Arms, Powder, balls and Loads of Cannon which are needed to complete the equipment and stores of the Companies; and two Memoranda of the Clothes, Foodstuffs and effects ruled necessary to Supply the troops which are to Guard the Channel, the Pobladores and their families, and in the Next year expected to arrive to this Province, and that it will be opportune to conduct by sea a Reconnaissance of the Channel for the purpose of marking the safest shelter for the landings.

My dear sir [Comandante-General de Croix], I convey to your Hands the enclosed report, which states the arms, Powder, and balls necessary to complete the Companies of these three presidios and their Stores; the Powder and balls and loads of Cannon are necessary, as likewise, the Stores belonging to the Troop which is to garrison the Channel of Santa Barbara, two Cannons of 4 for this Presidio and cartridges which for the present Supply it.

Likewise considering the necessities of the Troop, the Settlers and their families on their arrival, that they may be helped with Clothing, which has been destroyed during the long voyage, in order that they may not experience the need of the various effects and Food necessary, I have judged it necessary to direct to you the accompanying two memorials, in order that having it handy your excellency may condescend to take steps to remit the Supplies which they contain, from Mexico and San Blas in the Next year with the vessel which conveys the Pay of the Presidio de San Diego, to deliver it to Teniente Don Josef Francisco de Ortega in case that at their arrival here, the Channel is not occupied since they all ought to be transported there, with the two Cannons which you will be able to supply from the Department of San Blas.

In case this is carried out in this way the Commander of the Boat will find in the said San Diego, all the instructions that I may rule and can be useful in carrying out this Commission and it will be very opportune for me to bring the order to Inspect the coast of the Channel, to mark the shelter or bay which in relation to the Presidio, will allow the vessels to cast anchor and unload Food and effects which they may in the future contain.

Our Lord protect your Excellency many years. Monterrey, July 19, 1779.

I kiss the hand of your Excellency your
most Attentive and faithful servant,
PHELIPE DE NEVE [rubric].

Señor Comandante General Cavallero de Croix.

Correspondence Pertaining to the Reglamento and to Recruitment of Pobladores[1]

My Dear Sir [Comandante-General de Croix]: I have received, with Letter from yourself of last February 12, a Copy of the Reglamento which lately has been prepared by the Governor of Californias Don Phelipe Neve, altering the old one so that the affairs of this Peninsula may be regulated to course with more certain pulse; and so that every economy possible may be observed in the expenditures required for the Presidio de Santa Barbara, which has just been ordered, and those who prepare the employments which have been created for the better Service of His Majesty.

From the Context of this Reglamento one deduces that its object is directed toward good internal government, and the discipline of the Presidial Companies, the relief of the Troops, the benefit of that Peninsula, and the Security of the Interests of the Royal Hacienda. In this understanding you may soon proceed to dictate the Provisions required for its observance, in complete confidence that I am ready to Contribute on my part with those [provisions] which will further this intent, in which understanding I render a complete account [of these matters] to His Majesty so that all may be in accord with his gracious will.

May Our Lord guard you many years. Mexico, 19 May of 1780.

Your hands are kissed by your Most
Attentive and Devoted Servant,
MARTIN DE MAYORGA [rubric]

1. Provincias Internas Tom. 122, Archivo General de Mexico. Translated by Marion Parks. The original Spanish-language version of these documents can be found on pages 179–83.

Arispe July 15 of 1780.

To the Assessor-General in whose possession is the antecedent correspondence in consideration of which I have named the subaltern officers who are being added to the Presidios of Californias for Assistant inspector to the ranking Capitán Don Nicolas Soler.

DE CROIX [rubric]

Señor Comandante General [de Croix]:

By Royal Order of March 21, 1775, His Majesty was pleased to command that the Reglamento for the Peninsula of Californias be altered because of the defects which were noted in the one then in force; to which end Your Excellency ordered in a letter written by you on the 15th of August of '77 to Gobernador Don Phelipe Neve, that he inform you at length and in detail what he estimated necessary for its Reform, so that he might be placed in a position to act when he should find himself on the ground. Subsequently in a new Order which was passed on September 3 of the following year of '78; he was instructed to dedicate himself to the task of improving the Reglamento in Force; and in doing so Bearing in mind the new establishments, which at his suggestion Your Excellency had resolved to found on the Channel of Santa Barbara, he framed and Remitted the new Reglamento, which, under date of June 1, 1779, is found in the file.

Having considered and Examined it, you were pleased to reply on February 12 of this year, that nothing was left to wish for, since in every particular you found the objects of the Royal Service fulfilled, especially as to relief for the Troops, Economy and security of the interests of the Exchequer, and Advantages which they proportioned for the cost of defending, developing and maintaining the Territory. This opinion you transmitted on the same date to His Excellency the Viceroy, and reported to His Majesty soliciting his Royal Approval.

Effectively, on the same day you also sent a Copy [of the Reglamento] to the Viceroy, informing him that you considered it not only worthy of his Recommendation, but that its adoption seemed to you very urgent in order that the advantages it offered might soon be realized, and that the expenses occasioned by the New Establishments might be reduced; and that if it merited the same Opinion on part of His Excellency, you hoped to be so advised in order to make the necessary arrangements and proceed immediately to the reform of the employments of the Commissaries, and Warehouse Keepers, and to make further provisions looking toward its provisional Observance, until, account having been given to His Majesty, the Royal Approbation should arrive. To this the Viceroy replied on May 19 following that you might at once proceed with ordering the provisions necessary for putting the Reglamento in force, in the firm conviction that you were quick to contribute on your part with those things which would promote its intention, and in the understanding that you would give complete account to His Majesty in order that this Resolve might meet with his Royal satisfaction.

On February 23 of this same year you rendered account to His Majesty of all which you had ordered Relative to the Peninsula of Californias, and as a result of the Orders which its Gobernador Don Phelipe Neve had given. [You reported also] that having framed this the new reglamento, of which you had ordered ad interim observance, the advantages toward which it was directed would be brought about, adding that in the Following Post, you would Remit a Copy, which you lacked time and hands for getting into that one.

Thus, not only is the said new reglamento found approved by yourself, but His Excellency the Viceroy has condescended to approve its observance, offering to make provisions conducing to this end, and of everything account has been rendered to His Majesty; and his Royal approbation is awaited. In everything possible Government, discipline and management of interests of the Troops of that Peninsula, have been made uniform to those established for the Troops of these Provinces in the last Reglamento of September 10, 1772 – which is in force in them; and even if all the provisions and resolutions which have been ordered as a result of the revisions of Inspection [military orders] and expedients promoted in this one are not adaptable to that Country, there may be many conducive [to this end], and easy of execution, especially in regard to the paymasters, powers conferred on the Officers of the Companies, method of distributing supplies, and responsibility of the Captains. In view of which it seems to me advisable that at the same time these Orders be given to the Gobernador Don Phelipe Neve, he be sent also a Copy, or Certified Collection of the Resolutions both general and particular which have been dictated by Your Excellency for the better government, discipline and management of the interests of these Troops, so that comprehending all that has been disposed regarding them, he may adapt to those of that Peninsula such items as he will find convenient in the enforcement [of the new Reglamento] adding such items chapter by chapter to the said Reglamento and advising as to those which he has added so that there will always be a record of it in this Superior Government.

In official communication of Number 88, of June 6 of 1777, the Gobernador Phe. Neve, after describing in complete detail the places which had been examined from the Misión San Gabriel to the Presidio de Monterrey, the distances at which they lie one from the other, and those which have available land and water for sowing and tilling, proposed that for the Province itself to produce the seeds and grains necessary to provision the Troops and Settlers, no other means can be found than to recruit forty or sixty laborers, who would settle on the Rivers of Santa Ana, San Gabriel, La Porciuncula, and Guadalupe, or at least, that divided in two crews be established one on the River of Santa Clara and the other on that of the Porciuncula, with various auxiliaries to aid them, as he stated later in a separate Oficio dated April 3, 1779, designated as Number 69. He explained [therein] that twenty-four Pobladores would be sufficient, including among them one Mason, and one Blacksmith with the other auxiliaries which have been asked, and which were included in this number.

Having Acceded to this proposal and having made provisions to secure the recruits and other auxiliaries asked by Neve, you advised him that you were instituting measures in interest of the project; with which motive, in a new Oficio of April 22 of this year, Designated as No. 130, he explained that he had ordered reconnaissance of the region about the entrance of the Channel of Santa Barbara to the North and South, to see if in this area might be found a site adequate for Planting crops which being contiguous would suffice to Supply with Provisions the Presidios and Pueblos which need to be established in order to Occupy it [the channel]. This resulted in finding to the North an Abundant flow of water, which falls from the Mountain, and may be made available most easily, with spacious Lands for tillage, and although in the immediate Vicinity of the water supply the pasture does not appear to be of very good Quality, such is to be found at short distance, with abundance of timber, firewood and stone, and more than two leagues of plain, down to the Camino Real which goes from the Presidio de San Diego to that of Monterrey. At five leagues distance is the first rancheria of the Channel, called la Asunta. At seven leagues from the Opposite entrance, was found another abundant arroyo or spring with much and good land for tillage, but lacking in timber and firewood. These discoveries, with those which were made in the year of '77, have brought him [Neve] to the conclusion that it would be more Advantageous to Change the foundation of the Pueblo, which was proposed for the margin of the River of La Porciuncula, as when he formed this project he was not instructed that you had approved that of the Occupation of the Channel. It therefore seemed to him more useful to found the two Pueblos, one in the stated place five leagues distant from the first Rancheria de la Asunta, and the other in the place which would offer most opportunity between Misións San Juan Capistrano and San Gabriel; the first in order to supply the Presidio and guard of the Channel of Santa Barbara; and the Second in order to provide for that of San Diego; in the understanding that before Don Fernando Rivera arrived, he would go personally to investigate these places, and to examine whether the opportunities they offer corresponded to the information which he had been given by the Teniente Don Joseph de Ortega, and the Sargento Juan Josef Robles, in which case he would Divide the Twenty-four families in the two establishments. He was not without confidence of being able to add some other Poblador, and that this idea would produce good effects; but needing for its execution your approval, he hoped that you would be pleased to Communicate your Will, in order to make arrangements for all things Concerned, so that before long the families who are to be colonized could be Settled and there could be found for them livestock and other auxiliary Necessities, because he thought to establish at one time, the two Pueblos, the Misión San Buenaventura, and the Presidio of the Channel, and this finished, to go on to found the Misión la Concepcion.

And Granting that the Governor needs to go to reconnoitre personally those lands as he offered to do in his Oficio, no one is better able to determine with light and certainty than he, those which may be most suitable, and provide most opportunity for the foundation of the two Pueblos and to facilitate their progress. It seems to me that in this matter you can, if it Please you, leave to his judgment the Selection of the places in which they shall be established, charging him that he shall arrange if it be possible, to place the New Presidio, which must be Situated along the Center of the Channel, on suitable land with soil and Water for Tillage so that under its Protection in time there may be founded another Settlement, which is the Object with which His Pious Majesty generously erogates the Expenditures Occasioned by such establishments. In View of the fact that those ordered founded at the junction of the Rivers Colorado and Gila are equal in importance to these, and that in order to facilitate their progress you have ordered several measures very Helpful to the undertaking which can be no less adaptable to [the needs of] the Peninsula of

Californias, it seems to me that you can equally, if it suits you so to command, order that there be Remitted Certified Copies of all [of them] to the Gobernador Don Phe. Neve, in order that having them before him, and at once observing those which seem to him possible of execution, he may report on the rest, [as to] that which should be done and what he finds. Nevertheless, in all these foregoing matters, you will resolve Upon such conclusions as may be to your pleasure. Arispe September 18, 1780.

GALINDO NAVARRO [rubric]

Arispe, September 18 of 1780.

I concur in the opinion of the Assessor, and in consequence made reply to the office of the Governor of Californias, No. 130, of April 22 of this year, regarding the establishment of the two new Settlements, sending to him separately the Orders preparing for the ad interim observance of the new Reglamento from the first of January of the next year; And forwarding the replies to the Gobernador Intendente of this Province and to the Capitán Don Fernando de Rivera y Moncada, Commissioned for the recruiting of troops and additional Settlers; gave advice of all to His Excellency the Viceroy, and a report to His Majesty with copies of the *Expediente* and related documents.

DE CROIX [rubric]

Report was given in Letter No. 721 – February 28 of '82.

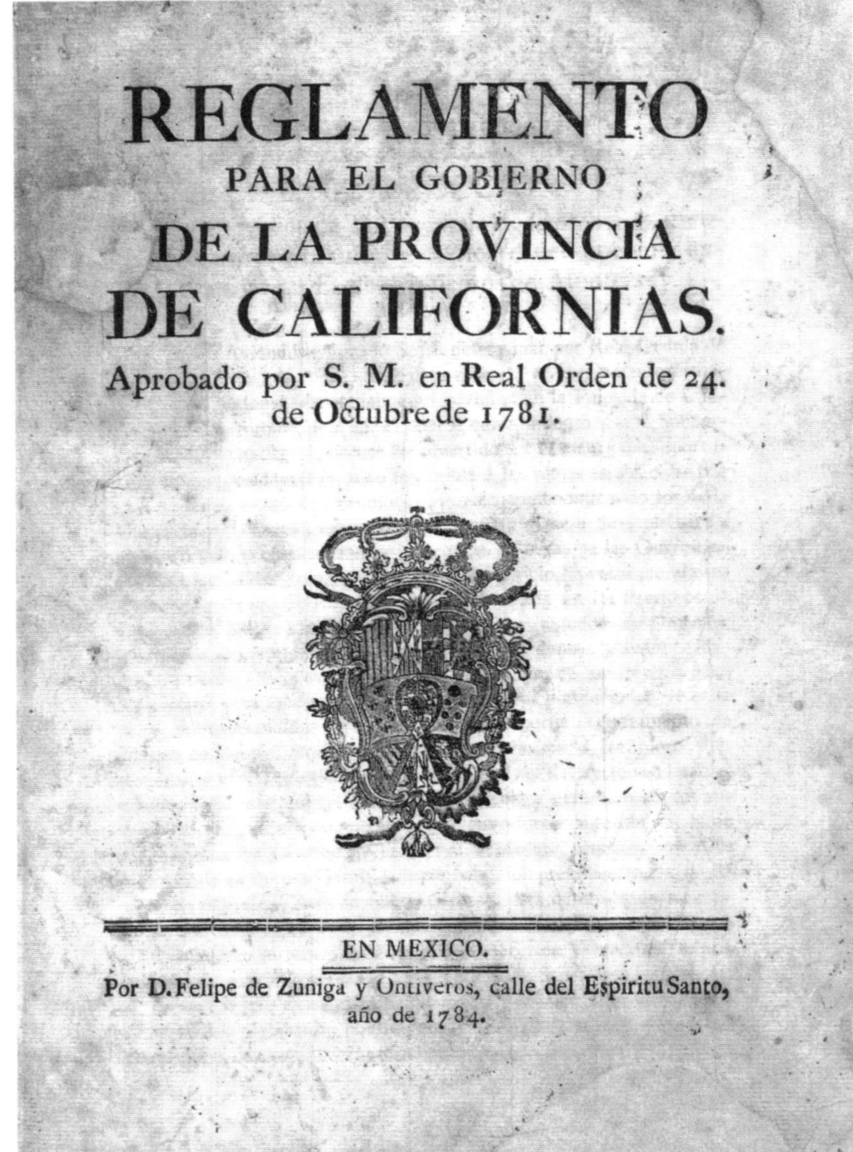

REGLAMENTO
PARA EL GOBIERNO
DE LA PROVINCIA
DE CALIFORNIAS.
Aprobado por S. M. en Real Orden de 24.
de Octubre de 1781.

EN MEXICO.
Por D. Felipe de Zuniga y Ontiveros, calle del Espiritu Santo,
año de 1784.

FIGURE 4. The first printing of the earliest collection of decrees and ordinances prepared for the government of Upper California, most authored by Governor Felipe de Neve. This title page is from the Thomas W. Streeter auction catalogue.

Reglamento

For the Garrisons of the Peninsula of Californias, erection of new Missions, and fostering of the colonization and extension of the Settlements of Monterey.[1]

His Majesty, having deigned to determine (by Royal Decree of March 21, 1775) to alter the provisional Regulations now in force in the Peninsula of Californias; in order to give due fulfillment to this Sovereign Resolve, has marked as the most opportune and suitable means their adaptation (so far as possible), to the rules established by the Royal Regulations for Garrisons, for the economical government of the [garrisons] of the Peninsula and their Troops; changing the footing, pay and management of interests in such manner as to make (by advantageously apportioning the force of the Posts for sallies and other functions of the Service) a saving in the present costs which the Royal Exchequer pays in the posts of Loreto,[2] San Diego, Monterey and San Francisco. [To] increase number of Officers, equalize and proportion the wages of Sergeants, Corporals, Soldiers, Surgeon, Master Mechanics and Colonizers, in such manner that the wages be such as are requisite for the subsistence, responsibility and heedfulness of each class. This includes the Subordinates of the small Department of Marine at Loreto; Stipends which have to be continued to Religious Missionaries; and the order in which new Reductions [centers for converting the Indians] should be located, Establishing rules which shall assure the encouragement, population and extension of the old and new settlements. With which important object, to secure communication and to draw to the true knowledge of Religion the

1. Original translation printed in *The Land of Sunshine*, VI (January 1897). Translated by Charles F. Lummis. The original Spanish-language version of this document can be found on pages 185–220.

2. Lower California.

numerous Gentiles that inhabit the indispensable strait and perilous pass of the Channel of Santa Barbara, it is decided to occupy it; establishing a Post and three Missions, with a Pueblo which, being nearby, can supply said Post and that of San Diego with Provisions from the product of its crops. And as it is not feasible that the Frontier Inspector of Posts review those of this Peninsula, since the sea-voyage and their enormous remoteness hinder, it is made obligatory upon the Governor to discharge the duties of Inspector (as he has done); heeding that the Government be purely Military, and that this Chief be not included as Captain of any of the Posts of his command. And if he is unable to discharge this duty personally, as is ordered, he shall (subject to Superior approbation) name and appoint an Aide, who shall, under his direction and orders, review the Posts to which he is destined, watch zealously the uniformity, service, discipline and subordination of the Troops as to the most exact observance of whatever is provided in the said Royal Regulations, without variation except as authorized by the following Titles.

FIRST TITLE.

1. As the present condition of the Peninsula does not permit change in the established order of transporting from New Spain [Mexico], at the cost and risk of the Royal Exchequer, of Clothing, Goods, Provisions and Troop Horses for the subsistence and alleviation of the Troops, Settlers and other Dependents of the Posts, this practice must be followed: the Agent of the Peninsula and the Commissary of San Blas forwarding their lists for the Requisitions which must be sent yearly by the Governor to the Most Excellent Viceroy, that he may deign to determine the purchase and forwarding [of supplies]. Excepting, the Post of Loreto, whose considerable remoteness forbids the sending of its Accounts in season; wherefore they must be sent by the Captain direct to His Excellency.

2. The Provisions, Uniform, Arms, Saddles, Clothes, Troop Horses and other articles sent from Mexico, San Blas or Sonora, must be received and distributed to the Troops at prices based on first cost, under which consideration the wages are fixed. Consequently there must be no intervention except the pay of the Individuals entitled to it and comprised in these Regulations.

3. As at present the Commissary of Loreto and the Storekeeper in other Posts has charge of the paying of Troops and Clerks and the receipt and distribution of the respective Requisitions, it will henceforth be in charge (under inspection of the Captain in Loreto, and of the Commandant in the Posts of

the new Settlements) of a Paymaster appointed from among the Subalterns of the Company under the rules hereinafter set forth.

4. The Payment of Allowances shall be continued from the Royal Chest in Mexico, in the same order as now; delivering to the Agent of the Peninsula, (as per Supreme Decree of the Most Excellent Sir Viceroy) of the amount fixed as sufficient to fill the Requisitions of goods. This shall include the sum to be remitted in pesos to each Post, likewise crediting to the Commissary of the Department of San Blas the funds necessary to purchase victuals and Articles for Rations; and whatever else, through Agency of said Commissary, is remitted him according to the Requisitions. As said delivery and purchases are made in the last months of the year, and received the following May or June, there should be no change in the established method of providing for the Troops, with reference to the balance that each individual deducts for his last year's settlement; providing, through the year, the Rations and other necessary expense of the Soldier or his family. For this reason the allowance of twenty-five reales daily for the support of Corporals and Soldiers is exempted; the Royal Exchequer paying the allowances at the end of the year they come due and paying the Troops the middle of the year following. With this knowledge and prudent regulation of the cost of the Provision, Uniform, Arms, Trappings, Clothing, Goods and Funds (counting the total sum of the Allowance for paying in pesos the Salaries of Officers and Surgeon, discounting that which they receive during the year and the balances left after supplying the Troops) the Paymasters will make out the Requisitions bearing in mind to deduct the residues, whether they arise from the delivery to be made of them, or as surplus from year to year; bearing in mind equally, that the cash to be asked must not exceed, at present, one-fourth of the Allowance, exclusive of the salary of the Governor and Aide (if that office is created), who shall receive theirs separately as suits them.

5. As prices of Clothing and Goods are subject to alteration, whenever for this reason, or because the Requisition amounts to more than one-half the Allowance, the assortment cannot be filled, the lack shall be supplied from the one-fourth part to be remitted in money; and since the remaining one-fourth is arranged to meet the cost of Provisions and Goods called for by the Requisition of San Blas, any deficiency will be covered in same manner.

6. Whenever the sowing, harvesting and storing of crops in the new Settlements is advanced so that the Garrisons can provide themselves in whole or in part with the needful Provisions, the Paymasters will ask for the sum of

money corresponding to their purchase price, above that already indicated, subtracting the equivalent from the San Blas Requisition for Seeds, and proportionately from the sum of supplying them.

7. The supreme difficulty and losses in transporting Troop Horses from Sonora to this Peninsula makes it necessary to supply each soldier with three or four, and to have in each Post, at cost of the Royal Exchequer, a drove of twenty-four or thirty mules to pack cargoes from the Ships, carrying Provisions for the Escorts and aid the Garrison, which, through the loss or considerable delay of a Vessel, might lack the most necessary seeds and Goods. For these reasons, that of the carrying of Rations to the Settlers of the new Town of San Jose Guadalupe and to the Town (if it is decided to found one) and for the other labors to be incurred in establishing the Post and Missions in the Pass of Santa Barbara – to which for the first year all food and other necessities must be carried by land – besides the need of hauling in wagons, henceforth, the produce of the Towns to supply the Posts; since it is impossible to put these Troops on a Cavalry footing like those of the Frontier until facilitated by the increase of the horse-herds in the Peninsula, it is proper that when the Herds of Loreto and San Francisco are filled to the number of twenty-four mules (each with its trappings) and that of San Diego with thirty mules, thirty others be supplied to the Post which must be located in the Pass equally equipped. All this at cost of the Royal Exchequer; their keep, the replacing of those that die or become useless, the repair of harness and other belongings, and the pay of one Muleteer in each Post, being charged to the allowance fund, as a general expense henceforth. If, owing to other uses to which it is destined, the fund will not cover this expense, let the deficit be charged to the General Fund of the Companies, which are at all times responsible for the stock of said Herds, that of Monterrey included, which now has forty pack mules.

8. It being indispensable to furnish the trades of Carpentry and Blacksrnithing to these recent acquisitions of Monterey, the two Master Mechanics, the Carpenter and three Blacksmiths now there shall remain, at the wages assigned them. This expense shall be included as part of the Allowance of Monterrey and San Diego to which they are set aside, this being the only one for this purpose to be met by the Royal Exchequer. Since all the tools and irons pertaining to those trades and that of Stonemason, which are included in the delivery to be made to the Paymasters, are to remain for the benefit of the settlements, the Paymasters are charged with their preservation and repair and with receipts for

the work done for individuals, applying any surplus to the wages or rations of four Apprentices, to be sought to learn these trades, whereof the due account must be kept. Meantime the continuance of these trades and the respective cost to the Royal Exchequer are to be understood.

SECOND TITLE.

Footing, pay and gratuities of the Companies and Dependents of Posts, and Marines of Loreto; posts covered by the Troops, and their distance apart.

1. The Company of the Post of Loreto, Capital of the old California, is and shall remain on the footing of Captain, Lieutenant, Ensign and forty-four Recruits, including two Sergeants and three Corporals. With this it should maintain the small Detachment of a Sergeant and six Soldiers in the Real [mining town] of Santa Anna of the South, distant one hundred [Spanish] leagues[3] [266 miles] from the Post. It covers with a subaltern Officer, two Corporals and twenty-three Soldiers, the three Missions of the North Frontier, which are at intervals in the two hundred thirty leagues [665 miles] between the last of them and Loreto. At Loreto must remain the Captain, one subaltern Officer (who must be the Paymaster), one Sergeant, one Corporal and ten Soldiers. It is distant three hundred fifty leagues [931 miles] from the following:

2. The footing of San Diego shall be of Lieutenant, Ensign and fifty-two Enlisted men, including one Sergeant and five Corporals, the rank of Ensign being added to the present footing. It should cover the three Missions of its district with one Corporal and five Soldiers apiece. Upon the founding of the new Pueblo it shall place therein a Safeguard of four Soldiers, who shall remain only the first two years. Thus the Garrison [San Diego] will be reduced to one Lieutenant, one Ensign and thirty men, including a Sergeant and two Corporals, wherewith it shall attend to the sorties and other duties of the Service. To the next is one hundred seventy leagues [452 miles].

3. That of San Carlos de Monterey shall be of the same number of Men as the preceding, adding to the Company a Lieutenant and Ensign. Three privates of its present footing shall be abolished. It shall continue the Escorts (of one Corporal and five Soldiers) in each of the three Missions of its territory. It has four Soldiers employed in the pueblo of San Jose; and there shall re-

3. A Spanish league was 2.66 miles. The distances given herein are not accurate.

main in the Garrison, for the duties of the Service, a Lieutenant, an Ensign, a Sergeant, two Corporals and twenty-seven Soldiers. It is twenty-seven leagues [71.9 miles] from the next.

4. That of San Francisco will consist of Lieutenant, Ensign, and thirty-one Men, including a Sergeant and four Corporals. An Ensign is added to its present footing, and three privates subtracted. It shall cover (with two Corporals and ten Soldiers) the two Missions in its scope; and will have left for the service of the Post, a Lieutenant, an Ensign and nineteen Men, including a Sergeant and two Corporals.

5. The Pass of Santa Barbara is seventy-four leagues [197 miles] from the Post of San Diego and seventy from that of Monterrey. It stretches between the Coast and the *Cieneguilla*[4] Range about twenty-six leagues [70 miles], its greatest width being half to three-fourths of a league. It is full of high hills, bluffs and profound clefts. In this indispensable pass are eight thousand to ten thousand Gentiles, who inhabit twenty-one Rancherias, situated at short distances on the heights and points contiguous to the Beach. Near the beach, sometimes on it and sometimes on the high ground, runs the *camino real*.[5] This evidences the risk to which small Parties are exposed on it; and that if some incident makes those Gentiles treacherous or hostile, communication with the old and new Settlements would be cut off. These urgent reasons have caused the determination to occupy this pass in the following form.

6. The Post which shall be established midway the Pass shall be manned by Lieutenant, Ensign and twenty-nine Recruits, including a Sergeant and two Corporals. It shall establish in its shelter a Reduction which afterward shall be removed to the neighboring spot which offers more land and sufficient water to irrigate the fields; and then it shall be given from the Garrison an Escort of a Corporal and five Soldiers. At the ends of said Pass, for its complete occupation, two other "Reductions" shall be placed, each garrisoned with a Sergeant and fourteen Soldiers. Said Recruits will be considered supernumeraries to the Company at the Post, while they secure these settlements peace and good admission among the Gentiles. Attaining this with the rapid progress that should be expected in the spiritual conquest, they shall be reduced proportionately to the regular Escort of a Corporal and five Soldiers each; the Sergeants shall be incorporated with the Companies of San Diego

4. Meadow.
5. King's Highway.

and Monterrey, and the sixteen remaining Recruits shall be destined to garrison other "Reductions" which it may be decided to found, in which case they shall be added to the Companies nearest the spot.

7. The annual Allowance of the Post of Loreto shall be 12,522.50; adding 1,996 (amount of the corresponding allowance for the Marine Department, which must be credited annually as extra to the Allowance of the Post) makes a total of 14,518.50 pesos,[6] divided thus:

Annual Pay of the Captain	1,500.00
Of the Lieutenant	550.00
Of the Ensign	400.00
Of each of the two Sergeants, 262.50	525.00
Of each of the three Corporals, 225	675.00
Of each of the thirty-nine Privates, 217.50	8,482.50
For Gratuities of 10 yearly per Private	390.00
Total for the Post	12,522.50
Marine Department of above Post.	
Yearly pay of one Ship-Carpenter	132.00
Of one Blacksmith	120.00
Of one Porter	120.00
Crew of the Sloop *Pilar*	
Annual Pay of the Master	120.00
Of the Boatswain	84.00
Of eight Sailors at 72 each	576.00
Crew of the Launch *Lauretana*	
Its Master, by the year	84.00
Six Sailors at 60 each	360.00
Annual cost of careenings, overhaulings and Masts for one Sloop and two Launches, allow	400.00
Total allowance for the Post and Marine	14,518.50

This Regulation abolishes the Crew of the Launch San Juan Nepomuceno,

6. The amounts shown are pesos.

which Boat must be kept ready to be fitted out whenever there is grave need (only during that urgency) of the three Vessels; and for this purpose, the actual Master will remain as Boatswain of the Sloop.

The annual allowance of the Post of San Diego shall be 13,162.50, divided as follows:

Annual Pay of the Lieutenant	550.00
Of the Ensign	400.00
Of the Sergeant	262.50
Of each of the five Corporals, 225	1,125.00
Of each of the 46 Privates, 217.50	10,005.00
For gratuities of 10 yearly to each Private	460.00
	12,802.50
One Carpenter by the year	180.00
One Blacksmith ditto	180.00
Total	13,162.50

The Annual Allowance of the Post which shall be established in the Pass of Santa Barbara shall be 7,577.50; adding 6,895 for the two Escorts, which must be provided temporarily, gives 14,472.50, divided thus:

Annual Pay of Lieutenant	550.00
Ensign	400.00
Sergeant	262.50
Each of two Corporals, 225	450.00
Each of 26 Privates, 217.50	5,655.00
Gratuities from general fund of 10 each	260.00
	7,577.50

Escorts

Two Sergeants at 262.50	525.00
28 Privates at 217.50	6,090.00
Gratuity at 10 each	280.00
Total	14,472.50

The Annual Allowance of the Post of San Carlos de Monterey shall be 17,792.50; divided in this manner:

Annual Pay of the Governor	4,000.00

Lieutenant	550.00
Ensign	400.00
Surgeon	450.00
Sergeant	262.50
Corporals at 225	1,125.00
46 Privates at 217.50	10,005.00
Gratuities at 10 each, yearly	460.00
	17,252.50
One Carpenter, by the year	180.00
Two Blacksmiths at 180	360.00
Total	17,792.50

The Annual Allowance for the Post of San Francisco shall be 8,027.50, divided in this form:

Annual Pay of the Lieutenant	550.00
Ensign	400.00
Sergeant	262.50
Four Corporals at 225	900.00
26 Privates at 217.50	5,655.00
Gratuity from common fund, 10 each	260.00
Total	8,027.50
To each Settler in each of the two first years, for pay and rations	116.37½
For rations in each of the three following years that they may be granted him	60.00

THIRD TITLE.

Uniforms.

1. As the Clothing and corresponding goods to uniform the Troops of these Posts have been included in the annual Requisitions, causing considerable delay to the Soldier, either because what was furnished him for uniform did not fit, or because of want of Tailors to make up the cloth they were long without the necessary skill or spoiled the cloth in cutting, henceforth the Paymasters shall order the uniforms for their Companies made in proportionate sizes, itemizing the individual measurements and garments. And while

the total of uniforms must conform to the provisions of the Royal Regulations, and likewise the distribution, it must be borne in mind that as a pair of Breeches (and sometimes the jacket) is not enough to last a year in the constant hardship of this service, it will be necessary to order extra garments in the required amount. Equally, that as the wooden one with double pouches is inconvenient, the Cartridge-Box should be made with one row of twenty-four receptacles, of tin covered with leather, to be attached firmly to the strap used as a belt, which is to be one and a half yards long and of corresponding width. The row of receptacles to be covered with a flap of soft leather, shall begin six inches from the buckle,[7] which shall be of brass, smooth, with two claws; and two pouches in the ends of the cartridge box, one of them with a small tin priming-horn.

FOURTH TITLE.

Armament and Horse-Trappings.

1. These must fully meet the provisions of the Royal Regulations. As it is not practicable to furnish the troops of this Peninsula eight mounts to the man, because of the difficulty of transporting horses, they shall be maintained with as many as may be, until by encouragement of stock-raising in the new settlements it shall become possible to Re-mount all the Posts.

2. As to maintaining the horse-herd in close proximity to the Posts, to be brought in, morning and evening (if the country is not exposed to surprises by the enemy), that a prompt sortie be not hindered by the way the horses are held together and tended, there shall be no change in the established practice of keeping four horses tied by day and eight by night, in the Garrison; and this number shall be increased whenever there is noticed any reason calling for it.

FIFTH TITLE.

Distribution of Funds, and order in which general and special accounts must be kept by the Paymaster.

1. Understood that during the year the Troops must be assisted by the Paymaster in the special expenses which befall individuals and families; that, as there is no commerce in the Peninsula, these (expenses) must be on credit

7. In the Spanish text, "Evilla" is used. The correct word is Hebilla.

in the respective Warehouses, the daily succour of twenty-five reales each to Corporals and Soldiers (as is practiced in the Frontier Posts) shall be dispensed with; though when some urgent need arises, and there is sufficient balance, with the knowledge and order of the Captain or Commander of the Company, twenty pesos or thirty pesos may be advanced; but in no case shall this be done for one who is not on the stipulated footing; and for this the Commander shall be responsible.

2. Recollecting that the collection of the Estimate for these Posts is made at the end of the year, and that the paying of the Troops is effected in the middle of the year following (by which means, at whatever time the Soldier may depart, since economy must be practiced, there will be sufficient balance above the value of the armament and horses) there shall be retained in the fund for Corporals and Soldiers only fifty pesos each; which shall be discounted in the first four years for the purposes set forth in Title 4, Article 2, Royal Regulations.

3. Of the discounts annually made for the balance-fund of the Company, the Paymaster must make the corresponding entry to Cash, with a List specifying the names of the Corporals and Soldiers, the amount retained for each individual and the sum total. For his safeguard, a copy of said List shall be signed (crediting the deposit of that amount in the Treasury) by the Depositary, who shall be the captain in Loreto, and the second Officer who does not act as paymaster in the remaining Posts. The second year, and thereafter, the introduction of the amount pertaining to this fund shall be made, with its respective settlement; the charge being made up from the balance in hand from the preceding year, and the amount of discounts of the present year; the payments made therein being shown, as also the total of said fund.

4. The settlement of the yearly account (making the preceding discounts and the two percent, which the Paymaster is to receive) must be made under the supervision of the Captain or second Officers mentioned in the preceding Article; and of the Interested person or Subject named to examine it; making good in ready money to each his dues, in the order fixed by the Royal Regulations.

5. The gratuity fund for the Garrison, at the rate of ten pesos per Man, is designated (outside the general expenses) to meet the cost of the rations wherewith must be assisted the Indian Prisoners, or those that come to treat under a truce. Also to meet the fitting-out of the Recruits, under the exact rules fixed in Art. 5 of this Title in the Royal Regulations; the salary of a Muleteer, the re-

pair and care of pack-saddles and other equipment and the replacing of pack mules that may die or become useless in each Post. The common fund of the Companies shall be responsible (as aforesaid) for any shortage in this fund; said Officers distributing pro rata whatever deficit may result; remembering that the pack-animals are destined for the benefit of the Companies, and that consequently these are always responsible for their keep, and that in no case must the Royal Exchequer be charged with any excess of cost in this or other matters to which the fund is applied.

6. The Paymaster must keep his accounts, supervised by the other Officers of the Post, with the utmost precision and equity. Each year there should be entered to Cash, with the Amount corresponding to this fund, its respective settlement, with the vouchers for the legitimacy of the expenditures, which must be agreed and determined by the Officers of the Company. They shall not fail of this duty nor delay to consult the Governor and await his decision, the very thing which must be observed by those who are not executive officers, as well as to give account of those who (being such) should do so. Nevertheless he must examine in the Reviews their good and legal government, to give account yearly of the amounts on hand and the costs, and other matters bearing on the condition of each Post and Company to the Sir General Commanding.

7. The general accounts shall be kept in a Book, to be called the Cash-book. Its first item of charge will be the amount on hand, by delivery or brought forward, of clothing, goods, victuals, money or horses; next, the amount of the requisitions received from Mexico and San Blas; the total of balances of the Company and dependents of the Post; and the amounts realized from colts, steers and other livestock which may have been distributed to the Troops during the year. These items are to come last in the charge, both in this account and the private ones. The aforesaid charges must be verified by the Inventory of stock on hand, which must be made out at the end of every year (under supervision of the Officers of the Post) and their respective account. The original Invoices from Mexico and San Blas, with copies of the corresponding Receipts given by the Paymaster; the private settlements and accounts of the Company and dependents of the Post, and the vouchers for the entries pertaining to the Royal Exchequer, which must be made out, for the livestock, separately; the items of credit do and must specify the payment of loans and wages, with the settlements and private accounts of the Troops and dependents of the Post; the posting in the cash-book of the amount corresponding to the gratuity fund, and the amount held back for Corporals and Soldiers,

to verify the estimated balance in their respective settlements; the debts-on-account of individuals of the Troops and dependents of the Post; and the sum of the stock on hand at the end of the year shall prove up with the Inventory, wherewith (deducting the total of debit from the total of credit) shall be shown the balance, surplus or deficit resulting.

8. The settlements and private accounts of Officers, Surgeon, Sergeant, Corporals, Soldiers and dependents shall be kept in a Memorandum Book arranged annually for that purpose. It shall begin with an Index, showing the name and page under which is to be found the account of each one, headed with his name and rank. This shall enter the item showing last year's credit or debit, which must be brought forward on the margin and underlined, to follow out the supplies to be furnished this year. The items must state the quantity, quality, price and total value of the goods, noting on the opposite margin the month and day of delivery. The prices must agree with those fixed in the original Invoices or Tariff, to be made up the last of December. The accounts are to be closed, deducting from the total delivered and owed that which is due, thus showing the balance resulting. This must be noted in the presence of the interested party, as already provided.

SIXTH TITLE.

Supply of articles of clothing and other necessaries to the outfitting of the families of the Troops.

1. As it is not feasible in these Posts to make the assortment from the Requisitions agree with the lists provided for by the Royal Regulations to be given to individuals of the Troops in clothing and goods they may need for their outfitting and that of their families (partly by the fact that a year or more elapses before their arrival and receipt, partly because the Soldier has no other means of assorting or providing than from a general stock, and would therefore fall short in the necessary memoranda – since, anxious to receive the remainder of his pay in money, he would prefer it to the forced maintenance of his wife, children and remaining family) it is necessary to change this custom in these Posts. Therefore such Lists shall be given only by the Officers, Surgeon and Sergeants, following in making Requisitions that which is set forth in Art. 4, Tit. 1 of these Regulations.

2. When it is possible to show that any of the articles or goods sent by the Agent are not absolutely up to specifications, if the deterioration has not been

caused by the voyage, it shall be charged back at the first opportunity – and, if possible, on the same vessel which brought it.

3. As it is inevitable that there will be damage to seeds and articles of food, after they are received – particularly Corn, which is generally landed wormy; Lard and cane sugar, which the heat of the holds melts and ferments; and the latter article remains fermented and even becomes watery by the frequent fogs and dampness of the climate; to which must be added the shrinkage and waste caused by retailing, and by the carrying of these articles, victuals and necessaries for the subsistence of such Troops as are on escort duty – the Paymaster should not report these losses, nor those in piece-cloths which by shrinkage fall short of their proper measure; it being proper that the Common Fund suffer these losses. To proceed with due equity, that there be not inconvenience and that the Paymaster be secured, it is to be observed that preceding nomination (by the Corporals and Soldiers of the Company) of two Proxies in the same manner to be provided in Head 9 of Tit. 13; in their presence and that of the Officers shall be made an average of one, two or three bolts of each cloth, measuring them by different hands. Having discovered how much lacks, and the number of yards in hand, this (shortage) shall be deducted from the Invoice of value of the bolts, comparing the price of each yard with that which shall be fixed by the cost of the other bolts of the same quality. The same (precaution) must be practiced with all the other goods which show variation; all those measured must be noted together, and marked by the Officers and Proxies, and (thus) shall be the Tariff of retail prices upon cloths and goods which show shrinkage. To cover loss in grains and articles for rations, one "*real*"[8] shall be added to the price of each *fanega*[9] of Corn, Beans, Peas and Lentils; one real to the price of each *arroba*[10] of Lard and Rice; two reales to that of each arroba of sugar cane. Wherewith the anticipated shrinkage and variations shall be at the charge of the Paymaster, as shall those resulting from carelessness in storage and care of whatever is entrusted to him.

8. 12½ cents or one-quarter of a peseta.
9. 1½ bushels.
10. 25 pounds.

SEVENTH TITLE.

Powder.

1. There must be scrupulous observance of the provisions of Articles 1, 2, 3 and 5 of this Tit., in the Royal Regulations; altering Art. 4, in that the store of Powder and Ball in each Post must amount to sixteen pounds per man; in view of the difficulty and risk of bringing them from Mexico, where must be made up any shortage shown in the special account which must be kept of the consumption of stores. This being approved by the Governor, and on his request, it shall be supplied by the Factory in said Capital, the Most Excellent Sir Viceroy deigning to assign it.

EIGHTH TITLE.

Conferment of Positions.

1. Under the rules established by the Royal Regulations under this Title, in case of vacancy in the Company of the Post of Loreto, the Lieutenancy or Sublieutenancy of the remaining (Posts) of the Peninsula, the Governor shall propose [names for] the aforesaid positions, directing his Nominations to the Sir General Commanding.

2. To provide a Lieutenant or Ensign for the Company of Loreto, the Captain shall propose three persons, having the necessary qualifications and who are actually in service; passing the nominations to the Governor, and the latter to the Sir General Commanding, with his approval or remarks.

3. To fill vacant Sergeancies, the Captain shall make similar nominations; as shall the Lieutenants in the remaining Posts where there is no Captain (and where the Lieutenants must in this and other matters discharge the functions of Company Commanders). [The nominations shall be] from among those who have most distinguished themselves for good conduct and bravery; taking care, so far as possible, that they shall know how to read and write. The Governor shall approve the one who seems to him fitting. Corporals shall be named by the Captain and by Lieutenants who command a Post, on their own account; with the difference that they must hand up the nomination to the Governor for his approval.

NINTH TITLE.

Monthly Reviews.

1. The Commander of each Post shall review the Company monthly, and shall draw up an abstract, with the names of Officers, Sergeants, Corporals, Soldiers, Surgeon and other dependents. For those present at the review he shall write in the margin a P: the occupation of each employee; and for vacancies among employees or men a V. Vacancies of the past month which have been filled shall be indicated by a note in said abstract. If the place was that of an Officer, it shall carry the date of the Commanding General's approval, and Certificate signed by all the Officers, as to date of taking possession. If of Chaplain, Sergeant or Corporal, it shall carry merely the Certificate. And if of a Soldier, it shall copy the record of enlistment, which must be written in the Roster; and the ten years' papers which must be given each man on enlistment.

2. To adjust departures, there shall be no variation from the provisions of the Royal Regulations under this Title, except such Departures as are verified by the retirement of Soldiers. Seeing that the vast distance of this Peninsula does not permit that other Departures be verified until the return of the vessels which arrive at the Posts with the Allowance, and from whose crews substitutes are sought, this being the only means available in these Posts; consequently this consideration makes binding upon the Reviews the Discharge papers of those who have finished their service, or for other cause are deemed proper to be retired from their Companies. Wherefore, having first secured leave from the Governor, the abstract shall give the date thereof, and the Officers shall certify the day on which the retirement took place, except on occasions when the Governor was present.

3. As it is proper to credit as an Extra to the Allowance of the Post of Loreto that of its small Department of Marine, the individuals of the latter shall be included monthly in the abstract of review, separate from, and following, the Company; observing with them respectively the formalities hereinbefore set forth for the registering of the places in the Roster, and noting the vacancies and replacements of Soldiers. With this difference, that the Captain may, of his own authority, give leave of absence to the Sailors, according to the needs of the service.

4. The Reviews must be held in all Posts from the first to the fourth of each month. The original abstract must remain in each Post; but two copies shall be taken with the same formalities, and these shall be forwarded from Loreto

and San Diego at the first opportunity; and from the other Posts monthly.

TENTH TITLE.

Behavior toward hostile or neutral Indians.

1. Since the Peninsula is in peace and quiet; and its numerous Gentiles (by virtue of the mildness of the punishments visited upon those that in different localities made disturbances causing hostilities and deaths; along with the good treatment, humaneness and gentleness experienced by the Prisoners) remain friendly, so that communication with the Posts and other settlements is kept open; therefore there should be no change in the rules formerly established according to those defined by the Royal Regulations under this Title. These must be obeyed exactly in all their parts, varying only according to circumstances that may arise.

ELEVENTH TITLE.

Function of the Governor as Inspector of Posts for the Peninsula.

1. These shall conform wholly, with respect to the Government Posts, to those exercised by the Commanding Post Inspector of the Frontier, as set forth in Tit. 12 of the Royal Regulations. The only variation is that the Post of Loreto should be reviewed every second year, because of its enormous distance and the roughness of the intervening road. Wherefore – and because he has to discharge the other duties of Government – he shall be furnished with an Aide, with the rank of Captain. In view of the expenses and constant journeys he has to make for the Reviews and other duties to which he may be commissioned, if his appointment be approved, I [de Neve] fix his annual salary at 2,000 pesos.

TWELFTH TITLE.

Functions and powers of the Captain and other Officers, Sergeants, Corporals and Soldiers.

1. These shall be in every respect equal to those defined for each class under Tit. 13 of the Royal Regulations; except the variation hereinbefore provided in case of Lieutenants Commanding Companies and Posts in the new settlements.

THIRTEENTH TITLE.

Obligations, appointment and Instruction of Paymasters.

1. The first obligation of the Official Paymaster is to prove himself worthy the election and confidence shown by his Company in entrusting to him the management, custody and distribution of its interests; proceeding in all things with the cleanness and honor inseparable from his profession.

2. He shall keep the general accounts of debit and credit with the utmost clearness, accuracy and order, as is provided; so that at the end of the year (when his accounts shall have been examined and approved by the Captain in the Post of Loreto, and, in the other Posts, which have no Captain, supervised by those Officers who are not Paymasters), they may be approved also by the Governor.

3. Likewise he shall keep, with the same detail and order the private account of each individual, informing himself frequently as to those of the Soldiers, in order to reduce the distributions made in the general and mid-year advances to the balance of each one's account; so that (except the Recruits) no one shall receive more than is due him; preferring, in the delivery, the articles of uniform, arms and horse-trappings necessary for the weekly Reviews which must be passed.

4. Whenever any Soldier shall die or be furloughed, in view of the urgency of buying his mounts and equipment to supply the Recruit who is to take his place, or to fill the shortage of others, after their just appraisement (supervised by his heirs, if present), the Paymaster shall take these articles and distribute them (in the order set for him by the Company Commander) at the same price at which he received them; following the same method in case of taking them for the fund, to settle what is owing the dead, retired or furloughed man.

5. Under the prohibition and penalty set forth in Art. 7, Tit. 14 of the Royal Regulations, Paymasters shall not be allowed to charge the Soldier (in supplying victuals, uniform and other articles) more than the first cost given by the respective Invoices, with no other increase of price than is expressed in the Tariff, and deducted by the operation provided in Art. 4, Tit. 6 of these Regulations. The penalty prescribed in said Title equally includes any culpable loss or embezzlement of funds.

6. Paymasters shall keep in correspondence with the Agent of the Peninsula and Commissary of San Blas, who will send them by the most direct way

the corresponding remittances, invoices and bills of lading. It shall be the care of the Agent to ask for the settlements which must be made out annually by the Royal Officers of the Treasury of Mexico, conformably to the abstracts of Review for each Post; and these he shall direct to the Paymasters who must archive them with the general abstracts, and make use of them for guidance as to the sums which may be received from year to year on account, or the balance left over.

7. It being for the present indispensable that Horses and Mules be transported from Sonora to maintain in effective state the Companies of these Posts, the corresponding superior order having been obtained, the necessary sum for their purchase shall be estimated ahead; and upon the arrival and distribution of saddle animals as destined for each Company, according to their number, quality and first-cost price, the Paymasters shall make their receipts. These must be passed to the Governor, that they may be directed by his hand to the Royal Officers of the Treasury in Mexico, that the proper charge may be made. It being understood that the animals which may die, be lost or become worthless after they have been delivered in the Peninsula, shall have their value charged pro rata upon the remaining animals, which shall be distributed at the resulting prices.

8. Although these Paymasters are not to make expenditures to supply victuals, clothing and other articles, being bound to the costs, responsibility and safe-keeping of the stores and their distribution at retail, the keeping of general and private accounts of the Troops and employees of the Post, shall discount to the Captain, Officers, Surgeon, Sergeant, Corporals, Soldiers and employees two percent for the service and costs of commission.

9. Whenever it may be necessary to name a Paymaster in the Post of Loreto, in consideration of there being no Chaplain in it or in the other Posts of the Peninsula, the lack of this vote shall be supplied by a second Proxy of the Company. Since 32 of its 44 men are occupied in the Detachments of the Real of Santa Anna of the South and the frontier of the North, the Captain shall provide, with proper announcement, that the Sergeants, Corporals and Soldiers, collectively in their stations, nominate two Proxies for the Company from among themselves. This accomplished, the votes shall be sent in writing by the Individuals of each rank, direct to the Captain. He shall cause the same course to be followed by the troops present in Garrison, with assistance of the Master of the Sloop and the Naval Officers of the Department of Marine, who are to vote for a Member of the Company. And when it is seen who have re-

ceived the plurality of the votes, if they are stationed with the Detachments they shall be relieved, that they may transfer themselves to the Post, the Captain ordering the designated Officer on the Frontier to remit his vote sealed. As soon as this is done, he shall summon to his house his Subaltern Officer and the Proxies of the Company. The vote of the absent Officer having been opened and seen in its proper turn; one of these subaltern Officers, and no other, will stand named as Paymaster.

10. If of the five votes there be two for one person and three for another, the two who were of the contrary verdict must conform and assume their share of the responsibility, the same as if they had voted for the person elected.

11. In the Posts of the new settlements in which there are but two subaltern Officers, the naming of the two Proxies in each Company shall proceed in the same method with the same notice as is already provided. This done, the Commander shall convoke the Ensign and Proxies to name one of said Officers, and no other, for Paymaster. In case the four votes be for one person, the election shall be consummated, he who was opposed being bound to conform and assume responsibility, the same as if he had voted in that person's favor. In case there are two votes for each person, the Governor shall decide.

12. As soon as the election is perfected, the Appointment and Authorization shall be committed to writing, whereof, a copy must be taken to be rendered to the Governor. Every three years there shall be nomination anew for Official Paymaster, whether to reelect the incumbent or to appoint someone else.

13. Consequent upon the aforesaid first appointments, the Commissary of the Post of Loreto and the Storekeepers of the Posts of San Diego, Monterrey and San Francisco shall make delivery to the respective Paymasters, by formal Inventories, of all the stuffs, victuals and goods on hand in the storehouses, with proper distinction of qualities, measure, weight and values on prices of first cost, and the sum total. In these must not be included the goods which have not been distributed to the Troops and Employees (Settlers included) since of these a separate Inventory must be drawn up, showing clearly, as far as possible, their condition and value; which thus performed, shall remain deposited in the power of the Paymaster until such time as, giving account to the Superior Government with said Inventory, the expenditure which should be devoted to this item shall be determined.

14. Since the Pack Mules with all that belongs to their trappings, the tools for Carpentry, Smithing and other[11] materials are to remain for the benefit of the Posts and Companies, which are responsible for their condition, as is al-

ready provided for the due faithfulness, the delivery of said utensils, cargo Mules, harness, panniers, pack-saddles and other gear shall proceed (after they have been appraised.) This, with the due specification of the condition, quality and value of each article, must be done by the experts to be named for this purpose by the Post Commander, who must superintend the delivery and valuation, signing with the Experts and Paymasters, Commissary or Storekeeper, the vouchers which must be filed with the Inventory.

15. As there is on hand at the Post of Monterey a Herd of Cattle which at present exceeds five hundred head of all ages, and another herd of Mares which counts up over one hundred seventy head, and about two hundred fifty head of sheep and goats, with some droves of Burros and Pigs; and in the Post of San Francisco there are one hundred twenty-four head of Cattle, all belonging to the Royal Exchequer, these must be included in the first Inventory of delivery, itemizing the kinds and ages of the cattle and the Mareherd. This is the duty of the Paymasters, who, under the orders of the Governor, shall carefully oversee the herding and care of said Herds, their increase, their distribution to Settlers as pay or reimbursement; and with care in breeding shall be kept the outgo of Colts, Bulls, Calves, Sheep, Geldings, Goats, Pigs and of the others that because old or barren should be constantly used up. The reckoning of these Herds shall be kept, to give annual account of their produce and increase to the Royal Exchequer, as hereinafter set forth.

16. The Commissary of Loreto and Storekeeper of the other Posts must so make up their accounts that hereafter the Paymasters be not responsible to the Royal Tribunal and Court of Accounts for the results of preceding accounts. Consequently no other Document should remain in their possession except a copy of the last settlement or account, and the Inventories of the turning over. And it shall be exclusively the duty of each Paymaster, and part of the pay of his respective Allowances, the sum in which the value of the chattels distributed and chargeable to the Troops, Employees and Settlers exceeds the value of his debits to the total of balances (payable from the year 1774, inclusive, to the day of giving possession) which must be paid in full to those Interested. But if, on the other hand, the item of balances exceeds that of debits and chattels, the residue shall be in favor of the Paymaster, and must be credited to him by the Royal Treasury of Mexico in the first settlement had with him, subtracting the respective interest.

11. "Obras" seems to be a misprint for "otras" in the Spanish text. It is corrected here in translation.

17. Whereas in the transportation of the annual remittances there occur (caused by the heat in the Holds of the vessels, and by other incidents) losses, damage and leakage – principally in the Lard, Sugar and Liquids – the delivery should be made to the entire satisfaction of the Paymaster, weighing and measuring the articles and he shall separate from the aforesaid that which is found proper. In case any bale or one-third of the box turns out to be damaged, broken or in bad condition, to determine if it is spoiled partially or entirely, he shall proceed with his formal inspection on board the Vessel, with the superintendence of its Captain and of the Post Commander; checking by the Invoice the goods and articles it contains. This done, the said Officers shall certify the deterioration or loss which may have been caused by the damage or other incident which must be specified. Having done thus, the Paymaster shall disembark and take charge of said Certification, which must be placed head by head upon the appraisement lists that are to be made in the Post under the supervision of the Captain and subaltern Officers, previous to the appointment of experts by the Commander. Comparing the prices and the Invoice with the damage caused (specifying the damage and the goods or articles affected by it), there shall be shown the just value to which the goods are reduced; and upon this valuation, without change, they must be distributed and charged to the Troops. The Paymaster shall charge the present net value of the damaged goods and articles, as well as of those not damaged, as fixed by the official inquiry; and leaving a Copy thereof certified by the Officers in the Post, the Paymaster shall forward the original documents to the agent, whereby to prove and credit the loss.

18. To avoid the confusion arising from the delivery and measuring of the Corn and Beans in the Holds or Storerooms of the Vessel, wherein there inevitably must follow shrinkage to the person delivering, if he gives good measure – since the rolling of the vessel shakes down the Grain in the measure – or to the receiver, because scant measure is given, or because the grain is spilled at the time of emptying the measure into the bags, on account of the haste and inconvenience with which this is done (and to this the Storekeepers attribute a large part of the shrinkage); to shun such difficulties henceforth, the measuring of grain shall be done ashore, either on the Beach or in the Posts near the landing place, as has always been done at Loreto, and sometimes at Monterrey, with little or no loss, while large losses were suffered under the contrary practice.

19. The Paymasters shall stipulate as well the Bales, Tierces[12] and Boxes forwarded from Mexico as the provisions and goods which arrive from San Blas, at the ends of the Bills of Lading, noting the shortages, losses or leakages discovered at the delivery, and the amount received of each Grain, Flour and article of provision. These documents, signed by the Paymaster, shall be delivered by the Person who comes in charge of the shipment, by whom must be signed, in the Bills of Lading that are sent in duplicate from the Commisariat of San Blas, the declaration of the delivery made in each branch or kind of goods contained in the Bills of Lading themselves, which must remain in keeping of the Paymaster to attest his receipt. To this end he should forward them (retaining a Copy certified by the Officers of the Company) to the Agent of the Peninsula that it be exhibited wherein they tally, and that from them may be made the due receipt, seeing that the charge entered against the Allowance was made according to the gross amount of the Invoices, on account of the unavoidable delays in the arrival of these vouchers.

20. Whereas, it has been for a few years the rule to make delivery of the general consignment to the Boatswains of the Vessels, and they, through lack of intelligence and of the proper assistance on board, cause delays in impressing the delivery upon their memories, henceforth the one who receives should be an Officer, it is expedient to change the practice; and if the Commander of the Vessel is not supercargo, the Pilot should be, as he has more fitness and responsibility for said commission.

21. Whereas, it has been enacted that the Captain of the Post of Loreto, as Lieutenant-Governor, give the Licenses to the Cruisers to engage in the Pearl fisheries on that Coast and its contiguous Islands, regulating the amount which each Canoe must pay in Fifths [the Royal share] which sum is now fixed at 100; in view of the scarcity to which the deposits have come, for which reason years have passed in which not a single Pearl Diver entered, and even now there are not more than two or three Canoes that do; and this sum, by order of said Captain, has been collected by the Commissary who has turned it over to the Royal Exchequer with the proceeds of the sale of Salt and some Bulls bought by the Troops and Citizens of the Mining Camp of Santa Anna; and whereas this practice should be followed henceforth by the Paymasters, these shall enter, each year, the proceeds of these branches, and others pertaining to

12. Containers of varying sizes.

the Royal Exchequer, in a separate account, supervised by the Captain. In this shall be noted the costs of careenings, overhaulings and masts for the Sloop and Launches of the Department; and this, with the corresponding vouchers of debit and credit, shall be sent to the Agent of the Peninsula to be presented in the Royal Court of Claims, for the charges or rebates which shall make it tally with the Allowance.

22. The Paymasters of Monterrey and San Francisco respectively must make up annually a debit and credit account of the Herds in their charge, itemized by kinds, showing the increase of numbers and the proceeds in pesos for those sold during the year, for which purpose they will follow the formula which will go at the end of these instructions.

23. In the same manner it shall be the duty of the Paymaster of a Post in whose vicinity or boundaries a new Pueblo of civilized People may be founded, to make a register and open an account with the Settlers, take charge of, and give proper vouchers for, the sums that were supplied them in Sonora to outfit them; likewise of the herds or tools that are sent from other Posts for the same purpose; to credit them with their respective property from the day of their arrival, and verify the collection of the subsidy which may be due each Settler and should be discounted for him; making an annual account, in which, with due clearness and attestation, shall be given the expenditures and receipts pertaining to the Royal Exchequer.

24. The registration which the Paymaster must make out for every Settler shall give his name, quality, condition, age, nationality, and the Pueblo in which he is enrolled as a citizen; and with equal detail shall give the name, quality and age of his wife, sons and daughters; the day, month and year in which he entered upon the enjoyment of the salary and rations allotted to each one, following in this part the provisions to be made in the Instructions for Settlement, when feasible under the conditions on which those who come from Sonora to populate these Settlements are registered.

25. The entry of a new Settler and the credit of his property in the private account which has been provided for, shall tally with the order which must first be had from the Governor, and the copy of the record of registration. The losses by death shall be verified by a copy of the record of interments; and stopping of pay or rations due each year shall be indicated in the record by noting separately the remainder that from one to another the individual has received in the year, as the proof will be deduced from the respective register since a copy of the register must always accompany the first account.

26. In the two first years the value of the tools they have received must be discounted to the Settlers; and in the following three years payment shall be made for all the other things supplied them for the outfitting of their labors, according to the provisions to be made in the corresponding Instructions.

27. The Corn, Brown Beans, Peas and Lentils produced by the harvest of the Pueblo (the citizens reserving what is necessary for their subsistence and planting) have not and cannot for the present be given, other use than to supply the Posts. Accordingly the Paymasters shall buy these grains at the prices now fixed or those that may be fixed hereafter, bearing in mind that they have to be transported upon the Pack beasts of the Posts.

28. If in the Post to which a Pueblo is added there be on hand any herd belonging to the Royal Exchequer, its account shall be added to that of the Settlement; in which the Paymaster shall make the corresponding charge of the proceeds of the animals distributed, and likewise shall embrace in it (with the proper attestation) the proceeds of whatsoever other article pertains to said Royal Exchequer. Bearing in mind that all the Esmiquilpa[13] sacks sent up from San Blas (except those for Flour, which are included in the value of each tercio, and the loads of sacks distributed to the Troops on account), as well as the Barrels, must be returned from year to year, by this means to avoid the repeated expense of them; as to the wraps and mattings on bales which come from Mexico, as well as the boxes, pains shall be taken to get some benefit from those that arrive in good condition; and those which by being rotten or broken have no use, like those headed with hide, shall be considered a legitimate expense on the Royal Exchequer. That which turns out thus shall be attested with a Certification signed by the Officers who supervise the Inventory of stock on hand at the end of the year, which is to be attached to the aforesaid private account. This must be sent annually to the Governor; and being examined, compared and approved by him, shall be forwarded to the Royal Officers of the Treasury of Mexico, that by it they may credit the expenditures pertaining to the Paymaster.

FORMULARY

Debit and Credit Account of the Flocks which are on hand in the Post of San Carlos de Monterrey belonging to the Royal Exchequer, entrusted to my charge as Company Paymaster; in which, by kinds, I present under their re-

13. A particular fabric used to make sacks for flour, grain, and sugar.

spective accounts the charge entered from the Inventory of delivery, the increase of the present year, the distribution of animals, the proceeds thereof in pesos, the amount on hand and increase at the end of December 1780.

	Head	Pesos
Account of Mares and Colts.		
First: Credit one hundred ninety head, which was distinguished by classes in the Inventory of delivery, remain on hand	190	
Debit thirty-two Colts of the increase of the present year	32	
Debit thirty-eight Fillies of the same crop	38	
	260	
Credit by kind, and proceeds in pesos.		
Credit twenty Colts, fit for breaking, distributed among the Company at six pesos each	20	120
Credit ten three-year-old Colts, sold to the Paymaster of the Post of San Francisco at the same price	10	60
Credit two Mares that died, whose brands were exhibited and burned	2	
Credit	32	
Debit	260	
On hand the last of December	228	
On hand the year before	190	
Increase and proceeds this year	38	180
Account of Cattle Herd.		
Debit five hundred seventy head, which, by classes as per Inventory were on hand	570	
Debit eighty-three Bull calves of the increase of the present year	83	
Debit one hundred six Heifer calves of said increase	106	
	759	

Credit by kinds and proceeds in pesos.

Credit forty-six four-year-old steers, sent to D… N… , Paymaster of …, to distribute to Settlers, of which charge there remains to be entered their amount at six pesos per head, to the Royal Exchequer	46	276
Credit ten Bulls, which were distributed to the Troops at five pesos	10	50
Credit four Cows, which were sold as aged at six pesos each	4	24
Credit two Bulls which were injured and their meat was distributed in twenty rations, each one, at twenty-five reales per ration	2	10
Credit three Bull Calves and two Heifer Calves which the Wolves killed	5	
Credit	67	
Debit	759	
On hand the last of December	692	
Amount on hand last year was	570	
Increase and proceeds the present year is	122	360

The accounts of the other Herds shall follow in this order, followed by a summary of the amounts they brought in pesos, to show their total. Against this shall be credited the items realized from the Herds given out to Settlers, satisfaction for which should be made by another Paymaster, and the only items of cost which should be offered for the wages of the Shepherd and fifty or seventy-five pounds of Puebla Hay which is to be asked for one or the other years, wherewith subtracting the credit from the debit account, there will be shown how it stands against him who presents the account. And balancing at the bottom the total debit and distribution of pesos, he shall date and sign.

FOURTEENTH TITLE.

Political Government and Instructions for Settlement.

1. Since the most important object for the fulfillment of the pious intentions of our Lord the King, and to perpetuate his Majesty's dominion over the extensive territory embraced for more than two hundred leagues by the new

Settlements and respective Posts of San Diego, Monterey and San Francisco; to advance the conversion, and to make this so vast Country as useful as possible to the State – inhabited by innumerable Gentiles (except one thousand seven hundred forty-nine Christians of both sexes at the eight Missions on the road between the first and the last Posts), erecting Pueblos of civilized people, who, being assembled, shall encourage tilling, planting and stock raising, and in succession the other branches of industry, so that in the course of a few years their produce may suffice to supply the Post-Garrisons with victuals and horses, thus making up for the distance of transportation [from Mexico], risks and losses at which these things are brought by the Royal Exchequer, with which fit idea the Pueblo de San Jose is already founded and settled, and the building of another is determined upon, for which Settlers and their families must come from the Province of Sonora and Sinaloa; whose progressive increase, and that of the families of the Troops will provide for the establishing of other settlements and for Recruits for the Post Companies, thus freeing the Royal Treasury from the forced costs which it is now under to meet these ends; and it is convenient to establish regulations which shall certainly bring this about, the following Instructions shall be observed.[14]

2. Since, until now, there were assigned to each Settler his rations, 120 in each of the two first years, and in the three years following the rations only, fixed at seventeen and three-quarter reales a day, exempt; hereafter they shall enjoy as an equivalent one hundred sixteen pesos and thirty-seven and one-half reales in each of the two first years, it being understood that the rations are included in this amount; and for the rations in the three years following, sixty pesos in each. Whereby the foregoing emolument is advantageously replaced, subtracting the increase with which it was paid and reduction with which have been issued the Rations. These goods, and others shall be received at cost as soon as these Regulations shall be approved and declared in force. Warning is given that the said five years' time is to be counted for their prerogatives from the day of actual giving possession of the House Lots and Fields to be given out to each Settler, as will be hereinafter set forth; the time between registration and taking possession, to run under the conditions of Contracts; and to avoid this cost it shall be so arranged that as soon as new Settlers arrive, they

14. This is kept unsplit, as a typical de Neve sentence. Elsewhere his breathless flights are cut into sections. Had he been no more governor than rhetorician, the Province would have died young.

shall be located and given said Possession without delay.

3. To each Settler and to the common fund of the Pueblo must be given (subject to replacing in the case of Mules and Horses, which may be given and received, and to payment in the case of other herds, cattle and sheep under the just prices which shall be fixed, and the tools at cost, as is ordained) two Mares, two Cows with one calf, two Ewes, and two she-Goats, all pregnant; and one yoke of Oxen or Bullocks, one Colter, one Hoe, one Spade, one Ax, and one Sickle, one Field-knife, one Lance, one Musket and one Dagger, two Horses and one cargo Mule. Likewise and to the common charge, shall be given sufficient fathers for the number of head of stock in each kind in the whole community; one master Burro, one common one and three she-Burros, one Boar and three Sows, one forge fitted with an anvil and other necessary belongings, six crowbars, six iron spades and the necessary tools for Carpentry and Wagon making.

4. The building-lots granted to the new Settlers must be fixed by the Government as to location and size according to the extent of land where the new Pueblos may be established. So that a plaza[15] and streets shall be left as provided by the Laws of the Realm; and correspondingly shall be marked out sufficient Room for the Pueblo to grow, and Pastures, with the suitable arable lands for Individuals.

5. Each allotment of Fields, both for irrigation and for dependence on the rainfall, shall be 200 *varas*[16] long and 200 wide, this being the area ordinarily taken by one fanega of Corn in sowing. The allotment to be made of said Fields, as of the Building Lots, in the name of our Lord the King, to the new Settlers, shall be made by the Government equitably in proportion to the amount of land which can be irrigated; so that, after first making the proper demarcation, and reserving vacant the fourth part of the fields counting the number of Settlers, if they will tally, there shall be allotted to each Settler two Fields of irrigable land and two more of dry. And of the royal lands shall be set aside such as is deemed proper for individuals of the Pueblo, and of the remainder grants shall be made by the Governor in the name of His Majesty to those who come newly to settle; and also of the respective Building-lots, particularly to the Soldiers who, by having served the time of their enlistment, or because of advanced age, are retired from the Service; as also to the families of those who die. These shall carry on their farming by means of the funds

15. Public square.

16. 550 feet. One vara is 2¾ feet.

each should have, without assistance from the Royal Exchequer in salary, rations or livestock, this favor being limited to those who with that provision emigrated from their own country to colonize this one.

6. The houses erected upon the Lots granted and set aside to the new Settlers, and the Fields embraced in their respective grants, shall be an inheritance in perpetuity to their sons and descendants, or daughters who marry useful Settlers and have no allotment of Fields for themselves; all such persons to comply with the conditions which will be set forth in these Instructions. And that the sons of the possessors of these grants may have the obedience and respect they owe their parents, the latter shall be free and empowered, if they have two or more sons, to choose which one they will (being secular and lay) for heir of their Houses and Fields. And likewise they shall be able to dispose that these fields be divided among the children – but not that one single Field be divided, for the fields must be, all and each, indivisible and inalienable forever.

7. Neither shall the Settlers nor their heirs be able to place a quitrent, entail, bond, mortgage nor other encumbrance whatsoever (though it be for a pious cause) upon the House and Fields granted to them; and if anyone shall act contrary to this just prohibition, he shall be irredeemably deprived of the property, and for the same act his endowment shall be given to such other Settler as is useful and obedient.

8. To maintain their herds the new Settlers shall enjoy the common privileges of water and pasturage, firewood and lumber from the Outer Lands, Forests and Pasture to be assigned according to Law to each new Pueblo. Each shall also have exclusively the grazing of his own lands; but on condition that – as he should have and breed all kinds of livestock, large and small, and it is impossible that each should by himself care for the few head consigned to him for a start, since that would lead to neglect of his crops and public duties – for the present the goats and sheep of the Community should be herded together, the pay of the Shepherd being a common charge; and for rounding up the cattle and horses and bringing them to the corral, as Mares and She-Burros, there should be two mounted Settlers appointed daily (or as often as seems best) from the community. Thus the herds will be cared for in their kinds, avoiding the risk of their being "lifted," and the fields and other duties of the community being attended to. Each individual shall mark his sheep and goats and brand his horses and cattle, for which the registers of branding irons will be given without any charge. Warning being given that henceforth no Settler

shall have over fifty head of each kind of stock; in order that the usefulness of the herds be distributed among all, and that the real wealth of the Pueblos be not monopolized among a few Citizens.

9. The new Settlers shall be exempt and free for the term of five years from paying tithes or any other tax on the fruits and produce brought them by the lands and herds with which they are furnished; on conditions that in the first year from the day they are allotted their Lots and Fields they shall build their houses as best they may, and dwell in them; shall open the proper ditches for the irrigation of their lands, placing on their boundary lines, instead of landmarks, useful fruit or forest trees, at the rate of ten to the Field; and equally that they shall open the *acequia*[17] or *zanja madre*,[18] build a reservoir and other public works necessary to benefit the crops. This should by preference be done in Common; and at the common charge must be built the Royal Buildings within four years, and in the third year a bin, large and adequate, for a Public Granary, in which must be guarded the communal crops. This communal sowing at the rate of one *almud*[19] of Corn per Citizen, must be made from the third year to the fifth, inclusive, in the land allotted to individuals of the Pueblo. All the work incidental thereto, up to storing the crops in the Public Granary, is to be done by the community, for whose exclusive benefit it shall serve. To regulate and increase this item, the Ordinances will be drawn up, in due time, and must be observed.

10. After the five years, they shall pay tithes to His Majesty, to be applied as may be his Royal pleasure; since they pertain wholly to him, not only by the absolute Royal Patronage which he has in these his dominions, but also as tithes from new broken lands, as they are to be produced in lands till now uncultivated and abandoned and now about to be made fruitful at the cost of the great expenditures made by the Royal Exchequer.

When the said term of five years is past, in recognition of the direct and supreme dominion which pertains to the Sovereign, the new Settlers and their descendants shall pay half a fanega of Corn per irrigated Field; and for their own benefit it will be an indispensable obligation upon all in common to repair the irrigating-ditch, reservoir, sewers and other public works of their Pueblo – including the Church.

17. Irrigation canal or ditch.
18. Mother ditch.
19. Three-quarters of a bushel.

11. When the droves of pigs and burros shall have multiplied, the necessary Burros having been adopted for service of the Mares, if the division of each of the two kinds be feasible, said division shall be made, by common consent of the Settlers, among themselves, as equitably as possible so that from the first herd each Citizen have two Head, a male and a female. This done the animals shall be marked and branded by their owners.

12. Within the aforesaid five years the new Settlers are all obliged to have two yokes of Oxen, two plows, two plowshares or points to cultivate the earth, two hoes, with the other necessary tools for farming. Their houses must be entirely finished within the first three years, and furnished with six Hens and a Rooster. It is absolutely prohibited that within the fixed term of five years settlers shall dispose, by sale, exchange or other pretext, or kill any animal of those supplied them or of those of their own raising – except the sheep and goats, which at four years must be crossed (since otherwise they die); and in consequence those of this age may be disposed of at the owner's will. But not the younger ones; under penalty for him who disobeys this provision (which is for his own good and the increase of his belongings) of being by the very act deprived for one year of his rations. And he who howsoever receives one or more head of said flocks within said period, in whatever state or condition, shall be obliged to give them back.

13. On completion of the term of five years – preserving the breed of all the kinds (except pigs and burros, of which each Settler will be obliged to keep but one Sow and one Burro or She-Burro) having their farms equipped with the yokes of Oxen or Bullocks indicated, being provided with a cargo Mule and the necessary Horses – the settlers shall be at liberty to sell the Bulls, Bullocks, Colts or Horses, Burros, Wethers, gelding Goats, Pigs and Sows. It being forbidden to kill a Cow unless she is old or barren; and Ewes and She-Goats under three years old; or to sell Mares or good breeders until such time as each Settler shall possess fifteen Mares and one Stallion, fifteen Cows and one Bull, twelve Ewes and one Ram, and the ten She-Goats with one Male.

14. It shall be forbidden to all Settlers or Citizens to sell Colt, Horse, Mule or Stud, or to exchange said beasts, except among themselves, being provided with those that are necessary, since the remainder are destined only for spare Mounts for the Troops of the Posts, and must be paid for at the just prices which shall be fixed (except all Horses and Mules of private ownership in the Pueblos themselves) under a fine of twenty pesos which shall be collected from whatsoever person shall disobey this law for every head of which he shall make

other disposal than has been stated, which shall be applied half to the accuser and half to the Public expenses.

15. The Maize, Beans, Peas and Lentils which are harvested in the Pueblos (the Citizens reserving what will be necessary for their subsistence and planting) shall be bought and paid for in cash at the prices which are established, or henceforth shall be established, for the provision of the Posts; and of its value the prudent discounts which shall seem proper shall be made to every Settler, to reimburse the Royal Treasury for the amount which for his equipment he has been supplied in coin, riding beasts, flocks, tools, seeds and other effects, so that in the five first years the pay shall be completed.

16. Every Settler and Citizen Head of family to whom has been granted, or in the future shall be granted, Building Lots or Fields and their successors, shall be obliged to keep themselves equipped with two Horses, a saddle complete, firelock and other arms which are mentioned, and must be furnished them at cost that they may defend their respective districts, and assist, without abandoning their first obligation, where with grave urgency they shall be ordered by the Governor.

17. Of the grants of the Building lots, Lands and Waters conceded to the new Settlers, or Citizens to whom such may be granted in the future, the corresponding patents shall be delivered by the Governor or Commissioner named for this purpose, whereof record must be kept (and of the registers of brands) in the general Book of the Settlement which must be made up and guarded in the Archives of the Government, in which will be put head by head a copy of these Instructions.

18. And it being essential to the good government of the Pueblos, administration of justice, direction of the public works, division of the "turns" of water, and to fulfill carefully the accomplishment of whatever has been provided in these Instructions, the Pueblos shall be given, in proportion to their number of inhabitants, Alcaldes of the first instance, and other Officials of the Council yearly. These shall be appointed by the Governor the first two years; and in the following years they shall nominate by themselves and from themselves the Public officials that shall have been arranged for. These elections must pass for their confirmation to the Governor, by whom said nomination shall be continued in the three following years if he deems it expedient.

FIFTEENTH TITLE.

Erection of New "Reducciónes."[20]

1. Since after the location of the three Reductions which are determined upon for the Channel of Santa Barbara, the Demarcation will be complete which has ruled from South to North the establishment of the eight previously founded on the road which leads from the Post of San Diego to that at Monterrey, and from this to the one of San Francisco; and consequently communication between the new Establishments is facilitated, as the eleven Missions and Posts are from thirteen to twenty leagues distant from one another (excepting the interval from San Antonio to San Luis, and from San Juan Capistrano to San Gabriel, which is reckoned at twenty-five leagues) it is of the greatest importance for advancing the conversion of the numerous Gentiles which inhabit this part of the Peninsula to change the establishment of the new Reductions to the opposite directions; proportioning them as the site will permit (in which must be sought the necessary qualities) in such a manner that each one of those which shall be in the future (and except one or two, the remainder shall be to the East) shall be at a distance of fourteen to twenty leagues from two of the old Reductions. By this means they will fill the gaps which are now between the old ones, will girdle the Rancherias of the Gentiles, will increase Christianity markedly, and will explore the Country.

2. It being understood that the line of the aforesaid Establishments is more than two hundred leagues long from Monterey, while the width of the country is unknown (but is presumed to be as great as the length, or greater, since its greatest breadth is counted by thousands of leagues) it is consequently made imperative to increase the number of Reductions in proportion to the vastness of the Country occupied, and although this must be carried out in the succession and order aforesaid, as fast as the older establishments shall be fully secure, decreasing the size of their Escorts that the remaining Troops may garrison the added establishments which must perforce be many and consequently will either be a considerable burden on the Treasury or will have to be erected slowly. To facilitate the matter it is advisable that (except the three Reductions which have to be located along the Santa Barbara Channel, which are to have two Priests each, for the local reasons already set forth) the rest that

20. Reductions or stations for converting Indians. The word mission was used in the Californias.

may follow shall be established under the old practice in this and the other Interior Provinces, with only one Priest, but without change from the aid of four hundred pesos a year which is assigned to each. In this sum, it must be understood, are to be included all the articles necessary to worship, as the temporal supplies for Mission work and farming in the one thousand pesos granted for each founding. It shall be permitted, for the more rapid increase of the new Missions, that the older ones help them with livestock and seeds (given so as not to run short in any variety, as the Reverend Father President of the Missions shall direct) and with one Priest in the first year of establishment.

3. The eight Missions already established shall retain the two Priests that each now has; but vacancies by death or retirement shall not be filled until they are reduced to one Priest apiece. Excepting, the Missions which are close to posts; in which must be maintained two Priests, one being obliged to serve the Post as its Chaplain, until it shall be decided to provide the Posts with secular Chaplains. Consequently if a vacancy occurs in these Missions, or in those of the Channel, a Priest shall come from the Misiónes de San Juan Capistrano, San Gabriel, San Luis, San Antonio or Santa Clara to fill it – or, as aforesaid, to aid in founding new Missions.

4. In the same order as explained by the second Article, the Curacies administered by the Priests of the Order of Santo Domingo in old [Lower] California shall be cut down to one Priest each. Excepting, the curacy of Loreto (in which two Priests must be kept; one of them as Chaplain of the Post) and the two most northerly curacies which now are or shall become the frontier Missions. And in all these, vacancies shall be filled from the second Priests of the other Missions, while they hold out. All shall be continued in the stipend of three hundred fifty pesos which is assigned to each. But the Prelates shall not have discretion, for any reason, to move the Priests from one Curacy to another, that the form of the Royal Patronage be preserved exactly and fully in all its parts and whatever case may arise.

5. It is understood that the Reduction of Our Lady of the Rosary at Viñadaco, and that of Santo Domingo, are the only ones yet founded that should be located according to the plan formerly agreed upon by the Royal Council of War and the Royal Exchequer, to cover the road from the Frontier to the Post of San Diego; as it is of the greatest importance to effect the erection of the remaining three, whereby communication between the old and new Establishments will be facilitated, this should be done with all possible promptness.

So much as I have set forth is that which the experience and knowledge acquired here, my zeal and love for the Royal Service, and the fulfillment of Superior Orders have dictated to me as most suitable for carrying out the Royal Resolution and the pious intentions of the King.

FELIPE DE NEVE

Royal Post of San Carlos of Monterrey, June 1, 1779.

This is a copy of the original, which remains in the Secretary's office of the General Commandancy, in my charge. Whereto I certify.

ANTONIO BONILLA.

Arispe [Mex.] February 1780

The King has seen the Regulations for the government of the Province of Californias, drawn up by the Governor thereof, Don Felipe Neve, by virtue of the dispositions of the Royal Decree of March 21, 1775 of the which Your Excellency forwards testimony with your Letter No. 856 of January 19 of this year. His Majesty has deigned to approve it, and of his decree I advise Your Excellency beforehand for your understanding and guidance. God guard Your Excellency many years.

JOSEF DE GALVEZ,
Sir Viceroy of New Spain.

San Lorenzo, October 24, 1781.

Mexico, March 26, 1782.

Let a certified copy of this Royal Decree be taken; and adding it to the Regulations to which it relates, in proof of its approval by His Majesty, let the corresponding copies be printed, and the necessary number be sent, with the respective Official Letters, to the Sir Commander-General of the interior Provinces, to the Royal Officers of this Treasury, to the Royal Tribunal of Accounts, to the Agent Don Manuel Ramon de Goya, to the Commissary of the Department of San Blas, and to the Governor of the Californias for their understanding and fulfillment in the part that relates to each. The which supplying with copies shall be acknowledged in response to said Royal Decree.

MAYORGA

Copy of the original, whereof I certify. Mexico, third of April, One Thousand, Seven Hundred and Eighty-two.

PEDRO ANTONIO DE COSIO.

For the government archives. Monterey, 18 of September 1781

PEDRO FAGES.

Correspondence Pertaining to the Instruction[1]

Letter to Capitán Fernando de Rivera y Moncada Accompanying the Instructions for Recruitment of the Pobladores for the Expedition of 1781

With the due aims of defense, conservation and development of the Province of Californias, toward which the service of God and King is especially directed, I have resolved upon Occupation of the Channel of Santa Barbara with a Presidio of this name, and three Missions; the erection of a Pueblo with the title of la Reyna de los Angeles on the River of the Porciuncula, and His Majesty has approved the one named San Joseph which I ordered founded on the margins of the river of Guadalupe.

In order to bring to happy success these important new establishments, the Señor Gobernador of that Province, Don Phelipe Neve, has deemed it expedient, and requested of me in various communications, that you join this party of Troops, and I having heartily consented, the time is now come for your zealous performance of the duties enunciated in the attached Instructions.

They refer to the advantageous Recruital of Families and Soldiers for Californias, so that this Province [Sonora] will not be laid open to risk by serious diminution of its already small Population; and to useful increase and requisite remount of Mules, Horses, Mares, etc., needed by both old and new establishments of the Peninsula.

Giving precedence to and with due reflection upon all things imposed by my instructions, you must inform me before your departure from this Capital, and during the time subsequently employed in your Commission, of the doubts and difficulties which confront you, in order that I may clarify and surmount them.

1. Provincias Internas Tom. 122, Archivo General de Mexico. The original Spanish-language version of these documents are on pages 221–24.

In Article 14 of the Instruccion I say to you that Recruits must not be deceived with offers of more than can be fulfilled, and realizing that this delicate Point requires the greatest clearness I advise you that the Poblador Recruit is to receive the monthly stipend of ten pesos and daily rations with the understanding that the payments will terminate at the close of three years exactly, which must be counted from the day of enlistment. That to each one will be given two Cows, two Oxen, two Mares, two Horses, one Mule, two ewes, two Goats, and the tools and utensils necessary for the Labors of the Field: And that for all these supplies and those of clothing and Riding Equipment which they now receive, they will reimburse the Real Hacienda (with exception of the amount of the monthly Stipend and the rations) with part of the crops and increase of the Herds, making allowance so that they shall not lack in whatever is requisite for their own subsistence and yet carry out reintegration as indicated.

As the Soldier Recruits enjoy a fixed position and better wages, and are governed by distinct regulations, they will, by means of prudent discounts, satisfy out of their income the expenses incurred in supplying them and their families with clothing, Accoutrements, Armaments, provisions and remount.

The false interpretation which the people have given to the Reglamento de Californias, persuading them of greatest detriments in the surcharges or discounts there made against the Salaries of Officers, troops and Pobladores, may prevent many from taking advantage of the opportunity which now is presented to them for gaining an honorable and happy berth and of performing a loyal service to the King which will merit in all times his sovereign pleasure and just remuneration.

In order to dispel these harmful impressions it is imperative that you strive to exercise prudence and skill, not lacking in the slightest degree the truth and probity which are the North star of my disposals, in the understanding that I am endeavoring seriously and efficaciously to find the remedy for the imagined detriments, which I am sure, partake more of appearance than of reality; for all those (detriments) which thus are experienced here on these frontiers, as on that of California, do not result actually from the provisions of the Ordinance but rather from the vicious mode in which it is being enforced, which difficulty is most easy of remedy through methodizing the rules, clarifying those which time and experience show to need some alteration, and zealously working for its exact and proper fulfillment.

I am certain that you will be scrupulously faithful to the important Commissions which I confide to you, as you need be in order that I may recommend to His Majesty this new special service so that he will deign to extend to you the favors of his Royal pleasure, and in this understanding advising you that I will arrange for the supplies of clothing, Accoutrement, remount, etc., for the recruits and families, of which Article 22 of the Instrucción treats, and as your first march must be to Los Alamos, I enclose the attached Passport so that you will not delay your Journey.

God and Country, Arispe, December 27, 1779.

[COMANDANTE-GENERAL TEODORO DE CROIX]

Señor Don Fernando de Rivera y Moncada.

LETTER TO COMANDANTE-GENERAL TEODORO DE CROIX ORDERING THE OCCUPATION OF THE SANTA BARBARA CHANNEL AND THE ESTABLISHMENT OF EL PUEBLO DE LOS ANGELES[2]

// 26

Your Excellency [Comandante-General de Croix]

My dear Sir: The Province of Californias is one of those placed especially in my charge by His Majesty in the Royal Instructions, and in consequence of orders from his Excellency the Viceroy, predecessor of yourself, and from me, the Gobernador Don Phelipe Neve has offered several suggestions relative to the better defense, conservation and development of that important Country.

Having examined in detail the Reports made by the Governor, and viewing them in the same favorable light as did the late Viceroy,[3] I have ordered the Occupation of the Channel of Santa Barbara with one Presidio of that name and three Missions; the establishment of a Pueblo with the title of la Reyna de los Angeles on the River Porciuncula; and His Majesty has deigned to approve the one named San Joseph, which has been founded on the banks of the Guadalupe.

These provisions require an increase in Troops as shown in the attached Statement No. 1 [not reproduced], to be distributed as provided in Document no. 2 [see below]. In order that [these plans] may prove effective it is neces-

2. Provincias Internas Tom. 122, Archivo General de Mexico.

3. Antonio Bucareli.

sary to recruit families of Settlers and Soldiers, assemble a remount, and secure various other auxiliary items which I will expound to Your Excellency in separate reports.

In order to facilitate the matters to which I refer herein, I have prepared the Instruction of which Copy is enclosed. I have charged Capitán Don Fernando de Rivera y Moncada with the responsibility of carrying out its provisions, and that Officer already has entered upon his duties. But as the gracious assistance of Your Excellency is necessary for the successful outcome [of the plan], I enclose the attached note No. 3 [not reproduced], which indicates the dispositions necessary on the part of Your Excellency. And while I have given the orders pertaining to the Account and Purpose of expenditures, which Comisionado Rivera is to present as soon as he concludes the Recruital of troops and families of Settlers and the assembly of remounts, my subsequent advices and the remittance to Your Excellency of Documents regarding the expenses and warrants in favor of the Presidios of Californias and for the families, and for the reimbursement of Advances made by the Royal Treasuries of Guadalajara and Alamos, must await his reports.

SEÑOR MAYORGA.[4]

Arispe, February 9, 1780.

4. Martín de Mayorga was successor to Antonio Bucareli as viceroy of New Spain, after the death of Bucareli in April 1779.

//29

No. 2. [Enclosure]

Distribution of Troops for Californias as Detailed by Governor Don Phelipe de Neve

Destinations	Captains	Lieutenants	Ensigns	Sergeants	Corporals	Soldiers	Total
Presidio de Loreto	1	–	1	1	1	10	14
Real de Santa Ana del Sur	–	–	–	1	–	6	7
Missions of the Northern Frontier	–	1	–	–	2	23	26
Presidio de San Diego	–	1	1	1	2	27	32
Missions of its [San Diego] District	–	–	–	–	3	15	18
New Pueblo de la Reyna de los Angeles	–	–	–	–	–	4	4
Presidio de Monterrey	–	1	1	1	2	27	32
Missions of its [Monterey] District	–	–	–	–	3	15	18
New Pueblo de San Josef	–	–	–	–	–	4	4
Presidio de San Fran[cis]co	–	1	1	1	2	16	21
Missions of its [San Francisco] District	–	–	–	–	2	10	12
New Presidio de Santa Bárbara and Central Mission	–	1	1	1	2	26	31
Mission San Buenaventura	–	–	–	1	–	14	15
Mision la Purisima Concepción	–	–	–	1	–	14	15
Totals	1	5	5	8	19[5]	211	249

Arispe, February 9, 1780.

5. In the Spanish text the mistaken figure of 18 is used.

Instrucción

Instructions for the Recruitment of Soldiers and Settlers for the California Expedition of 1781[1]

Teodoro de Croix to Fernando de Rivera y Moncada

Instruction to be observed by Capitán Don Fernando de Rivera y Moncada in the Recruiting and equipment of *familias pobladoras*[2] and troops, assembling of mounts, and transportation of these, and further auxiliaries solicited by and granted to Coronel Don Phelipe Neve, Governor of Californias, for the defense, benefit and conservation of the new and old establishments of that Peninsula.

1.

As it has been resolved to add two Subaltern Officers to the Presidio de Monterrey, one Ensign to that of San Francisco, the same to that of San Diego; and to name one Lieutenant, one ensign and three Sergeants for the new Presidio de Santa Barbara, which is to be erected midway of the Channel of that name, I have sent provisional commissions as Lieutenants to the Alferezes Don Alonso Villaverde, and Don Diego Gonzalez; and as Alferezes to Sargento Don Mariano Carrillo and to the Cadetes Don Manuel Garcia Rovi [Ruiz] and Don Ramon Laso de la Vega, reserving decision on the commission for the officer lacking in this class pending advice from the Governor of the Province of Californias. By the same order, three Sergeants, two Corporals and 20 volunteer

1. Provincias Internas Tom. 122, Archivo General de Mexico. Translated by Marion Parks. Old style of spelling and capitalization has been retained throughout the translation. The original Spanish-language version of this document can be found on pages 225–35.

2. Settler families

Soldiers of the Presidial Companies of this Province have been withdrawn so that they may continue their service in the said Province of Californias.

2.

Of the Cited Individuals two are in the Peninsula, and the rest must assemble on the first day of February next in San Miguel de Orcasitas, enjoying from the same day the Salaries and supplies pertaining to their new employments, according to the Reglamento which governs in California.

3.

I select this Rendezvous so that Capitan Don Fernando de Rivera may appoint from the Officers, Sergeants and Corporals under his immediate command those whom he considers best fitted to aid him in the discharge of his duties.

4.

As, in discharging these duties, the principal *comisionado*[3] as well as those who will assist him, naturally will need some supply of Money for their subsistence and marches, the former will request of me the amounts which he considers necessary for each one, in order that I may draw against the Real Caxa de los Alamos[4] advances on the respective Salaries and Supplies.

5.

With these foregoing matters completed, Capitan Rivera will dispatch his people to the proper destinations, and having requested the Necessary Passports, will leave without delay to prosecute the recruital of Troops and families, and the assembling of Mules and Horses to the number specified in the attached documents numbers 1 and 2.

6.

Provisions for the Recruital. For the recruital and gathering of the remount, I do not limit the territory, but assign to the Comisionado the Provinces of Ostimuri, Sinaloa and the rest which extend to Guadalajara inclusive. In those which are not recognized by the Comandancia General as in my charge, he

3. Commissioner

4. Branch of the Royal Treasury at Los Alamos, Sinaloa

will proceed in virtue of permission which I have asked of His Excellency the Viceroy. Since the requirements for the recruital and for securing the remount are distinct, I will make provision for them separately.

7.

Twenty-four families and 59 Men are at present needed in Californias to erect a new Presidio and Town, but if this number is taken from the territories under my charge, there will be a scarcity [of people] what with the number which already has been taken out, and with the numbers which in future may be withdrawn, for the necessary repopulation of Sonora; which is equally to the interest of California, since the two Provinces should be united and have communication one with the other through the establishments on the Rivers Colorado and Gua. And while it is expedient for them and for those of the Peninsula to secure Recruits in these interior Territories, it is also certain that there are not enough people for the two enterprises [there] and that it will always be necessary to apply to the neighboring Provinces, commonly called *tierra afuera,*[5] in consideration of which the Comisionado must direct careful attention to the object of accomplishing an advantageous Recruital for California without greatly affecting the Population of Sonora and in everything possible acting in accordance with the points prescribed in the following Articles.

8.

In order to direct his course to the City of Guadalajara Capitan Don Fernando de Rivera must travel perforce through all the Provinces subject to the Government of Sonora. In these he has a free hand to recruit the families as well as the Soldiers, but as he will not be able to complete the Recruital of volunteers [there] it will be necessary that he conclude it in Guadalajara, and by this means the withdrawal of People from Sonora will be minimized.

9.

Three Sergeants, two Corporals and 20 Soldiers already have been taken from the Presidios of this frontier, and since their Places are being kept vacant so that they may be filled by an equal number of Recruits of similar rank, whom Capitán Comisionado will have to bring from Guadalajara, it follows that for

5. Outlying territory

the Presidios of Californias he will only have to recruit 34 Men. If he secures all of them in the Provinces of the Government of Sonora, he will not continue the Recruital in Guadalajara, as also in the case of familias pobladoras; but, the success of this being doubtful, el Comisionado will bear in mind the number of People which he may recruit in the territorios internos, in order to complete in those *de afuera* the number needed and prescribed for California.

10.

Recruital of the 24 familias Pobladores. The Head or Father of each family must be a Man of the Soil, *Labrador de exercicio,*[6] Healthy, robust, and without known vice or defect that would make him prejudicial to the Pueblos. For these will be situated in the midst of a numerous population of Gentiles, [who are] docile and without malice but susceptible, like all Indians, to the first impressions pf good or bad example set by the Spanish who settle among them aiming to civilize them with good treatment and to win them happily through the practice of true justice and good deeds to a knowledge of our Sacred Religion, and the Sweet Dominion of our Catholic Monarch.

11.

Among the said families must be included a Mason, a Carpenter who knows how to make Yokes, ploughs, *Rodadas*[7] and Carretas, and a Blacksmith, who will do if he knows how to make ploughshares, pick-axes, axes and Crowbars.

12.

Recruital for the Presidios of California. The Soldier Recruits for California must be Married, and of the same Qualities and conditions as must be the Settlers, adding those of greater strength and endurance for the hardships of the frontier service.

13.

Recruits for the Presidios of Sonora. All those recruited for the Presidios de Sonora must be Bachelors, Young Men not over 25 or 30 years of age, and not under 18 and who are at least two yards tall, healthy, robust, of good presence, and without defect of body or face.

6. A worker in the fields
7. Solid wooden wheels.

14.

No recruit must be forced to enter but must volunteer, and he must not be deceived by offers of more than can be fulfilled, and you will emphasize this Instruction.

15.

From the day on which enlisted, the Recruits must receive [as follows]: those *who are destined for Californias and Sonora*, the Goods allotted to them respectively according to the Reglamentos of that Province and *of these frontier* Provinces; and the *vecino* Poblador[8] his salary of ten pesos a month and the customary rations; while each Recruit *without exception* will receive the daily stipend of two Reales in cash, where he can use it in maintaining himself, and provisions when traveling through unpopulated places or on the frontier where money is of no use to him, reserving the rest of his pay to cover the costs of the march and equipment.

16.

All Recruits without exception will be enlisted for ten years, which will be counted from the day of the date of their affiliations.

17.

The Soldiers' enlistments will be formalized as prescribed by the general ordinances of the army, except with the general provision that they must join one of the Presidios de California *or Sonora*. The comisionado must deliver the registers of enlistments *to the military Governor of the latter* [province] *Don Jacobo Ugarte y Loyola* and to Don Phelipe Neve [military governor] of the former in order that these Chiefs may assign the Recruits to the presidial Companies as they see fit.

18.

As to the vecinos Pobladores they shall enlist in the proper mode and for the same period of ten years, for either the Pueblo de San Joseph de Guadalupe or of La Reyna de los Angeles de la Porciuncula, adding after their own declarations those of their Wives, sons, daughters and Sisters or Unmarried Female

8. Stipend.

relatives who of their own will desire to accompany them, for to these latter there offers the possibility that they may marry Members of the troops who remain Single in California for lack of Spanish Women, according to the notices communicated to this Superior government.

19.

It will be advisable for the Commissioner to take with him in his company from San Miguel de Orcasitas three Officers or two officers and one sergeant, and also a small party of troops, charged solely with looking after the Recruits.

20.

During his march to the boundaries of the Jurisdiction of the Viceroyalty of New Spain, it is very likely that he will make some Recruitment of Soldiers and settlers for Californias, and as these will have to be assisted with their daily rations, they will have to be habilitated and escorted, the Comisionado will appoint one of the officers who accompanies him, with a detail of troops, to return from the Place in the Provincia interna where the last Recruit is enlisted, to pick them up and conduct them to the Real[9] de los Alamos.

21.

During the time consumed by the return of the Oficial comisionado, the *Justicias*[10] will be careful to supply the Recruit or Recruits with the daily allotment of two Reales, Capitan Don Fernando de Rivera leaving in their charge [for this purpose] the small sum he judges sufficient according to the time that the return of the Subaltern charged with assembling the Recruits is expected to take.

22.

No expenditures for the recruits should be made by the Subaltern Officer other than for the daily Provisions, baggage, and incidentals requisite for the march to the Real de Los Alamos. There, where the resources are greater, the recruited Soldiers, Pobladores and families will be equipped with all Clothing, Arms, Riding Equipment, and Animals stipulated for them.

9. An encampment or village, originally a mining camp.
10. Village magistrates.

23.

For the said expenses of daily provisions and transportation of Recruits, Capitán Don Fernando Rivera will Require the advance of some money, but since I cannot determine the correct amount myself, the said Captain will inform me how much he estimates as sufficient so that a warrant may be drawn for him by the Gobernador Intendente of this Province, Don Pedro Corvalan. In case the expenses be greater than the amount now delivered, the warrants of Capitán Rivera will be honored and paid in the Caxa de los Alamos, he giving a statement explaining with detail and clarity the ends for which he may have used the money drawn; and the Royal Officials of that Caxa will forward their report to me by way of the Gobernador Intendente.

24.

From the Boundary of these Provinces to Guadalajara Capitan Don Fernando de Rivera will continue the Recruitment of Pobladores and Soldiers for Californias. He will conduct the recruits to that city in his Company or entrust to some Subaltern official their transportation and the responsibility of providing them with the daily allowance of two Reales, as well as care of the Baggage and other impedimenta necessary to the march.

25.

As soon as he arrives in Guadalajara he will present himself to the Señor Regente, and delivering to him the attached document, will request lodging for the Recruits mentioned in the preceding Article, for the officers and troops of his Party, *and for the People who are to be recruited in said City and* are to be destined for the Presidios de Sonora.

26.

If the Captain shall not have been able to complete the Recruitment for Californias during the march, he will finish the quota in Guadalajara, and will present the enclosed document to the Royal Officers of that Caxa so that in compliance with the orders which His Excellency the Viceroy will soon communicate to them they will deliver the sums necessary to supply the Recruits with Clothes and Riding Equipment in accordance with memorandum number 3 [not enclosed].

27.

The Recruits, Soldiers and Pobladores whom the Comisionado shall enlist for the Peninsula from the Boundaries of these Provinces to Guadalajara will have to be transferred to California by way of San Blas. In this understanding, the Recruits and their families, being furnished with what they may need in Clothing and further supplies as provided in Memorandum no. 3, will proceed to their destination when ordered by el Señor Regente, under the command of another Subaltern Officer to whom Capitan Don Fernando de Rivera will give written Instructions as to what he must do, it being understood that until the day of the embarkation of Recruits at San Blas they must receive the daily socorro in money or provisions as circumstances dictate.

28.

To cover the socorros of these Recruits and expenses of the march to Guadalajara, Capitán Comisionado will inform me as to the prudent sum which should be advanced to him by the Caxa de Alamos, and he will present his request for what he may need to meet similar expenses on the march thence to San Blas, to the Royal Officials of Guadalajara.

29.

I have stated in Article 26 that these Señores Ministers will deliver to Capitan Don Fernando de Rivera the Funds necessary for supplying the said recruits for Calif ornias with Clothing and other supplies stipulated, but it will be understood that the distribution must be made under the supervision and with consent of the said Ministers and that it must appear in the reports covering this subject, which the Capitan Comisionado will prepare and forward to me.

30.

He will receive in addition [to the amount drawn] from the Real Caxa de Guadalajara and with obligation to reimburse [la caxa de] Alamos, the money which he may need to supply the Soldier Recruits of Sonora, to pay the expense of their Baggage, and to fulfill the pledges of Clothing and riding equipment prescribed in Memorandum no. 4 [not enclosed].

31.

Having completed and equipped this recruitment, and dispatched by way of San Blas [the recruitment] for California, he will entrust to the other Subaltern Officer the march of the first with part of the members of the detail of troops and taking the rest [of the troops] the Captain will go forward in order to carry out the task of securing the Remount.

32.

All of this is completely expressed in Memorandum no. 2. If [the Comisionado] delay, all his care will not avail to control circumstances so that the several auxiliaries may arrive approximately at the same time in Californias, and many days will be lost.

33.

In order to take advantage of every day, at the same time that the Capitan Comisionado on his march to Guadalajara discharges the duty of Recruiting, he may address himself also to securing the remount, having someone to help him in its care and gathering, and for this he will make use of the rest of the officers and Sergeants provided for Californias, and of the Corporals and Soldiers who will rendezvous in Orcasitas.

34.

I may omit advising the Capitan Don Fernando de Rivera of the Places where he can secure the remount and best arrange to assemble it, for he has a rich knowledge of the territory; the same is true as to the quality of the Mules and Horses, since he already knows that for this Stock to be useful in California it must have in addition to the conditions of strong health, of Robust–ness, sound bone, and normal stature, that of *newness*, for the Old Beasts become useless on protracted marches, and it is not possible to restore [their strength] in whatever length of time. And finally, I realize it is unnecessary to remind the Comisionado of the care that he must observe in concluding the purchases [to secure] them under advantageous conditions, and [to observe] economy in the adjustment of prices, for these are points which will attest to his zeal, intelligence and faith to his obligations; but I do advise him that in case the remounts do not have to be assembled, if that be possible, in any particular place *until* the arrival of the Recruits, he will try to stipulate with the venders of the stock that the Horses, Mules, Mares and the rest must be maintained at the venders' cost and risk in their summer Pastures until the Officers and troops enlisted by the Capitan Comisionado return, gathering the animals and transporting them to the Place of Reunion which he will designate as expedient. This must not be omitted, so that the farmer or rancher vender may receive without delay the value of the Beasts which he sells, on condition that he enters into formal obligation to deliver them in the complete number and of the Quality and conditions stipulated, and to bear the cost and risk of those [animals] which die, are lost, or become useless or are stolen by Enemy Indians up to the day of the delivery to those Commissioned to assemble the remount.

35.

In order to gather them up, Capitan Don Fernando de Rivera will inform me as to what funds he will need and if it be preferable that his warrants to the Farmers for the price of the Beasts needed, be paid from the Real Caxa de los Alamos.

36.

As prescribed above, the Soldiers and Pobladores destined for Californias who are Recruited in the interior must go to the Real de los Alamos and in charge of one Subaltern Officer. Those who are recruited for the same Province in outlying territories must be transported to Guadalajara, and from there to San Blas for embarkation as soon as convenient, under orders of another Subordinate officer. The Recruits destined for the Presidios de Sonora who are enlisted in Guadalajara must be conducted under another Officer by the most direct road to San Miguel de Orcasitas. On his march, with a complement including the rest of the Officers, Sergeants, Corporals and Soldiers, the Capitan Comisionado will devote himself to finding, contracting for and purchasing the remount, and on his return [will attend] to assembling and transporting [the animals] to the place found convenient for their assemblage.

37.

I must advise el Comisionado that this Place must be selected by the good judgment of the Comisionado taking into consideration the fact that the entire Remount has to be transported by way of the Rivers Gua and Colorado, and that I will provide the necessary requirements for its custody up to the day on which the Expedition starts out, and at that time such assistances as necessary for the successful conduct [of the Expedition].

38.

In order to prevent delay to the march overland, it may be desirable to transport by Sea the familias Pobladoras and the Troops for Californias which are to rendezvous at los Alamos. The Comisionado will inform me what circumstances present themselves and what he thinks on this point, in order that I may formulate my instructions.

39.

All Persons who exercise any Commission delegated by the Capitan Don Fernando de Rivera must keep account and a clear and formal record of the Funds that they receive and the objects for which they are disbursed, in order to satisfy themselves as well as to render accounts to their Commander who must approve them if they are meritorious, and use them to balance his general accounts.

40.

Four [records] must be rendered by the Capitan Don Fernando de Rivera: first of the remount, second of the Poblador families, third of the Soldiers recruited for Californias, and fourth of those destined for the Presidios of this Province, according to the forms which will be handed to him by the Gobernador Intendente, to whom he will deliver the records so that the latter may examine them, add his comments, and put his approval on them, and report to me.

41.

Everything cannot be held in mind, nor is it feasible to give a minute and prolix account of all the new situations with which the carrying out of these Commissions naturally will be confronted, therefore the Comisionado will [be depended upon to] surmount with his own zeal, action and experience the difficulties [that may arise].

42.

Finally, from whatever place where there may be provision for a Post, he will advise me of the condition of his Charge, and if any grave matter or new

thing arise which makes Superior aid or orders urgent, he will dispatch his Letters to me by message sent from camp to camp and thus his difficulties will be known and I shall be able to make contingent decisions.
Arispe, December 27, 1779.

No. 1. [Enclosure]

Statement of the Number of Families for the new Pueblo de la Reina de los Angeles, and of the number of Soldiers for Californias to be recruited by Capitan Don Fernando de Rivera y Moncada in the Places, and of the Character and Conditions prescribed in the accompanying Instructions of this date.

Recruits	Number
Families of Settlers	24
Soldiers for Californias	59
Total	83

Note: Among the twenty-four Poblador families must be included one Mason, one Carpenter, and one Blacksmith.

EL CABALLERO DE CROIX [rubric].

Arispe, December 27, 1779 (4 Copies).

No. 2. [Enclosure]

Statement of the remount to be procured by Capitán Don Fernando de Rivera y Moncada for the Province of Californias in accordance with the provisions made in the attached Instructions.

		Mules	Horses
For the Four existing Presidios de Loreto, San Diego, Monterey and San Francisco		350	130
For the new Presidio de Santa Bárbara		153	102
For the 24 Settlers of la Porciúncula		48	24
For the Pueblos de San Joseph, and of that planned for la Porciúncula	Mules	551	256
	Horses	256	
	Brood Mares	60	
	Iden. Burros	80	
	Donkeys	6	
	Stallions	4	
	Geldings	4	
	Grand Total	961	

Arispe, December 27, 1779 (2 Copies).

Correspondence Pertaining to the Pobladores[1]

May 16, 1781 San Gabriel
Neve to the Comandante-General

DEPARTURE OF FAMILIES WITH SOLDIER ESCORT.

To the effect that on 12 March seventeen families under command of the Alferez Ramon Laso [de la Vega] left Loreto for the bay of San Luis [Gonzaga] where they arrived April 24, and that they continue their march to this place, and that José Zúñiga follows with the rest of the families. That Sargento Juan José Robles will set out with 12 soldiers for the Colorado to meet Capitán Fernando de Rivera whom he asks, if assured of the safe conduct of his entire expedition, to send them back.

1781 San Gabriel
Neve to the Comandante General
July 13 – in which he reports on smallpox contracted in Loreto.

July 14 –
To the effect that the Teniente Diego Gonzalez and the alféreces José Argüello and Cayetano Limon with 35 recruits and 30 of their families, arrived today at this Mission. That in the short interval which will remain from the time the mules will regain their strength until the beginning of the rainy season, which in this country starts in November, it will not be possible to transport with the 62 pack mules brought by the expedition the families and 750 fanegas of grain and baggage of the troops in 7 months or more. And anticipating that the rains will cease in February, the roads will be impassable for pack animals for more than a month thereafter; and as it is not possible to build warehouses for storage of everything where for lack of wood they have to be built of adobe, there-

1. Bancroft Library transcripts. Translated by Marion Parks. The original Spanish-language version of these documents can be found on pages 237–39.

fore the founding of the Presidio of the Channel will not commence until next year as soon as the rains terminate. That the decision of Fernando Rivera to remain on the Colorado prevents auditing the accounts of recruits and settlers.

Dispatch of documents.

August 29 (two documents) Military register. Dispatch of documents.

September 10 [1781]

To the effect that the Alferez Cayetano Limon returned to this Mission [San Gabriel] with all speed from the Colorado where he went to join Fernando Rivera, discovering there that the Gentiles had killed the Capitán Fernando Rivera y Moncada with all his troops, and even also the religious, the troops and settlers of those Establishments. And that at a short distance from them death had been dealt the Cabo Pascual Bailon, nine soldiers, one poblador and a muleteer who transported supplies and livestock for the said establishments. That Limon examined the corpses both in the pueblo and nearby on the banks of the river, and from the state of destruction and the dryness of them inferred that the deed had been perpetrated some 40 days before his arrival on the twenty-first of this month [August] at the Colorado, and that he himself was attacked by a considerable force of Indians who fired on him for more than 4 leagues, killing two of his soldiers, and wounding him with a ball which pierced his side under the left arm.

That he [Neve] has taken the necessary steps to prevent transmission of this news to the natives of these establishments [in California].

October 28 [1781] (6 documents)

He remits 52 accounts which because of loss of the original records have been made up for 52 recruits enlisted by Fernando Rivera, according to their own statements and to information from other sources. He knows that some through malice or forgetfulness have not declared some of the supplies of clothes or money which they received, and it being not easy to ferret out these last, as far as the clothes are concerned the records can be cleared up if the merchants of Los Alamos have retained their memoranda of what they severally distributed.

Dispatch of documents.

Id. (2 documents)

Id. (2 documents)

October 29 [1781]

That for the basis of the Santa Barbara Company one corporal and seven soldiers have been withdrawn from the Companies of Monterey and San Diego. This leaving them ten, which he considers a sufficient number so that the Company will soon be in condition for service. That it has been necessary to construct 40 small houses of palisades and mud so that these troops and their families may pass the rainy season in comfort.

That having arrived at this Mission on August 18, the Teniente José Zúñiga provided that the recruits, pobladores and families which he brought, under his charge, should camp at a distance of one league [from the Mission] because of the fact that some children among the party had but recently recovered from the smallpox. From [their camp] they went to establish themselves on the ground where they are founding the pueblo of Los Angeles, and now having finished the zanja madre they are continuing with building their houses and also the corrals for the stock. The latter has not as yet been distributed because they are concentrating their efforts on finishing the pueblo and when it is completed, they begin to plow the fields for the sowing of the wheat. That to this pueblo there arrived but 11 pobladores, and of these eight alone are of any use.

Although the funds allocated for goods for these Presidios have not arrived, the Presidios can be supplied until next April. The Santa Barbara and San Francisco companies will have all allocated funds for next year available and Santa Barbara will receive the balance of the account at the end of this December. Monterey and San Diego will have about 17,000 pesos available during that month and Loreto will have more than 21,000 pesos available without relying upon the long held account balances of these last three presidios, that amount to more than 20,000 p.v.

Even though Loreto did not receive provisions from San Blas, 98 fanegas of corn were supplied to the frontier as aid.

On the 5th of last June, Alférez José M. Estrada was appointed paymaster in Loreto and Comisario Francisco Alvarez Osorio supervised the delivery of the documents that were in disarray. He ordered that they be arranged correctly.

Outfits for Soldiers, Settlers, and Families[1]

Statement of the clothing and riding equipment to be supplied to the soldiers and settlers and their families recruited from the Real del Rosario to Guadalajara.

OUTFIT FOR A SOLDIER

One jacket of blue wool [shag] or Querétaro cloth, with cotton facing reverse side, lapels and collar of second grade cloth, dyed red; blue wool buttons, cotton lining, epaulets of wool; yellow buttons with loop. One pair of breeches of blue wool, cotton lining, knee-strap of the same woolen [shag], and yellow button; a black Campaign Hat; one cape of blue Querétaro cloth, with reveres lined with red baize; one black Barcelona silk handkerchief; one good linen shirt; one shirt of puebla cotton; two pairs of underdrawers of puebla cotton; two pairs of woolen hose, double [knitted] of fine thread of the country [local manufacture]; one pair of buckskin boots; two pairs of shoes with half-gaiters; two blankets; ribbon for hat and hair. One cowhide saddle with the requisite accoutrements, all of good quality, but with wooden stirrups and without cover or fringe; one horse and one mule bridle; one pair of cowboy spurs, but small, as is the usage according to regulations on these frontiers; one sweat-cloth or saddle-blanket of coarse frieze; a large sheath case for musket; some saddle bags; a cartridge-box for 21 to 24 charges, for cannons and other [guns] as requested by the Governor of the Province.

OUTFIT FOR A SETTLER

One jacket of blue Querétaro cloth, lined with cotton, trimmed with white or yellow buttons, but without insignia; one pair of woolen breeches like those of the soldiers; one tie or kerchief of linen as a neck piece; two cotton shirts;

1. Translated by Thomas Workman Temple II. The original Spanish-language version of this document can be found on pages 241–42.

two pairs of under drawers; the same of woolen stockings, buckskin boots, shoes with half-gaiters, blankets, and ribbon for hat and hair as for the soldier.

OUTFIT FOR A FAMILY

For a woman: Three chemises; three pairs of skirts, some of serge, the others of baize and *faldellin*;[2] two varas of linen for jackets; two pairs of Brussels stockings; two pairs of understockings; two pairs of shoes; two shawls; one hat; six varas of ribbon.

For a boy: One jacket of Querétaro cloth; one pair of breeches of the same; two cotton shirts; two pairs of cotton under drawers; one pair of woolen stockings; two pairs of shoes; one hat; one blanket.

For a girl: Two linen chemises; two pairs of cotton skirts; one kerchief to be used as a shawl; one pair of baize skirts; one underskirt; two pairs of hose or under-stockings; two pairs of shoes; one blanket.

Note: In addition to the endowments provided in the above account, the Capitán Comisionado may secure for the recruits others which he may consider of precise necessity, the royal officials of the cajas de Guadalajara supervising the purchases and distribution, as well as the accounts of these subministrations.

Copies of the originals which I certify, Arispe, February 10, 1780.

ANTONIO BONILLA [rubric]

2. A particular kind of cloth.

Supplies Purchased for the Pobladores

Carrying out his instructions, Capitán Fernando de Rivera y Moncada apparently kept a careful record of moneys expended and supplies purchased for the settlers from the time they started out on the long journey to Los Angeles. Then his memoranda perished with him on the banks of the Colorado, strewn on the sands or cast into some fire, out of the pockets of the uniform in which his Yuma slayer strutted – *quien sabe?*[1]

It remained for Lieutenant José de Zúñiga to replace Rivera's memoranda with the following documents, compiled from memory and with aid of the notebook kept by Alferez Don Mañuel Ruíz, sworn to by the pobladores and marked with the "VB"[2] or "OK" of Felipe de Neve.

So picturesque and packed with human interest are these unadorned bookkeeping records that they provide an absorbing revelation of the conditions under which the pobladores made ready to come to Los Angeles, the kind of people they were, and the customs of their day.

It will be noted that the statements are prefaced with the explanation "copy of his account starting June 4, 1780, taken from his memorandum book," referring to the notes of Alferez Ruíz; and that a little below appears the record of purchasing the notebook itself, under "June 4 – 2 pesos worth of rations and 6 reales for memo book."

The entries which follow after are veritable little vignettes of the pobladores, which show their tastes and inclinations and even tell of incidents in their lives, as in the case of Alejandro Rosas (Account No. 74), who "in the first place admits having taken as a first entry in the Villa de Sinaloa, 25 pesos for the expenses of his marriage." Account No. 72, with the entry "12 reales expenses as padrino at wedding ceremony," indicates that Antonio Villavicencio must have stood sponsor on this occasion, which was perhaps the first event to give the

1. Who can say.
2. Visto Bueno

newly assembled pobladores a sense of the bonds of fellowship which would draw them closer and closer into a community as they traveled to the frontier of empire. It will also be noted in the record that this Villavicencio was a Spaniard, and judging by the quality of his purchases, a man of somewhat cultivated tastes.

These documents were brought to light in the Archivo General de Mexico during 1931 by Vernon D. Tate and are here published for the first time. Obviously, since they number 71 to 75, they constitute only a portion of a series of which the remaining items are yet to be found. Doubtless the memoranda of supplies issued to the pobladores were combined with those made up for the recruits and mentioned by Neve in a letter of October 28 [1781], as being sent in place of those compiled by Rivera and lost.

In these translations, the society is indebted to Mr. Temple for an unusually painstaking task, as the problem was one not only of translating numerous obscure and obsolete words written with a maze of abbreviations, but also of first transcribing the Spanish from photographs of minute and perplexing manuscript. – EDITORS

No. 71[3]

ANTONIO MESA, negro, 38, native of el Real de los Alamos, married, his wife is Anna Gertrudis Lopez, native of said Real, mulata, 27. Two children, Antonio Maria, 8, and Maria Pascuala, 10. He enlisted as a Settler for the New Establishments of Monterey, at la Villa de Sinaloa, on June 4, 1780, and is a resident in el Pueblo de la Reina de los Angeles.

In the first place, he received at the hands of Capitan Don Fernando de Rivera, the following on account.

	Debit		
	Ps.	Rls.	Grs.
1 Saddle with its tree and bows, from the House of Don Prudencio worth 13 pesos, 4 reales	013	4	0
1 pair of Armas de montar[4] at 20 reales	002	4	0
1 set of tools for the saddle, at 12 reales	001	4	0
2 bridles and a pair of spurs, at 9 reales each	003	3	0
2 pair of Reins and a Halter, worth 10 reales	001	2	0
2 cruppers, at 3 reales	000	6	0
1 leather water Bag	001	0	0
3 pesos for a pair of riding Boots	003	0	0
2 Hats at 18 reales	004	4	0
1¼ varas of Coarse linen wrapping for portmanteaus, at 6 reales	000	7	6
1¼ varas of Rouen linen cloth, at 6 reales	000	7	6
2 pair of women's shoes and a pair of men's shoes, worth	001	7	0
1 bed blanket from the House of Comes, at 4 pesos, 4 reales	004	4	0
1 reel of thread for sewing	000	1	0
94 daily rations at 2 reales each, from November 1, 1780, until February 2, 1781, when he left completely outfitted from Los Alamos	023	4	0

Copy of his account starting June 4, 1780, taken from his memorandum book, in Alferez Don Manuel Ruiz's hand.

June 4th, 2 pesos worth of rations and 6 grs. for memo book	002	0	6

3. Provincias Internas Tom. 199, Archivo General de la Nacion. Translated by Thomas Workman Temple II. The original Spanish-language version of these documents can be found on pages 243–55.

4. Leather aprons or chaps for riding

June 5th, 3 pesos for a silk handkerchief	003	0	0
" 13th, 2 pesos worth of rations	002	0	0
" 14th, for Provisions and rations on the march to Los Alamos	003	6	0
" 29th, he charged 3 pesos (for supplies)	003	0	0
Item, 10 reales for Freight or baggage to el Fuerte	001	2	0
July 8th, 12 reales for fresh meat	001	4	0
" 9th, 1½ Almudes of corn at 6 reales	001	1	0
" ½ [almud] of beans at 3 reales	000	3	0
" 15th, ½ almude of corn	000	3	0
" 2 almudes of the same	001	4	0
" 2 reales for Cigars	000	2	0
" 22nd, 1 almud of corn at 6 reales	000	6	0
" 1 almud of beans at same price	000	6	0
" 2 reales of Soap	000	2	0
" 24th, 4 reales for medicine	000	4	0
" 28th, ½ almud of corn	000	3	0
" 29th, 2 Almudes of corn	001	4	0
" " 2 reales worth of Soap	000	2	0
August 5th 2 Almudes of corn and beans at 6 reales	001	4	0
August 5th, 1 pair of women's shoes at 6 reales and 2 reales of soap	001	0	0
August 5th, 12 reales worth of provisions	001	4	0
" 9th, ½ almud of beans at 3 reales	000	3	0
" 12th, 1 almud of beans and 2 reales in silver	001	0	0
" " 6 reales in silver for corn	000	6	0
" 17th, 1 almud of corn and beans	000	6	0
" 19th, 2 almudes of corn and 2 reales worth of soap	001	6	0
" 22nd, ½ almud of corn	000	3	0
" " 1 almud of corn at 6 reales	000	6	0
" 27th, 2 almudes of corn and beans	000	6	0
" " 2 reales in silver	000	2	0
September 2nd, 2 almudes of corn and beans, at 6 reales	001	4	0
September 2nd, 2 reales in silver	000	2	0
" 9th, 2 almudes of corn and beans, and 2 reales in silver	001	6	0
" 16th, 14 reales in silver for Rations	001	6	0
" 23rd, 14 reales in silver for rations	001	6	0
" 30th, 14 reales in silver for Rations	001	6	0
October 7th, 14 reales in silver for rations	001	6	0

" 14th, 14 reales in silver for rations	001	6	0
" 18th, he Charged 42 pesos, value of effects supplied in clothing as found in detail in memo book	042	0	0
On same day he charged 48 pesos, 4 reales, 8 grs. value of items furnished his wife as per memorandum	048	4	8
On the same day he charged 26 pesos, 1 grano value of items furnished to his children, as per memorandum.	026	0	1
October 21st, he charged 20 reales worth of rations until the end of said month	002	4	0
October 24th, 1 pair of Cordovan shoes, worth 6 reales	000	6	0
Having read his account in full, and having received all items as found therein, he made his mark. Alferez Josef Arguello signed for him.			
To Credit Don Fernando Rivera	231	3	3
Total	231	3	3
To this amount should be credited the daily rations in his favor from June 4, 1780, when he enlisted as a settler, until February 2, 1781, when he left Los Alamos completely outfitted, in the value of	061	0	0
Also he is credited with 10 reales, value of transportation at his expense from la Villa del Fuerte to los Alamos	001	2	0
	62	2	0
Total sum charged against the Settler	169	1	3

This agrees with the account rendered this Individual, and his Declarations, and the investigations made, by reason of the originals, which were in the hands of Capitan Fernando Rivera y Moncada, having been lost at the time of his death on the Colorado River. Mision San Gabriel, September 18, 1781.

O.K. JOSÉ DE ZÚÑIGA. [rubric]

NEVE [rubric]

No. 72

ANTONIO VILLAVICENCIO, Spaniard, 38, native of La Villa de Chihuahua, married. His wife is Maria de los Santos Severina, native of el Real del Rosario, Indian, 26 years of age. One daughter, Maria Antonio Josefa, mestiza, 8. He enlisted as a Poblador for the New Establishments of Monterey, at la Villa de Sinaloa, on June 6, 1780, and is a resident of el Pueblo de la Reina de los Angeles. [Fig. 5]

	Debit		
	Ps.	Rls.	Grs.
In the first place he admits having received 20 pesos which he thinks were paid the late Don Miguel Aviles, a miner from Severifoa	020	0	0
Also he received at said Villa, 4 varas of fine Brittany linen at 7 reales each, for his wife's chemises	003	4	0
6½ varas of serge at 12 reales each, for Skirts	009	6	0
1½ varas of Glazed Linen for lining, at 2½ reales	000	3	9
1¼ [varas] of silk and 4 varas of ribbon at 1 rl. ea.	000	6	6
7 varas of Revecillo [lining] at 1 real each and 12 reales for tailoring	002	3	0
8 varas of domestic Cotton Shirting, at 4 reales	000	4	0
13 reales Expenses as padrino at wedding ceremony	001	5	0
1 pair of silk Stockings, worth 3 pesos, 4 reales	003	4	0
2 loads of Baggage from Sinaloa to Los Alamos at 2 reales per league	005	0	0
1½ varas of Queretaro cloth for a Jacket	003	0	0
4 varas of second-grade Cotton Shirting for lining, 3 reales each	001	4	0
1/4 ounce of silk, and 14 reales for tailoring	002	0	6
1½ dozen Buttons at 3 reales a dozen	000	4	6
2½ varas of woolen cloth, at 2 pesos each, for Breeches	005	0	0
¼ ounce of silk and a dozen buttons, all for 5½ reales	000	5	6
1 Peso, 2 reales of tailoring and 3 varas of cotton shirting for lining, at 3 reales each	002	3	0
6½ varas of Queretaro cloth, at 2 pesos each for a Cape	013	0	0
¼ ounce of silk, and the tailoring	001	2	6
1½ varas of Castillian Baize for linings worth 20 reales each	003	6	0
1 black Campaign hat, worth 18 reales	002	2	0
16 varas of cotton shirting for two changes of clothes, at 4 reales each	008	0	0
½ ounce of silk, worth 5 reales	000	5	0

FIGURE 5. The document No. 72 listing the items issued to Antonio Villavicencio, his wife, and young daughter, recruited settlers for the new pueblo of Los Angles.

Supplies Purchased for the Pobladores

N.o 72

Antonio Villavisencio Español de 32 años natural de la Villa de Chihuahua casado su muger Maria de los Santos Severina Natural del R.l de [illegible] India de edad de 26 años, una hija Maria Antonia de edad de 8 años se registró de Poblador para los nuevos Establecim.tos de Monterrey en la Villa de Sinaloa en 6 de junio de 1780 y queda avecindado en el Pueblo de la Reina de los Angeles ... // Deve

Primeram.te declara haver tomado 20 p.s q.e se pagaron de [illegible] al Difunto D.n [illegible] Aviles [illegible] ... 20..0..0
Y tomó en la citada Villa 4 varas de Bretaña a 7 r.s para camisas a su mug.r ... 3..4..0
6½ v.s de [illegible] a 4 r.s para Naguas ... 3..6..0
1½ var.s de [illegible] a 2 r.s p.a forro ... 0..3..9
½ [illegible] de seda y 4 var.s de liston [illegible] ... 0..6..6
7 v.s de [illegible] a 1 r.l y 12 r.s de echura al Sastre ... 2..3..0
8 v.s de manta Sanguina a 4 r.s ... 4..0..0
13 r.s de las Arras quando fue padrino ... 1..5..0
1 par de medias de seda en 3 p.s 4 r.s ... 3..4..0
2 Bagajes desde Sinaloa a los Alamos a [illegible] r.l p.r legua ... 5..0..0
1½ var.s de Paño Queretano para chupa ... 3..0..0
4 varas de manta de 2/3 para forro a 3 r.s ... 1..4..0
½ de seda, y 1 p. 4 r.s de echura ... 2..0..6
1½ doz.a de Botones a 3 r.s ... 0..4..6
2½ v.s de [illegible] a 2 p.s p.a Calzon ... 5..0..0
½ de seda, y una doz.a de boton.s en 5½ r.s todo ... 0..5..6
1 peso y 2 r.s de echura, y 3 var.s de manta a 3 r.s p.a forro ... 2..3..0
6½ v.s de Paño de Queret.o a 2 p.s p.a Capa ... 13..0..0
½ de seda y la hechura al [illegible] ... 3..2..6
1½ varas de Bayeta de Castilla p.a forro a 20 r.s ... 3..6..0
1 somb.o negro de Tarea en 18 r.s ... 2..2..0
16 v.s manta de 7/8 p.a 2 mudas de Ropa a 4 r.s ... 8..0..0
½ [illegible] de seda en 5 r.s ... 0..5..0
1 vara de Bretaña p.a pañuelos en 6 r.s ... 0..6..0
2 Pañitos Poblanos en 5 r.s ... 0..5..0
2 par.s de Zapatos a 5 r.s ... 1..2..0
2 [illegible] de Cabrestos a 4 r.s ... 1..0..0
3 p.s p.a un par de Botas ... 3..0..0
1½ var.s de liston a 2 r.s ... 0..3..0

A la Vuelta ... 102..1..3

De la v[uel]ta ... 31 . 2 . 1 . 3

1. p[ie]za de [illegible] en 6 p[eso]s para camisas ... 0 0 0 6 . 0 . 0
1. par de Naguas de Bayeta az[u]l de la q[u]e dio el Alf[érez] Roy[z] en el R[ea]l de los Alamos en 3 p[eso]s 2½ r[eale]s ... 0 0 0 3 . 2 . 6
1. faldellin de paño de Queretaro de lo q[u]e dio el d[ic]ho ... 0 0 0 7 . 2 . 6
2. Armadores de [illegible] de lo q[u]e dio el d[ic]ho ... 0 0 0 2 . 7 .
2. par[e]s de calzetas a 4 r[eale]s ... 0 0 0 1 . 0 .
3. pares de Naguas blancas Poblanas a 15½ r[eale]s ... 0 0 0 5 . 6 . 6
2. Pares de Medias de Nimes a 14 r[eale]s ... 0 0 0 3 . 4 .
2. Pares de Zapatos p[ar]a mug[e]r a 6 r[eale]s ... 0 0 0 1 . 4 .
2. Nuevos a 11½ r[eale]s ... 0 0 0 2 . 7 .
1. somb[rer]o negro de Tarea en 18 r[eale]s ... 0 0 0 2 . 3 .
6. v[aras] de liston a 8 r[eale]s ... 0 0 0 . 6 .
1. frezada ½ camera en 4 p[eso]s 4 r[eale]s ... 0 0 0 4 . 4 .
5. var[a]s de Coleta p[ar]a camisa a 5 r[eale]s ... 0 0 0 3 . 1 .
6. v[ara]s Manta Sanquina a 4 r[eale]s ... 0 0 0 3 . 0 .
1. Panito de Rebozo chico en un peso ... 0 0 0 3 . 0 . 0
1. Onza de Seda ... 0 0 0 1 . 2 . 0
1½ var[a]s de Bayeta az[u]l a 6 r[eale]s ... 0 0 0 1 . 1 . 0
1. d[ocen]a de [illegible] en 7½ r[eale]s ... 0 0 0 . 2 . 6
2. var[a]s de Liston ... 0 0 0 . 2 .
2. r[eale]s de seda, y 6 r[eale]s al sastre de la hechura ... 0 0 0 1 . 0 .
1¼ var[a]s de Paño az[u]l Queretano a 2 p[eso]s p[ar]a faldellin ... 0 0 0 2 . 4 .
2. var[a]s de liston, 2 r[eale]s de seda, y 6 r[eale]s de la hechura al sastre ... 0 0 0 1 . 2 . 0
1. frezada Pastora ... en 8½ r[eale]s ... 0 0 0 1 . 1 . 6
2. Par[e]s de Zapatos de muchachita a 4 r[eale]s ... 0 0 0 1 . 0 .
1. Silla de [illegible] en 13 p[eso]s 4 r[eale]s ... 0 0 13 . 4 . 0
1. par de Armas de Montar en 20 r[eale]s ... 0 0 0 2 . 4 . 0
1. terno de fierros de Silla en 12 r[eale]s ... 0 0 0 1 . 4 . 0
1. Cavrest[o] en 3 r[eale]s ... 0 0 0 . 3 . 0
2. Par[e]s de Riendas a 3 r[eale]s ... 0 0 0 . 6 .
2. frenos, y un par de Espuelas a 9 r[eale]s p[ie]za ... 0 0 0 3 . 3 . 0
3. Pesos, para un fuste, y Estrivos ... 0 0 0 3 . 0 . 0
2. botas p[ar]a Agua ... 0 0 0 2 . 0 . 0
1¼ var[a]s de Cotense p[ar]a cavalera ... 0 0 0 . 7 . 6
3 par[e]s de Zapatos a 5 r[eale]s ... 0 0 0 1 . 7 . 0
Un par de los a mug[e]r en 6 r[eale]s ... 0 0 0 . 6 . 0
Por 341. Diarios a 2 r[eale]s desde el 6. de Junio inclusive q[u]e tomó partido, h[as]ta el 2 de febrero de 1784 q[u]e valió socorrido del R[ea]l de los Alamos ... 0 0 85 . 2 . 0

Y haviendole leydo las partidas de ... 254 . 5 . 3

su quenta á este Yndividuo, Dijo estar conforme y ser las mismas que tiene recevidas, las señaló con una cruz, y firmó á su ruego el Alfz. Dn Ramon Lasso.

Suman el frente, hasta el Capn. Moncada 325. 5. 3

Sele revonan a. Contenido Veces que tiene Cargados el Ymporte de 2 bagages en que se transporto con su Muger de la Villa de Sinaloa a el de los Alamos 0 5. 0. 0

Ydem 2 1/2 a 2 rr. con que sele socorrio desde el 6 de Junio de Bochavia el 3 de febrero de 81 con Racion .... 60. 2. 0 | 00. 65. 2. 0

Resulta liquido en contra del Poblador 3 2 8 6. 3. 3

Concuerda Con la Cuenta, que se le a formado al Contenido, Conforme a su Declaracion, e Informe que se han tomado no Caresa de haverse perdido las Originales que existian en poder del Capitan D. Ferndo. Moncada, en su Muerte hacaenda en el rio Colorado. Mision de San Gavriel y Febre 13 de 1781.

Jose de Zuñiga

V. B.
Neve

1 vara of Brittany linen for Handkerchiefs, worth 6 reales	000	6	0
2 puebla cotton drawers worth 5 reales	000	5	0
2 pairs of Shoes at 5 reales each	001	2	0
2 pairs of Hose at 4 reales each	001	0	0
3 pesos for a pair of Boots	003	0	0
1½ varas of ribbon at 2 reales each	000	3	0
1 bolt of Brittany linen for his wife's chemises, worth 6 pesos	006	0	0
1 pair of blue Baize Skirts, of the lot which Alferez Ruiz distributed *at el Real de los Alamos*, worth	003	2	6
1 petticoat of Queretaro Cloth, of the same lot, worth	007	2	6
2 linen jackets of the same lot as distributed	002	7	0
2 pairs of hose at 4 reales a pair	001	0	0
3 pairs of white Puebla cotton skirts, at 15 reales a pair	005	6	0
2 pairs of Nimes stockings, at 14 reales each	003	4	0
2 pairs of women's shoes at 6 reales a pair	001	4	0
2 rebozos at 11½ reales each	002	7	0
1 Black Campaign hat, worth 18 reales	002	2	0
6 varas of ribbon at 1 real each	000	6	0
1 bed blanket, worth 4 pesos, 4 reales	004	4	0
5 varas of Linen for Shirts, at 5 reales each	003	1	0
6 varas of domestic Cotton Shirting, at 4 reales each	003	0	0
1 small Rebozo, worth 1 peso	001	0	0
1 ounce of silk, worth 10 reales	001	2	0
1½ varas of blue Baize, at 6 reales each	001	1	0
1 vara of glazed linen, worth 2½ reales	000	2	5
2 varas of Ribbon	000	2	0
2 varas of silk and 6 reales for tailoring the material	001	0	0
1¼ varas of blue Queretaro Cloth at 2 pesos each for underskirts	002	4	0
2 varas of Ribbon, 2 reales worth of silk and 6 reales for tailoring same	001	2	0
1 Small blanket, worth 9½ reales	001	1	6
2 Pairs of Shoes for the little girl, at 4 reales each	001	0	0
1 Saddle from the House of Don Prudencio, at 13 pesos, 4 reales	013	4	0
1 pair of leather "Chaps" for Riding, worth 20 reales	002	4	0
1 set of saddle tools, worth 12 reales	001	4	0
1 Halter worth 3 reales	000	3	0
2 pairs of Reins, worth 3 reales each	000	6	0

2 Bridles and a pair of Spurs, at 9 reales apiece	003	3	0
3 pesos for a saddle tree and stirrups	003	0	0
2 leather Water bags	002	0	0
1¼ varas of Coarse Linen for wrapping	000	7	6
3 pairs of shoes at 5 reales a pair	001	7	0
1 pair of women's shoes worth 6 reales	000	6	0
231 daily rations at 2 reales each, from June 6, 1780, when he enlisted, to February 2, 1781, when he left el Real de los Alamos completely equipped	060	2	0
	251	5	3
Having read the entries of his account to this individual, he remained satisfied that they were the same as those received, and made his mark Alferez Don Ramon Laso signed at his request.			
To credit Capitan Moncada	251	5	3
To this sum should be credited 5 pesos, value of 2 loads of baggage, charged against his account, with which he transported himself and family from el Real de Sinaloa to los Alamos	005	0	0
Also value of 241 daily rations furnished him from June 6, 1780, to February 2, 1781	060	2	0
	065	2	0
Total sum charged against this Settler	186	3	3

This conforms with the account rendered this individual and agrees with his testimony and the investigations made by reason of the original accounts, which were in Capitan Fernando Moncada's hands, having been destroyed at the time of his death on the Colorado River. Mision San Gabriel, September 13, 1781.

O.K. JOSÉ DE ZÚÑIGA. [rubric]

NEVE [rubric]

No. 73

JOSEF VANEGAS, indian, 28, Native of el Real de Bolanos, married, his wife is Maria Maxima Aguilar, native of el Real del Rosario, indian, 20. One son Cosme Damien, a year and 2 months old. He enlisted as a settler for the New Establishments of Monterey, at el Real del Rosario, on August 11, 1780, and is at present a resident in el Pueblo de la Reina de Los Angeles.

	Debit		
	Ps.	Rls.	Grs.
In the first place he admits having received from Capitan Don Fernando Moncada, at el Real del Rosario, 6½ varas of serge from the store of Josef Maria Farro, at 12 reales each	009	6	0
1½ varas of glazed linen for lining, at 2½ reales ea.	000	3	9
4 varas of Ribbon at a real each, and ½ vara of silk	000	6	6
7 varas of Lining, at a real each	000	7	0
1 piece of common Brittany linen	006	0	0
1 ounce of silk, worth 10 reales	001	2	0
1 Rosario Saddle, worth 10 pesos, 4 reales	010	4	0
1 pair of new Saddle-bags, worth 3 pesos, 4 reales	003	4	0
1 Set of saddle irons, worth 12 reales	001	4	0
2 bridles and a pair of spurs at 9 reales apiece	003	3	0
2½ varas of blue woolen cloth, at 20 reales each	007	4	0
3 varas of Cotton Shirting (second grade), at 3 reales for lining	001	1	0
1 quarter of silk and 10 reales for tailoring	001	4	6
1 dozen Metal Buttons worth 3 reales	000	3	0
6 varas of Queretaro Cloth, at 2 pesos each for a Cape	012	0	0
1 quarter ounce of silk, hand tailored	001	2	0
1½ varas of Querétaro Cloth, at 2 pesos each	003	0	0
4 varas of cotton shirting, second grade, at 3 reales each, for lining	001	4	0
1½ dozen Buttons for the jacket, at 3 reales a dozen	000	4	6
1 quarter of silk and 14 reales for tailoring	002	0	6
1 hat worth 18 reales	002	2	0
3 pair of Hose at 4 reales each	001	4	0
16 varas of Cotton Shirting at 4 reales each for 2 changes of underwear	008	0	0
½ ounce of silk worth 5 reales	000	5	0
1 vara of fine Brittany linen for handkerchiefs, at 1 peso	001	0	0

Supplies Purchased for the Pobladores

2 Blankets at 2½ reres each	000	5	0
2 Pair of men's shoes, at 5 reales each	001	2	0
1¼ varas of Ribbon for the hat, worth 3 reales	000	3	0
4 reales for a pair of boots bought at San Sebastian	001	6	0
1 piece of Brittany linen, worth 6 pesos	006	0	0
2½ varas of baize at 6 reales each	001	7	0
1 vara of Glazed Linen for lining, worth 2½ reales	000	2	6
3 varas of ribbon at 1 real each, and ½ vara of silk	000	5	6
6 reales for tailoring a pair of Skirts	000	6	0
1 ounce of white silk	001	2	0
9 varas of Rouen linen, at 6 reales each	006	6	0
1 pair of Women's stockings, worth 3 pesos, 4 reales	003	4	0
2 varas of Linen for Jackets, at 5 reales each	001	2	0
2 pair of hose at 4 reales each	001	0	0
2 rebozos at 11½ reales each	002	7	0
1 hat worth 18 reales	002	2	0
6 varas of ribbon at 1 real each	000	6	0
2 pair of Women's Shoes worth 12 reales	001	4	0
1 bed blanket worth 4 pesos, 4 reales	004	4	0
1 coarse blanket for his son, worth 9 reales	001	1	0
1¼ varas of Coarse Linen Wrapper for portmanteaus, at 6 reales each	000	7	6
6 reales for a pair of stirrups	000	6	0
3 varas of Rouen linen for handkerchiefs, at 6 reales each	002	2	0
3 varas of Linen for the little girl, at 5 reales each	001	7	0
1 pair of Reins from the House of Don Prudencio, worth 3 reales	000	3	0
2 Headstalls at 3½ reales and 2 Halters at 3 reales	001	5	0
1 leather Water Bag, worth 1 peso	001	0	0
1 quarter pound of leather, worth 5½ reales	000	5	6
1 real for a sweat pad for the saddle	000	1	0
3 Cruppers at 3 reales each	001	1	0
1 silk handkerchief worth 18 reales	002	2	0
2 loads of baggage from el Real del Rosario to Los Alamos, a distance of 120 leagues, 15 pesos	015	0	0
176 daily rations at 2 reales each, from August 11, 1780, till February 2, 1781, when he left Los Alamos fully equipped	044	0	0
	194	6	3

The account having been read in full to this individual, he expressed his satisfaction that the entries of Merchandise and other effects therein contained are the same as he has received, and he made his mark,

Alferez Don Ramon Laso signing at his request.

To Credit of Don Fernando Rivera y Moncada's account	194	6	3
From this sum should be subtracted the value of 2 loads of baggage with which he conducted himself and family from el Real del Rosario to Los Alamos, at ½ real per league	015	0	0
Also he is credited with 176 daily rations at 2 reales each charged against him from the 11th of August 1780 to the 2nd of February 1781, when he eft fully equipped from Los Alamos	044	0	0
Credit	059	0	0
Net sum charged against the settler	135	6	3

This agrees with the account rendered this individual, and conforms to his testimony and the investigations made because the original accounts which were in the hands of Capitan Don Fernando Rivera y Moncada were lost at the time of his death on the Colorado River. Mision San Gabriel, September 20, 1781.

O.K. JOSÉ DE ZÚÑIGA. [rubric]

NEVE [rubric]

No. 74.

ALEJANDRO ROSAS, Indian, 19, native of el Real del Rosario, married, his wife, Juana Rodriguez, native of San Blas, coyota, 20. He enlisted as a Settler for the New Establishments of Monterey, in the Villa of Sinaloa, on November 7, 1780, and continues a resident in el Pueblo de la Reina de los Angeles.

	Debit		
	Ps.	Rls.	Grs.
In the first place he admitted having taken as a first entry in la Villa de Sinaloa, 25 pesos for the Expense of his marriage	025	0	0
1 pound of wax, worth 5 reales	000	5	0
1 pair of silk stockings, worth 4 pesos	004	0	0

6½ varas of serge for Women's Skirts	009	6	0
1½ varas of glazed linen for lining, at 2½ reales	000	3	3
¼ [ounce] of silk, worth 2½ reales, and 7 varas of Lining at 1 real	001	1	6
4 varas of ribbon at 1 real each	000	4	0
2 pesos for Tailored goods	002	0	0
1 piece of ordinary Brittany linen, worth	006	0	0
1 ounce of silk, worth 1 peso, 2 reales	001	2	0
2 pair of Hose, at 4 reales each	001	0	0
2 pair of shoes at 6 reales each	001	4	0
2 rebozos at 11½ reales each	002	7	0
1 vara of Linen for a jacket, worth 5 reales	000	5	0
1 hat, worth 18 reales	002	2	0
1½ varas of ribbon for a hat band, at 2 reales	000	3	0
2½ varas of blue Woolen Cloth, at 20 reales each for breeches	007	4	0
3 varas of domestic cotton shirting, of ⅔, for lining, at 3 reales	001	1	0
1 quarter of silk worth 2½ reales	000	2	6
1 dozen Buttons, which, with the tailoring, amounts to 11 reales	001	3	0
16 varas of Domestic Cotton Shirting, at 4 reales each	008	0	0
1 [ounce] of silk, worth 10 reales	001	2	0
1 Crupper, worth 3 reales	000	3	0
3 varas of ribbon, at 1 real each	000	3	0
1 piece of Brittany linen, that he got at los Alamos, worth 6 pesos	006	0	0
6 varas of Queretaro Cloth, at 2 pesos each, for a Cape	012	0	0
¼ [ounce] of silk, and 1 peso for tailoring	001	2	6
2 pair of hose, at 4 reales each	001	0	0
2 pair of men's Shoes at 5 reales each	001	0	2
1¼ varas of Coarse Linen Wrapper for making Portmanteaus	000	7	6
1¼ varas of Rouen Linen for handkerchiefs	000	7	6
1 real worth of silk for sewing same	000	1	0
1 vara of Brittany Linen for handkerchiefs	000	6	0
1 Bed blanket, worth 4 pesos, 4 reales	004	4	0
1 Black work hat (de Tarea), worth 18 reales	002	2	0
1 saddle complete, with tree and all, from el Rosario	010	4	0
1 set of saddle irons, worth 12 reales	001	4	0
2 bridles and a pair of Spurs, at 9 reales each	003	3	0
1 pair of Reins worth 3½ reales	000	3	6
1 leather water Bag, worth 1 peso	001	0	0

1 Rosarian women's Saddle, worth 10 pesos, 4 reales	010	4	0
2 loads of Baggage, at 1 real per league from el Rosario to el Real de los Alamos	015	0	0
1 pair of women's shoes on leaving los Alamos	000	6	0
88 daily rations at 2 reales each from the 7th November, 1780, when he enlisted, till the 2nd of February, 1781, when he left fully outfitted	022	0	0
1 pair of saddle bags, worth 3 pesos	003	0	0
	178	6	9

Having read this account to the Interested party he approved of same with his Mark, and Alferez Don Josef Arguello signed for him.

Sum in favor of Capitan Don Fernando Rivera y Moncada	178	6	9
From this sum should be subtracted in favor of said party, 15 pesos, value of 2 loads of baggage, with which he brought himself and family from el Real del Rosario to Los Alamos	015	0	0
Also the value of 88 daily rations which he received, at 2 reales each, and are charged against his account supra, from the 7th November, 1780, till the 2nd of February, 1781	022	0	0
	037	0	0
Net sum charged against this Settler	141	6	9

This agrees with the account rendered this individual, and conforms to his declarations and the investigations made, because the original accounts, which were in the hands of Capitan Don Fernando Moncada, were lost at the time of his death on the Colorado River. Misión San Gabriel, September 18, 1781.

O.K. JOSÉ DE ZÚÑIGA. [rubric]

NEVE [rubric]

No. 75.

PABLO RODRIGUEZ, Indian, 25, native of el Real de Santa Rosa, in the jurisdiction of Volanos, married to Maria Rosalia Noriega, native of el Real de Panuco, in the jurisdiction of Rosario, indian, 26. One child, Maria Antonia, a year old. He enlisted as a Settler for the New Establishments of Monterrey at el Real del Rosario on August 13, 1780, and continues a resident of el Pueblo de la Reyna de los Angeles.

	Debit		
	Ps.	Rls.	Grs.
In the first place he admits having received a peso in reales from Capitan Don Fernando for medical services at Rosario	001	0	0
3 varas of wide Brittany linen, bought at the House of Don Lorenzo Moro, at 10 reales each	003	6	0
1 black Work hat, worth 18 reales	002	2	0
1 pair of women's shoes	000	6	0
1 pair of men's shoes	000	5	0
1 pair of spurs worth 9 reales	001	1	0
1 Rosarian saddle completely accoutred	010	4	0
2 bridles, at 9 reales each	002	2	0
1½ varas of Queretaro Cloth, at 2 pesos each for a Jacket	003	0	0
4 varas of domestic cotton shirting for linings, at 3 reales each	001	4	0
1½ dozen Buttons, at 3 reales each	000	4	6
1 quarter [ounce] of silk and 14 reales of tailoring	002	6	0
2½ varas of Woolen Cloth for Breeches, at 2 pesos each	005	0	0
3 varas of cotton shirting for lining, at 3 reales each	001	1	0
1 quarter of silk and a dozen buttons	000	5	6
1 peso for tailoring	001	0	0
16 varas of Lanquina shirting, at 4 reales each	008	0	0
1 [ounce] of silk, worth 10 reales	001	2	0
2 pair of hose, at 4 reales each	001	0	0
2 pair of men's shoes, at 5 reales each	001	2	0
2 small Puebla Handkerchiefs, at 2½ reales each	000	5	0
1 vara of fine Brittany linen, worth 6 reales	000	6	0
6½ varas of cloth for a Cape, at 2 pesos each	013	0	0
1 quarter [ounce] of silk, and 1 peso for tailoring	001	2	6
3 pesos, 4 reales, for a pair of boots	003	4	0

1 piece of fine Brittany linen for Shirts	006	0	0
1 pair of silk stockings, worth 3 pesos, 4 reales	003	4	0
1 Marca [a frontier province] silk handkerchief	002	2	0
6½ varas of serge, at 12 reales each	009	6	0
1½ varas of Glazed Linen for lining, at 2½ reales each	000	3	9
1 quarter [ounce] of silk, worth 2½ reales	000	2	6
4 varas of ribbon at 1 real each and 7 of revecillo [lining]	001	3	0
2 pesos for tailoring	002	0	0
2 varas of linen for jackets	001	3	0
1 ounce of silk, worth 10 reales	001	2	0
3 varas of blue Baize for Skirts, at 6 reales each	002	2	0
1 vara of glazed linen at 2½ reales	000	2	6
¼ of silk and 3 varas of ribbon at a real each	000	5	6
2 pair of shoes, worth 6 reales	001	4	0
1 bed blanket, worth 4 pesos, 4 reales	004	4	0
1 halter worth 3 reales, and a Headstall at 3½ reales	000	6	6
1 leather Water Bag, worth 1 peso	001	0	0
1 set of saddle irons, worth 12 reales	001	4	0
1¼ varas of coarse linen for Wrapping, at 6 reales each	000	7	6
1¼ varas of Rouen pack thread for hand cloths	001	1	6
4 varas of cotton goods for child's diapers at 3 reales each	001	4	0
2 varas of blue baize for mantillas at 6 reales	001	4	0
For 2 loads of baggage from Rosario to Los Alamos at ½ real per league	010	0	0
For 173 daily rations at 2 reales each, from August 13, 1780, to February 2, 1781	043	2	0
Also for 1 rebozo that he received at Los Alamos	001	3	6
	168	4	3

Note. That although this person brought two loads of baggage, he was not paid for one of them from a distance of 20 leagues from Rosario to Sinaloa, which amounts to 80 leagues, and he is credited with forty reales accordingly. Having read his account, he admitted that the entries were regular, and the same that he has received, in evidence of which he made his Mark. Alferez Josef Arguello signed at *his request.*

Sum in favor of Capitan Don Fernando Rivera y Moncada	168	4	3

Said person is credited with the 10 pesos charged against him, value of the transportation of himself and family from Rosario to Los Alamos	010	0	0
Also he is credited with the 173 issues of rations charged against him, and which he received from August 13, 1780, to February 2, 1781	043	2	0
	053	2	0
Net sum charged against this Settler	115	2	3

This conforms with the account rendered this individual and agrees with his declarations and the investigations made by reason of the originals, which were in Capitan Rivera's hands, having been lost, when he was killed on the Colorado River. Mision San Gabriel, September 18, 1781.

O.K. JOSÉ DE ZÚÑIGA. [rubric]
NEVE [rubric]

Governor Neve's Order for the Founding of Los Angeles[1]

For the establishment of the Pueblo de Los Angeles, near the Río Porciúncula, and on the land designated for this purpose, there shall be included all the lands that may be benefited by irrigation. There shall be marked out the best place to construct the dam in order that the water may be distributed to the largest extent of land.

The site where the Pueblo is to be established shall be marked out, on land slightly elevated, exposed to the North and South winds. Measures shall be taken to avoid the dangers of floods; the most immediate vicinity to the river or vicinity to the principal zanja shall be preferred; taking care that from the Pueblo the whole or greatest portion of the planting lands may be seen.

The Plaza ought to be 200 feet wide by 300 long; from said Plaza four main streets shall extend, two on each side; and besides these, two other streets shall run by each corner. The four corners shall look towards the four cardinal points, for the reason that said streets being prolonged in this manner from the Plaza they shall not be exposed to the four winds, which would be a great inconvenience. Taking this into consideration and the gradual increase of population there shall be marked out the convenient lands to establish said Pueblo; and for the purpose of building there shall be marked out as many building lots as there may be suertes of land susceptible of irrigation. Also, a tract of land 200 varas wide between the planting lands and the Pueblo shall be left vacant. [Figs. 6 and 7]

Every building lot shall measure 20 varas wide by 40 varas long.

Every suerte of land, either susceptible of irrigation or not, ought to be 200 varas long by 200 wide, on account of this being the size of a tract of land usu-

1. This is a portion of the order. It is from a certified traced copy from the Surveyor-General's office, filed as evidence in Los Angeles District Court, Case no. 1344, March 11, 1869. There is no copy of the original Spanish-language document in existence.

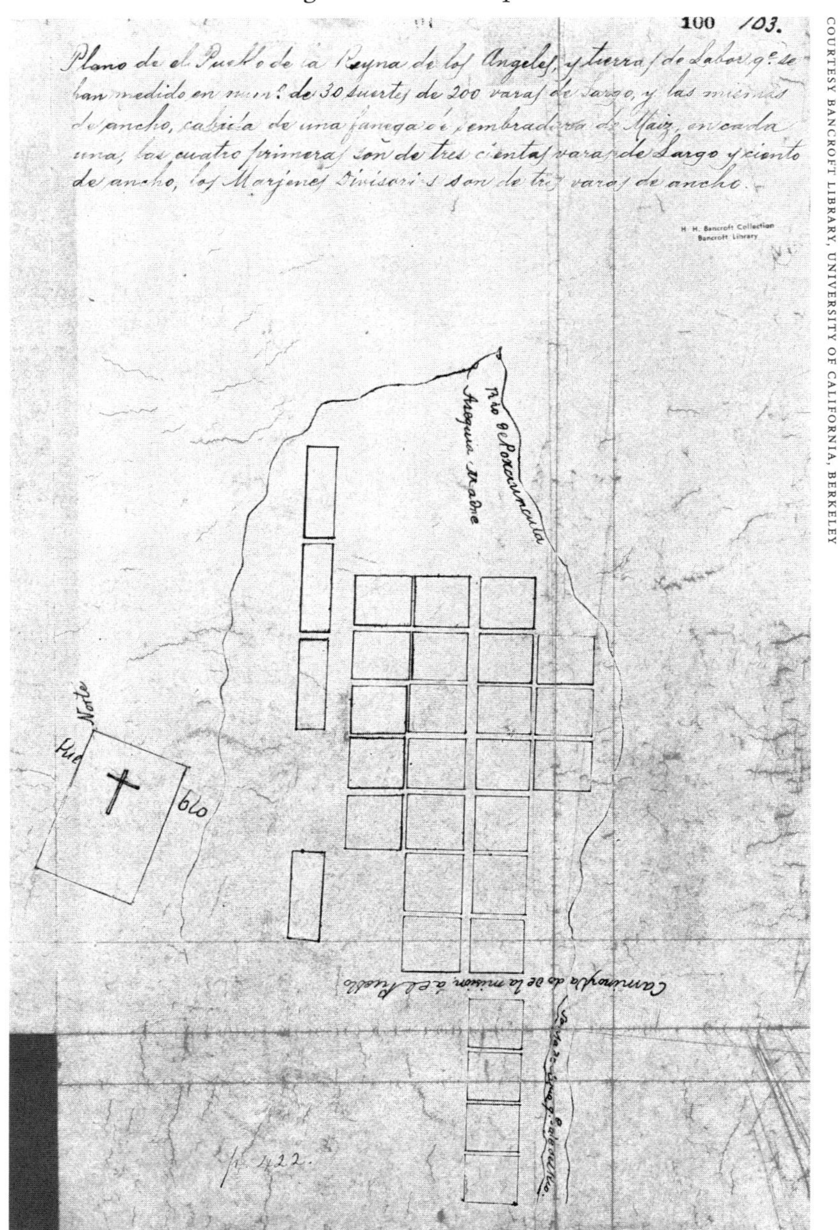

FIGURE 6. The 1785 map of the pueblo of Los Angeles showing the allotment of lands to the pioneer settlers.

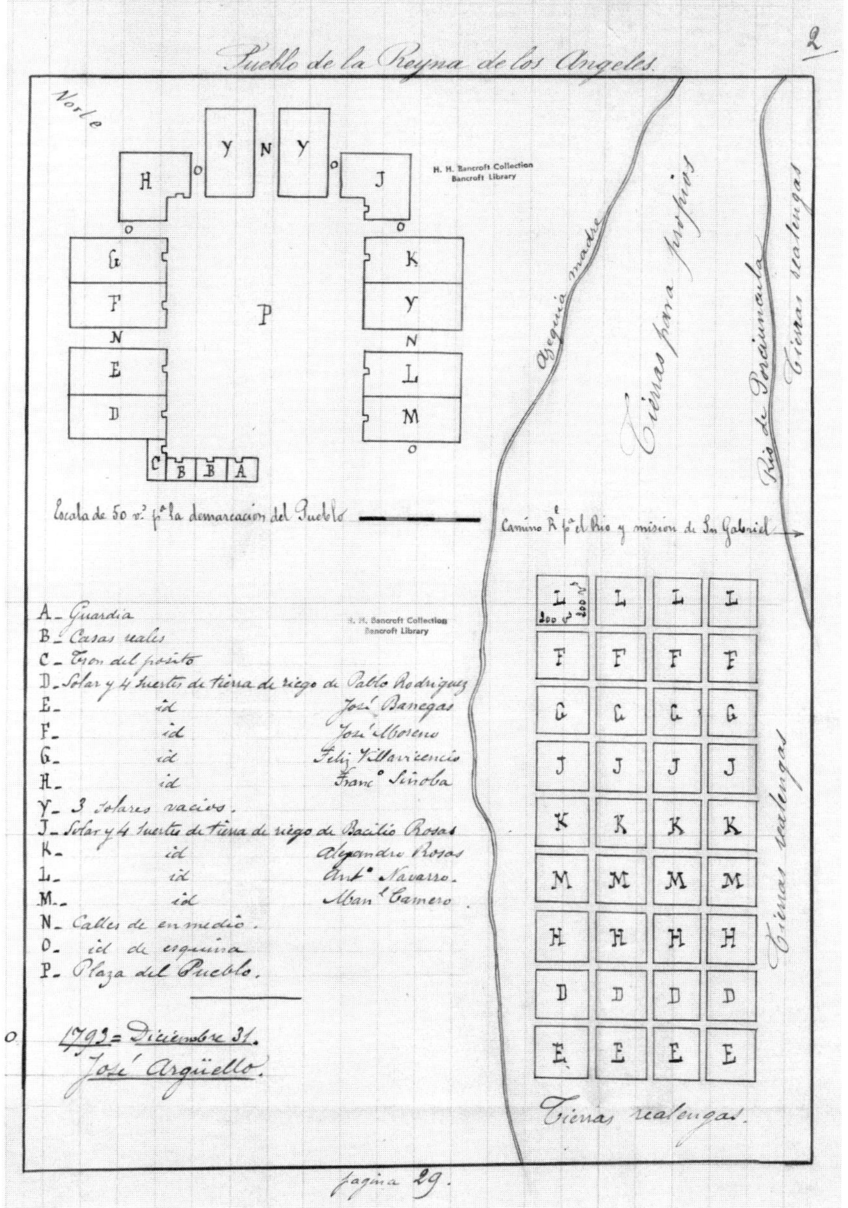

COURTESY BANCROFT LIBRARY, UNIVERSITY OF CALIFORNIA, BERKELEY

FIGURE 7. A map drawn in 1792 which details the pueblo of Los Angeles, including land plots, but also the river and early irrigation system which were the life blood of the fledgling community.

ally employed in planting one bushel of corn. The distribution of said building lots and planting lands shall be made in the name of the King – equally and proportionately to all new settlers – in such a manner that after measuring the land susceptible of irrigation there shall be reserved as *baldios*[2] the fourth part thereof counting the number of population. There shall be distributed to each settler two suertes of land susceptible of irrigation and two suertes of land not susceptible of irrigation. The remainder of said lands shall be reserved for *propios*[3] of the Pueblo and the *realengos*[4] shall be awarded gratuitously to new settlers. An equal rule shall be observed in the granting of building lots to settlers, marking out the proper site for the Church, government buildings, etc.

The front of the Plaza looking towards the East shall be reserved to erect at the proper time the Church and Government Buildings and other public offices, and the adjoining lots shall be allotted to settlers.

On the main portion of said proposed buildings the proper site for the Guardhouse shall be marked out. Well understood that in the distribution of suertes every suerte shall be marked out separate and distinct from each other, designated by stakes, leaving the proper divisor margin between each suerte.

The suerte shall be numbered beginning by those nearest the town. The settlers shall draw lots therefore, the one obtaining the 1st number shall be awarded the 2d; and the person obtaining the 3d shall be awarded the 4th. In this manner the inconvenience resulting to them of having intermediate suertes distinct from those corresponding to each settler, shall be avoided.

Misión San Gabriel, Aug. 26, 1788.[5]

PHELIPE DE NEVE.

Note: As stated in Note 1 on page 157, there is no known extant copy of the original Spanish-language document. This is why there is no Spanish text presented in Part III. – EDITOR

2. Uncultivated land, uncultivated common land.
3. Lands that belong to a city or town and are used to pay for public expenses.
4. Unappropriated lands.
5. Evidently a copyist's error; it should read 1781.

Padrón of Los Angeles[1]

Peninsula of California

Census of the population of the City of the Queen of the Angels, founded September 4th, 1781, on the banks of the Río Porciúncula, distant 45 Leagues [120 miles] from the Presidio de San Diego, 27 leagues [72 miles] from the site selected for the establishment of the Presidio de Santa Barbara, and about a league and a half [4 miles] from the Mision San Gabriel; including the names and ages of the residents, their wives and children. Also an account of the number of animals and their kind, as distributed; with a note describing those to be held in common as Sires of the different kinds, Farming implements, forges, and tools for carpenter and cast work, and other things as received.

1 Lara, Josef de, Spaniard, 50
Maria Antonia Campos, Indian Sabina, 23
Josef Julian, 4
Juana de Jesus, 6
Maria Faustina, 2

2 Navarro, Josef Antonio, Mestizo, 42,
Maria Rufina Dorotea, Mulata, 47
Josef Maria, 10
Josef Clemente, 9
Maria Josefa, 4

3 Rosas, Basillio, Indian, 67
Maria Manuela Calistra, mulata, 43
Josef Maximo, 15
Carlos, 12
Antonio Rosalino, 7
Josef Marcelino, 4
Juan Esteran, 2
Maria Josefa, 8

1. Provisional State Papers, Missions and Colonization, Tom. 1, pp. 101–02. Translated by Thomas Workman Temple II. The original Spanish-language version of these documents can be found on pages 257–60.

4 MESA, ANTONIO, Negro, 38
Ana Gertrudis Lopez, Mulata, 27 — Maria Paula, 10
Antonio Maria, 8

5 VILLAVICENCIO, ANTONIO, Spaniard, 30
Maria de los Santos Soberina, Indian, 26 — Maria Antonio Josefa, 8.

6 BANEGAS, JOSEF, Indian, 28
Maria Maxima Aguilar, Indian, 20, — Cosmé Damien, 1

7 ROSAS, ALEJANDRO, Indian, 19
Juana Rodriguez, coyote Indian, 20

8 RODRIGUEZ, PABLO, Indian, 25
Maria Rosalia Noriega, Indian, 26 — Maria Antonia, 1

9 CAMERO, MANUEL, Mulato, 30
Maria Tomasa, Mulata, 24

10 QUINTERO, LUIS, Negro, 55
Maria Petra Ruvio, Mulata, 40 — Maria Concepcion, 9
Josef Clemente, 3 — Tomasa, 7
Maria Gertrudis, 16 — Rafaela, 6

11 MORENO, JOSEF, Mulato, 22
Maria Guadalupe Gertrudis, 19

12 RODRIGUEZ, ANTONIO MIRANDA, Chino, widower, 50
Juana Maria, 11

Note: That in addition to the Cattle, horses, and mules, distributed to the first 11 settlers, as set forth, they were granted building lots on which they have constructed their houses, which for the present are built of Palisades, roofed with earth; also 2 irrigated fields for the cultivation of 2 fanegas of Corn to each settler; in addition, a Plow Share, a Hoe and an Axe: and for the community, the proper number of carts, wagons, and breeding animals as set forth above, for which the settlers must account to the Royal Exchequer at the prices fixed: with the corresponding charges made against their accounts, as found in the Book of Poblacion, wherein are also to be found the building lots, planting fields, Farming utensils, and Animals belonging to the Settler Antonio Miranda Rodriguez, which will be granted to him, as soon as he appears at said Pueblo: San Gabriel, November 19, 1781.

Map of the Pueblo de la Reyna de los Angeles and agricultural lands that have been surveyed into 30 suertes. Each suerte measures 200 varas long by 200 wide, an area of land on which a fanega of corn can be sown. The first four suertes are 300 varas long by 100 varas wide. The borders dividing each suerte are 3 varas wide.

PUEBLO DE LA REYNA DE LOS ANGELES

Extract of the Review which I, Don José Francisco de Ortega, Teniente and Comandante of the Company which is to Garrison the Presidio de Santa Barbara, made of the settlers, who enjoy wages and draw rations, in said Pueblo, on December 2, 1781.

Feliz Villavicencio,
Antonio Mesa,
Jose Lara,
Jose Vanegas,
Pablo Rodriguez,
Manuel Camero,
Antonio Navarro,
Jose Moreno,
Basilio Rosas,
Alejandro Rosas,
Antonio Rodriguez, absent in Loreto,
Luis Quintero.

Total –	
With wages and rations	11
1 absent at Loreto	1
	12

Note: That had been included in the Regimental Register.

Note regarding the previous passage. Having apprehended the deserter Rafael Mesa, who recently arrived, and who claims to have enlisted as a soldier; [let it be known that] he enlisted as a Settler, and is therefore excluded from the company, having been a Settler from 12 June 1780, until 10 October of said year when he deserted.

There is in accordance with the review I have conducted, and based on that, I have notified the settlers who are currently living in the aforementioned pueblo about the precise day, month, and year, which I have certified.

JOSEPH FRANCO. DE ORTEGA.

NOTE ON RACES AND CASTES OF MEXICO

Intermarriage among the native Indians and the several races brought into Mexico as a result of the Conquest produced a multitude of castes. During the sixteenth century these were distinguished by an extensive nomenclature both in official records and in popular usage. Some of these terms were used in identifications of the founders of Los Angeles, among them the mysterious and much-discussed "chino." The following list is taken from "Mexico a traves de los Siglos," vol. II, p. 471.[2] – EDITORS

Español	Spaniard
Criollo	Child born in Mexico of Spanish parents
Mestizo or Coyote	Child of Spanish father, Indian mother
Castizo	Child of Mestizo father, Spanish mother
Español	Child of Castizo father, Spanish mother
Mulato	Child of Spanish father, Negro[3] mother
Morizco	Child of Mulato father, Spanish mother
Salta-atras (literally "throw-back")	Child having negro characteristics but born of white parents
Chino	Child of a Salta-atras and an Indian
Lobo	Child of a Chino and a Mulata
Gíbaro	Child of a Lobo and a Mulata
Albarrazado	Child of a Gíbaro and an Indian
Cambujo	Child of an Albarrazado and a Negress
Zambo-prieto	Child of a Cambujo and an Indian
Zambo-prieto	Child of a Negro and an Indian
Zambo-prieto	Child of a Negro and a Zamba
Calpan Mulata	Child of a Zambo and a Mulata
"Tente en el aire" (literally "up in the air")	Child of a Calpan Mulata and a Zamba
"No te entiendo" (literally "I don't understand you")	Child of "Tente en el aire" and Mulata
"Ahí te estas" (literally "there you are")	Child of a "No te entiendo" and an Indian

2. The reference is to a published book.

3. Negros were introduced as slaves into the Spanish West Indies as early as 1516, and subsequently were brought to Mexico in large numbers.

Confirmation of Titles to Pueblo Lands[1]

PEDRO FAGES: DISTRIBUTION OF TOWN LOTS AND TRACTS OF LAND FOR IRRIGATION AND DRY PLANTING

MONTEREY, AUGUST 14, 1786.

Inasmuch as, in Article 14 of the Royal Regulations, which rule in this Peninsula, provision is made for the arrangement, method, and order in which the town lots and tracts of land for irrigation and dry planting are to be distributed, with everything else pertaining to the cultivation of farms, raising of Cattle, and the encouragement of the Pueblos of White people situated in the territories adjacent to the Presidios of these new establishments, and since it is necessary for the formalities required to give possession to the citizens of the Pueblo de la Reyna de los Angeles shall be put into effect, in order that they may live in quiet and peaceful harmony: I therefore Commission the Alferez of the City of Santa Barbara, Don José Argüello, to go to the said Pueblo and, in accordance with the cited Royal Regulations, give possession in the name of his Majesty (whom God preserve) to each one of the Settlers to the tracts of land and town lots which are assigned to them, by means of legal writs, which will follow at the end of this order, preparing for each interested person a warrant, including a copy of this *Expediente* and the Measures respecting each one. These papers he will send to be ratified (so that they may serve as Titles) to this Governor, so that, after examining them, he may decide what is best. Care must be taken to make it clear that the citizens understand what pertains to the royal government and what is held in common, such as the Crops, water, pastures, and wood, which must be stated in

1. Archives of California, State Papers, Missions and Colonization, Tom. 1, Bancroft Library. Translated by Phil Townsend Hanna. The original Spanish-language version of these documents can be found on pages 261–64.

each warrant or act of Possession, which they accept, under the conditions and penalties provided in the abovementioned Instruction, as well as the privileges, exceptions, and favors with which the sovereign gives them this grant. They, or some other person at their request, will sign these papers before the commissioner and witnesses. Finally, record shall be made in the Administration book of each of these acts of Possession, as well as of the branding irons which are given to them for marking their Cattle; and there shall be a copy made of everything, to be placed in the archives of the aforesaid Presidio de Santa Bárbara.

ACT OF OBEDIENCE

In the Pueblo de La Reyna de los Angeles, on the 4th day of the month of September, 1786, I, Don José Argüello, Alferez of the Company of the Royal Presidio de Santa Bárbara, in consequence of the preceding order from Señor Teniente Coronel Don Pedro Fages, Governor of the Peninsula, Declared that proceedings should be started for the exact fulfillment of giving possession to the citizens of the aforesaid Pueblo de la Reyna de los Angeles, in the name of his Majesty (whom God preserve), of the town lots and sections of land which are assigned to them in accordance with the orders in the instruction which is inserted in the Royal Regulation of this Province for the Pueblos of White People. And, after they had been informed of its articles, with the rest pertaining to the literal contest of the cited expediente, I ordered that as soon as these measures were completed, with the necessary formalities and requisites, in the presence of two witnesses, the papers should be sent (conformable with orders) to the said Señor Governor for his validation, or whatever may seem best to his Superior judgment; and that a copy should be made of them to be placed in the archives at the Royal Presidio de Santa Bárbara. I so directed, ordered, and signed, to which I make oath.[2]

JOSEF ARGÜELLO.

2. This document may be regarded as an additional confirmation of September 4, 1781, as date of founding of Los Angeles. See Section 2, Fourteenth Title, *Reglamento*, warning the "said five years' time [of probationary occupation] is to be counted … from the day of actual giving possession of the House-Lots and Fields."

NOMINATION AND ACCEPTANCE OF TWO WITNESSES

In the said Pueblo, on the aforesaid day, month and year, I, the above-mentioned Alferez-Commissioner, in view of the act which precedes, it being necessary to appoint 2 witnesses to be present at the subsequent proceedings, for this purpose ordered to appear before me Corporal Vicente Felix, and the soldier Roque de Cota (of the Presidio de San Diego) who, when the nomination was made known to them replied that they accepted it, and promised to be present punctually whenever they were required during these proceedings. And they signed it with me, to which I make oath.

JOSÉ ARGÜELLO – VICENTE FELIX – ROQUE DE COTA.

ACT OF GIVING POSSESSION TO THE FIRST SETTLER, FELIX VILLAVICENCIO, OF HIS RESPECTIVE LOT

In the aforesaid Pueblo, on the day, month, and year mentioned, I, the above-mentioned Alferez-commissioner, in continuation of these proceedings, ordered to appear before me and the witnesses, the 2 Settlers, including the son of Antonio Navarro, who represents his Father during the latter's absence. All being present, I gave possession of his respective lot, 20 varas wide and 40 long, to the Settler Felix Antonio Villavicencio. I explained to him, and he replied that he understood, the Privileges, exceptions, and favors with which the sovereign makes him this grant, under the penalties imposed upon the disobedient. Being asked if he accepts his act of possession, he replies that he accepts it, obligates himself, and promises to fulfill the obligations pertaining to his establishment. Not knowing how to write, he made the sign of the Cross. I signed it with my witnesses, to which I make oath.

JOSÉ ARGÜELLO – X – VICENTE FELIX – ROQUE DE COTA.

ACT OF POSSESSION OF FOUR TRACTS OF LAND BELONGING TO THE SAID VILLAVICENCIO

In the said Pueblo, the day, month, and year cited, I, the aforesaid Alferez, accompanied by the witnesses and Settlers, went to the farm lands, where, after making the necessary measurement of 200 varas square for each lot of land, I gave possession to the said Felix Antonio Villavicencio of the 4 lots pertaining to him, all irrigated, in view of the fact that there were sufficient of this kind. The said Possession having been effected with the same formalities and proceedings as are described in the preceding measure, and the settler having been satisfied and informed of everything, not knowing how to write, he made the sign of the Holy Cross, and I signed it with my witnesses, to which I make oath.

JOSÉ ARGÜELLO – X – VICENTE FELIX – ROQUE DE COTA.

MEASURE TO CONFIRM THE BRANDING-IRON OF THE AFORESAID VILLAVICENCIO

In the said Pueblo, the same day, month, and year, I, the said Alferez, having the Settlers and my witnesses before me, delivered to the above-mentioned Villavicencio his corresponding branding iron (the design of which is shown in the margin), he having been informed that it was the same with which he would have to brand his Cattle. The iron was registered without any charge, according to the provision of Article 8 of the aforesaid Instruction. Not knowing how to write, he made the sign of the Holy Cross. I signed it with my witnesses, to which I make oath.

JOSÉ ARGÜELLO – X – VICENTE FELIX – ROQUE DE COTA.

[Then follow acts of lots and branding irons, with slight variation of language, to the following settlers: José Vanegas, Pablo Rodríguez, Mañuel Camero, Antonio Clemente, José Antonio Navarro, José Moreno, Basilio Rosas, Alejandro Rosas, and José Sinova. None was able to write and all had to sign with their mark. – EDITOR]

ACTS TO ASSIGN LANDS TO INDIVIDUALS AND THE ROYAL GOVERNMENT FOR IRRIGATION, PASTURE, ETC.

In the Pueblo de la Reyna de los Angeles, on the 5th day of the month of September, 1786, I, Don José Argüello, Alferez of the Company of the Royal Presidio de Santa Bárbara, commissioned for these measures, declared the acts of possession of the town lots and tracts of land corresponding to each one of these settlers concluded. I then went with them and the witnesses to the lands that were not yet assigned. Having made the necessary measurement from near the dam as far as the dividing boundary of the lands already partitioned, the measurement resulted in a length of 2,200 varas from north to South for those which have been assigned to individuals of the Pueblo; leaving for the government all the land on the opposite side of this river and

Pueblo, over 2,000 varas long. Those which are not comprised in the aforesaid lots of Possession, nor of individuals, I assigned to them, together with sufficient pasture land for their cattle. I caused them to be informed of all of this, and also that they were to enjoy the right to maintain their cattle from the community supply of water and Pasture, wood and Timber, with everything else pertaining to the Spirit of the aforesaid Instruction for Pueblos or White People, to all of which they replied that they understood and agreed. Not knowing how to write, they made the sign of the Holy Cross, and I signed it with my witnesses, to which I make oath.

JOSÉ ARGÜELLO – X – VICENTE FELIX – ROQUE DE COTA.

At the Royal Presidio de Santa Bárbara, on the 18th day of the month of September, 1786, I, Don José Argüello, Alferez de la compañia of the said Presidio and commissioner in the present proceedings, in view of their conclusion, and having made a record of each of the respective possession and their lands in the book of Settlements in charge of the Comandante of that Presidio, Don Felipe de Gycoechea, for whom a copy was made of everything to remain in the archive, I directed that the originals should be sent to the Superior Governor of this province, as is required in their heading. I so provided, ordered, and signed, to which I made oath.

JOSÉ ARGÜELLO.

PART III

LOS DOCUMENTOS FUNDARON DEL PUEBLO DE LA REYNA DE LOS ANGELES

Cuatro Informe por Gobernador Neve[1]

No. 82. // 78

FABRICAS.

Se de cuenta a S. E. de aver encontrado redificada la Mision de Sn. Diego y concluida la de Sn. Juan Capiſtrano. fundado el fuerte de Sn. franco. la ymediata mision de su nonvre y la de Sta. Clara, y q allandose sin resguardo dho fuerte, como eſte presidio sea dado providencia para que se serquen y conſtruian conforme a lo dispueſto en el Rl. Reglamento. de presidios, para cuia obra quedan acarreandose Materiales en Monte Rey.

Exmo. Sor. Señor

Doi quenta a V. E. que a mi Arrivo a eſtos nuevos eſtablecimientos, se allava ya redificada la Mision de Sn. Diego y concluida la fundacion de Sn. Juan Capiſtrano en el mismo paraje en que fue yniciada, aviendo en una y otra precavido sus fabricas del Ynsencio? cuvriendolas de Terrado. ygualmte. se allava fundado el fuerte de Sn. franc. y su ymediata Mision de el mismo Nombre, el primero ymediato al fondeadero del Puerto, y la segunda a diſtansia del fuerte de sinco cuartoa de legua contigua á la leguna de Nra. Sra. de los Dolores, uno y otro sitio fueron ocupados el 27 de Junio, y convienen ser el // de la Mision abundante de Agua leña y Piedra para fabricas, con tierras proporcionadas para sienvras, y con la ventaja de un Manantial que tiene mui ymediato y de no difisil saca que conseguida lograra veneficiar con riego vaſtante sienbra.

La segunda Mision á que se puso el Nre. de Sta. Clara fue cituada el dia quatro de Eno. ultimo, a 15 leguas de diſtancia del fuerte al sueſte y Margen del Rio de Nra. Sa. de Guadalupe, tiene segun se me ha ynformado, muchas tierras de sinebra á una y otra parte de el Rio, de riego, y vmedad, y mui facil la

1. Provincias Internas Tom. 121, Archivo General de Mexico. The English-language translation of these documents can be found on pages 57–63.

saca del Agua, vien que espuesta la mision y tierras de lavor (segun temen los R. R. P. P.) alas ynundaciones que puede causar de que no se tiene esperiencia por seguir el ano con la mor. escasez de Aguas que sea esperimentado, la Gentilidad que puebla aquel //79 Terreno se asegura mui numerosa; luego que me desenvarase, y regresen las partidas que se allan fuera de este Presidio, pasare a Reconoser dhas. Misiones, y fuerte, de que ynformare a V. E. con mas Yndividualidad: añadiendo tengo prevenido al Tente. Dn. Joseph Joáquin de Moraga disponga lo conveniente á sercar el fuerte, conforme alo prevenido por el Rl. Reglamto. de Presidios? alo que tengo dado prinsipio, y continuare asta su conclusion, en este, por allarse como aquel formado de Barracas, o chosas, y sin ningun resguardo, exectuada la pequeña casa del Comte. y el Almacen que son de adove y ia se avrian desplomado ano averse apuntaldo en el año pasado, como anteriormte. sucedio ala Capilla, de que sirve en el dia un pequeño jacal, y como para fasilitar el todo dela obra se ase presiso enplear la Tropa con los pocos // sirvientes del Presidio, lo represento esperando dela Venignidad de V. E. ade conseder á estas Conpañias la gratificasion que sea de su Superior agrado.

Nro. Sor. Gue.: la Exma. Persona de V. E. ms. as. Monte Rey 25 de febrero de 1777.

Exmo. Sor.
PHELIPE DE NEVE [Rúbrica].

Exmo. Sor. Bo. f Dn. Antonio Bucareli y Vrzua.

No. 83 //59

TROPAS

Se da cuenta a S. E. del estado en que existen las Conpañias delos tres presidios dela California Septentrional en Bestuario Montura Armamento, y Cavallers. con exprecion del numero de mulas y Cavallos que se regulan presisos, y acompañandose Relaciones de las prendas de Vestuario Montura, y Armamentos que se nesesitan.

Exmo. Sor.

Señor: El tres del presente mes llegue á este Presidio, no aviendome permitido verificarlo con mor. prontitud la considerable distancia, y conservasion de la cavallerias que me trasportaron.

Ami paso por el Presidio de Sn. Diego reconosi el estado de la Tropa de su guarnision, como lo ejecute a mi trancito, de los Cavos y Solds. enpleados en las escoltas delas Misiones, como de la Conpañia de eſte Presidio. a vnos, y otros, he allado en el mas deplorable eſtado, asi de Veſtuario, como de Armamento, y Montura; lo primero sobre no averse seguido uniformidad, yndistintamte. usan casaquilla corta, chupa, o chaleco de diversos colores, son raros los que tienen capa y los reſtantes mangas y muchos tan deteriorados que tocan // en yndesencia.

El Armamento, sobre ser de desigual calivre al prevenido por ordenanza las escopetas, son las mas desconpueſtas y de ninguna seguridad. las Espadas (a exesion de las que en el año pasado se remitieron a Sn. Diego) enteramente ynutiles, por su mala calidad, cortas, o rotas, siendo varios los que no la tienan, ygualmte. que Lanzas, allandose quasi todas los Solds. desaviados de su Montura que sobre ser mui vieja, son pocos los que no eſtan faltos de alguna de las prendas que la conponen.

Las Cavallerias que tiene la Tropa de eſtos presidios consiſten en 70 Mulas y 37 Cavallos, el de Sn. Diego, diſtrivuidas en las 43 plazas de su antigua Dotacion (excluidos los 25 Reclutas de Aumento que eſtan desmontados) 86 Mulas y 41 Cavallos, el de Monte Rey. Repartidas en 45 Plazas de que conſta su guarnision, yncluzas 20 qúe cubren las escoltas de las tres Misiones de S. Luis. S. Ano. y el Carmelo. 31. Mulas y 57 ca //60 vallos, el de Sn. Franco. repartidos en las treinta y quatro Plazas de que oi conſta su Conpañia escluido el Tente. en cuio numero de cavallerias puede considerarse una quinta parte de desecho.

En eſta Atension doi quenta á V. E. aconpañando dos Relaciones, vna del Beſtuario y Prendas de Montura que se necesitan para las Conpañias de dhos. Presidios segun el pie que oi se allan, y otra del Armamento, Polvora, y Balas correspondients. á cada una, asi para su respectivo Armanto. como para el que deve exiſtir de Repueſto, a fin de que siendo de la aprovasion de V. E. se Digne mandar remitir en primer ocasion las prendas de Beſtuario, Montura, Armantos. y Municiones que expresan á cada uno delos Referidos Presidios.

Ygualmte. devo Representar a V. E. que sin envargo de que las Armas que actualmte. tienen eſtas Conpañias, (exectuadas las de veinte Soldas. de la de Sn. franco.) son pro // pias de la tropa por averseles cargado su valor, es conveniente se recojan y depositen en los Almancenes para obiar por eſte medio el grave ynconveniente de que las vendan a los Gentiles, que con ansia Solicitan prinsipalmente. ojas de espada, pedanzos de hellas, moarras de Lanzas belduques, y todo genero de Ynſtrumtos. Cortantes, de que he viſto Armados muchos Gentires [sic] en la Canal de Sta. Barbara, siendo admirable el primer conque asicalan, y asen un agudo puñal de un pedazo de espada. por lo que siendo del Superior agrado de V. E. podra distiruvuirse el nuevo Armamén-to, sin cargo de su Valor al Soldado, que solo quedara responsable á su reparo, y entregarlo en extado siempre que se Lisencie ó Muera.

Por lo respectivo a Cavallerias siendo las Plazas que en el dia tienen las tres conpañias, (escluidos oficiales) 147 y las Bestias cavallars., y Mulares que exis-ten 322 a que agregadas, las ochenta Mulas y 26 Cavsa., //61. que proximamte. deven venir de Loreto resultan 438 que corresponden a tres cavallerias por Plaza, con falta de tres vestias, y sin contar con las que en aquel no. se con-prehenden de desecho por Viejas e ynutiles con las que no es posible se aga el servisio sin tan considerable atraso como el que se esperimenta de sufrir la fatiga, aquellos Solds. que se allan en major estado para las salidas, o prestan-dose los unos, alos otros, quedando quasi desmontados los que quedan en el Presidio; con cuia consideracion y la de que las Requas de este Presidio y el de Sn. Diego, se allan tan deterioradas que para socorrer este, con sinquenta y dos cargas de maiz. dela frontera de Velicata, y Mision de Sn. Luiz me a sido for-zoso valerme de 12 mulas dela Mision de Sn. Diego y 23 dela Requa del Pre-sidio de Sn. franco. no aviendo podido aprontarse en tal vrjencia mas de 17 Bestias delas dos restantes; por lo que para poner en estado de servisio la tropa de estos Presidios, contando con lo q ha de dilatarse el resivo de las // Vestias, y predidas que qn de ocurrir en las existentes regulo son presisas doscientas Mulas y trecientos Cavallos, cuia conducion unicamte. podra aserse por tierra siguiendo el derrotero de Dn. Juan Bautista de Anza, sin la perdida de Cava-llerias y cresido atraso de años que causaria su envarco, y dilatada marcha, viniendo por Loreto. Todo lo que represento á V. E. en desenpeño de mi obli-gacn., esperando dela yntegridad de V. E. determinara como conviene.

Nro. Sor. Gue. la Exma. Persona de V. E. felizes as. Monte Rey 26 de febrero de 1777.

Exmo. Sor.
PHELIPE DE NEVE [Rúbrica].

Exmo. Sor. Bo. f Dn. Antonio Bucareli y Vrzua.

No. 71

REGLAMTO.

Se da Cuenta de lo vrgente que sera nonbrar un Ayudante que exersa. en los

5 presidios de Californias las funciones que los de Ynspector, en los de frontera en el caso de aprovarse las reglas propuestas para el nuevo Reglamto.

Mui Sr. mio. paso a Representar a V. S. que asi para desempeñar los Establecimientos. de Presidio y Misiones que han de cituarse en el canal de Sta. Barvara y Pueblo que deve fundarse contiguo al Rio de Porsincula como tiene V. S. determinado, como ygualmente oara establecer el nuevo pie y reglamto. que tengo propuesto, para los Presidios de hesta Peninsula, uniformando en todo lo adactable su govierno a lo prevenido por el Rl. Reglamento de Presidios, siendo ynescusable (de ser aprovado este proiecto) o que se Nombre ynspector para estos o que exersa aquellas funciones el Govor. atendidas la enorme estencion de la Provincia y a la que estan sus Presidios, no es asequible que ninguno pueda dar cumplimto. a ello, sin el Auxilio de un Ayudante, y menos yo que he de formalisar y Radicar esta nueva planta, llamado de aquellas atenciones, quando mi devilitada Caveza me ynpide sufrir aquella mediana aplicasion y Ma // terial travajo conque pude dar expediente a los asumtos que se me fiaron en otro tiempo, y allandome al presente en un destino en que no tengo ni a quien fiar la copia de una carta.

En cuia atencion lo hago presente. a V. S. Suplicando que de ser aprovadas las reglas propuestas para la variacion de Reglamto. en esta Peninsula, se digne V. S. Nombrar un Ayudante que exersa en estos Presidios lás funciones que los de Ynspector en los de frontera, cuio acenso podra recaer en un Tente. de conosida ynteligencia y conducta con el Sueldo que V. S. tenga a vien consignarle.

Nro. Sor. Gue. a V. S. ms. as. Monterrey y Abrl. 3 de 1779.

Blmo. de V. S. su ms.

Atento Sergro. Servor.
PHELIPE DE NEVE [Rúbrica].

Sor. Comte. Genl. Cavallero de Croix.

No. 92. // 48

TROPA Y ESTABLECIM.

Seda cuenta con extado de las Armas Polvora balas y Cartuchos de Cañon que para conpleto delas Conpañias y correspondientes Repuestos se necesitan. y dos Relaciones delas Ropas Viveres y efectos que se regulan precisos para para

[sic] Socorrer la tropa que ha de Guarnecer el Canal, los Pobladores y sus familias, en el Ymediato año, supuesto lleguen en el a esta Provincia, y que sera conbeniente se execute por mar el Reconocimiento del Canal para demarcar el surgidero mas seguro para las embarcaciones.

Mui Sr. mio, pazo a Manos de V. S. el adjunto extado, que manifiesta las armas, Polbora, y balas que para conpletar las Caomanias de hestos tres Presidios y sus Repuestos; el de Polbora y balas y cartuchos de Cañon se necesitan, como assi mesmo, los Repuestos que corresponden para la Tropa que ha de guarneser el Canal de Sta. Barvara, dos Cañones de 4 para este Presidio y cartuchos que por aora le Regulo.

Ygualmte. con conciderasion de la necesidad conque ha de llegar dha. Tropa, los Pobladores y sus familias, de que se les socorra, con Ropas, por lo que ha de destruirle tan dilatado viaxe, para que no experimenten su falta y la de varios efectos y Viveres necesarios, he jusgado preciso dirigir a V. S. las dos memorias que aconpano, a fin de que teniendolo V. S. por conbeniente, se digne providenciar se remitan los Surtinientos que contienen, de Mexico. // y Sn. Blas en el Proximo ano, con la embarcasion que condusga el Situado, del Presidio de Sn. Diego, a entregar en el al Tente. Dn. Josef franco. de Ortega, en el cazo de que a su arribo alli, no se halle ua ocupado el Canal, pues de estarlo devera trasportarse todo a el, con los dos Canones que podran facilitarse del Departamento de Sn. Blas.

De verificarse assi allara en dho Sn. Diego el Comte. del Vuque, todas las prevenciones que yo Regule puedan conbenirle al desempeno de su Comision, ye sera muy oportuno, traiga la orn de Reconoser la costa del Canal, para demarcar el abrigo, o encenada que con mas proporcion al Presidio, permita fondear las enbarcasiones, praacer las descargas de Viveres y efectos que alli condusgan en lo subcesivo.

Nro. Sor. Gu. a V. S. ms. as. Monterrey 19 de Julio de 1779.

Blmo. de V. S. su ms.

Atento. Sro. Cor.

PHELIPE DE NEVE [Rúbrica].

S Comte. Genl. Cavallo de Croix.

Correspondencia Tocante al Reglamento[1]

N. 37 // 1.

Mui Señor Mio: He recivido con Carta de V. S. de 12 de fevrero ultimo Copia del Reglamento que nuebamente ha formado el Governador de Californias Dn. Phelipe Neve, para que con bariacion del antiguo se rijan los asuntos de eſta Peninsula con mas acertado pulso, se economicen en el modo posible los gaſtos que demanda el Presidio de Santa Barbara, que se acaba de erejir, y los que preparan los empleos que se han creado para el mejor Servicio de S. M.

Del Contexto de eſte Reglamento se deduze que su objeto es dirijido ál buen govierno interior, y disciplina delas Compañias Presidiales, al alivio dela Tro- // pa, el beneficio de áquella Peninsula, y la Seguridad delos Ynteresses de Rl. Hacienda en cuio Concepto puede V. S. proceder desde luego á dictar las Consiguientes Providencias para su observancia, bajo la firme persuasion de que eſtoy pronto á Contribuir por mi parte, con las que Conduzcan al intento, en inteligencia de que de todo doy Cuenta á S. M. por si fuese de su agrado resuelto.

Nro Señor Gue á V. S. ms. as. Mexico 19 de Mayo de 1780.

Blmo. á V. S. su mas Atto. Sego. Servor.
MARTIN DE MAYORGA [Rúbrica]

Arispe 15 de Julo, de 1780.

Al Asesor gl. donde se hallan los antecedentes en el concepto de qe. hé nombrado los oficiales subalternos que se aumentan en los Presidios de Californias para Ayudte. inspector al Capitan graduado Dn. Nicolas Solér.

DE CROIX [Rúbrica]

1. Provincias Internas Tom. 122, Archivo General de Mexico. The English-language translation of these documents can be found on pages 65–70.

Sor. Come. Genl.

Por Rl. Orden de 21 de Marzo // de 1775, se sirvio S. M. mandar que se Variase el Reglamento formado pa. la Peninsula de Californias pr. los vicios que se notavan en el qe. entonces governava; a cuio fin mando VE. en la que dirijio á 15. de Agto. de 77. al Governador D. Phe. Neve, que informase con extension y menudamente, quanto eſtimase necesario a su Reforma, de //2 vn. modo, que le pusiese en eſtado de determinar, quando se hallase sobre el terreno; y poſteriormente, en nueva Orn que se le pasó a 3. de Septire. del siguiente año de 78; se le previno que se dedicase a formarle, mejorando el Actual; y en su Cumplimiento, teniendo presente los nuebos eſtablecimientos, que a su proposicion havia VS. resuelto hacér en el Canal de Sta. Barvara, formó y Remitio el nuevo reglamento, que con fha de lo. de Junio de 1779. se halla en el expediente.

Reconocido y Examinado por VS, se Sirvio conteſtarle en 12 de febrero de eſte año, que nada le dejava que apetecer, pues en todos sus puntos hallava atendidos los objetos del Rl. Servicio, con particular alibio de la Tropa, Economia y seguridad delos intereses del Erario, y Ventajas, que proporcionaban el fomento, defensa y conservacion del Territorio, y que eſte Concepto lo trasladava VS. con igual fha al Exmo Sor. Virrey, y daua cuenta á S. M. Solicitando Su Rl. aprovazion.

Con efecto, en el mismo dia Remitio VS. Copia al Sor. Virrey, manifeſtandole que no solo lo considerava digno de su Recomendacion, si no es que le parecia mui vrgente su practica // para que desde luego se disfrutasen las ventajas, que ofrecia, y fuesen menores los gaſtos qe. Ocasionasen los Nuevos Eſtablecimtos y que si mereciese igual Concepto á S. Exa, esperava se lo havisase para arreglar sus disposiciones, y proceder inmediatamente á la reforma delos empleos de Comisarios, y Guarda Almacenes, y á tomár las demas providencias conducentes á su Observancia interina, haſta qe. dando cuenta á S. M. llegase la Rl. aprovazon. a que conteſtó en 19. de Mayo proximo, que podia VS. proceder desde luego á dictar las providencias consiguientes a su Observancia, bajo la firme persuasion, de que eſtava pronto á contribuir por su parte con las que condujesen a su intento, y en la inteligencia, de que de todo daua cuenta á S. M. pr. si fuese de su Rl. agrado eſta Resolucion.

En 23. de febrero de eſte mismo año dio VS. cuenta á S. M. de todas las providencias qe. hauia dictado, Relatibas a la Peninsula de Californias, y en Consequencia de los Oficios qe. le havia pasado Su Governor. D. Phe. Neve //3 y de que haviendo formado eſte el nuevo reglamento, que havia mandado observar interinamente, se consiguirian por Su medio las ventajas á que se dirigia, añadiendo que en el Siguiente Correo, se Remitiria Copia por havér faltado tpo y manos pa. sacarla en aquél.

De forma, que no solo se halla aprovado pr. VS. el citado nuevo reglamento, sino es qe. el Exmo Sor. Virrey há condescendido a su observancia, ofreciendo contribuir con las providencias que conduzgan á ella, y de todo se há dado cuenta á S. M.; y se espera su Rl. aprovacion: En todo lo posible, se ha procurado Vniformár el Govierno diciplina y manejo de intereses, de las Tropas de aquella Peninsula, al establecido para las de estas Provins. en el ultimo Reglamento de 10. de Sepre. de 1772 – que govierna en ellas; y quando no sean adaptables á aquel Pais, todas las providencias y resoluciones, que se hán dictado de resultas delas revistas de Ynspon.; y expedientes promovidos en este, puede haver muchas que sean conducentes, y de facil execucion, expecialmente las relatibas a los Avilitados, facultades // qe. se les Confieren en los Poderes de sus Compañs. metodo en que deuen hacer las Subministraciones, y Responsavilidad delos Capitanes, por la intervencion qe. les Corresponde tenér en ellas, Por lo qual me parece, que al mismo tpo se pase la Correspondiente Orn al Governor Dn. Phe. Neve, para que desde luego proceda ala Execucion y observancia interina del expresado nuevo reglamento, se le remita igualmente vna Copia, o coleccion Certificada de las Resoluciones generales y particulares dictadas pr. V. S. para el mejór govierno diciplina y manejo delos intereses de estas Tropas, a fin de que Reconociendo lo dispuesto acerca de ellas, adapte a las de aquella Peninsula, las que hallare no tener incombente. en su ejecucion, añadiendo las que econtrare de esta clase, por Capitulos del mismo Reglamto. y havisando las que fueren para qe. siempre conste en esta Superioridad.

En oficio de 6. Junio de 1777. Señalado con el No. 88, despues de informar el Governor Dn. Phe. Neve con la maior prolixidad; los parages que hauia Reconocido, desde la //4 Mision de Sn. Gabriel, hasta el Presidio de Monterrey, las distancias en que se hallavan vnos de otros, y los que tenian proporcion de tierras y aguas para Siembras y labores, propuso, que para que en aquella Peninsula se cojiesen las Semillas y granos, que se necesitavan, para provehér la Tropa, y Pobladores, no halla otro Arvitrio, que el de que se Reclutasen quarenta o Sesenta labradores, que poblasen los Rios de Santa Ana, Sn. Gabriel, La Porciuncula, y Guadalupe, o a lo menos qe. diuiliendose en dos quadrillas, se estableciese la vna en el Rio de Santa Clara, y la Otra en el de la Porciuncula, facilitandoles varios auxilios, que expresó con indiuidualidad posteriormente por nuevo Oficio de 3. de Abril de 1779. Señalado con el No. 69. expuso que vaſtarian Veinte y quatro Pobladores, incluiendo entre ellos vn Arbañil, y vn. Herrero con los demás auxilios, que tenia pedidos, y qe. fuesen respectibos á eſte numero.

Haviendo VS. Accedido á eſta proposicion y tomado las providencias Correspondientes pa. facilitar los reclutas y demas auxilios // pedidos por Neue, se le dio oportunamente aviso, para que en su inteligencia fuese dando las disposiciones Conducentes a su logro; con culo motibo en nuevo Oficio de 22 de Abril de eſte año Señalado con el No. 130., expuso que havia echo reconocer las inmediaciones de la entrada de la Canal de Santa Barvara, al Norte y Sur, para vér si en ella se encontrava sitio proporcionado para hacer Siembras, que con la posible inmediacion baſtasen á Surtir de Viueres los Presidios y Pueblos, que deuen eſtablecerse para Ocuparlo de que resultó encontrar ala parte del Norte vn Caudaloso trozo de agua, que se desprende de la Sierra, con facilisima toma, y dilatadas Tierras para labór, y aun que en la Cercania de la Saca, manifeſtava no ser el paſto de mui buena Calidad, lo havia a corta diſtancia, y abundancia de madera leña y piedra, con mas de dos leguas de llanura, haſta el Camino Real, que bá del Presidio de Sn. Diego, al de Monterrey, quedando a cinco leguas la primera Rancheria del Canál llamada la Asunta; que á siete leguas dela entrada Opueſta, se halló otro //5 abundante arroyo o manantial con muchas y buenas tierras de labór, pero escaso de madera y leña; y que eſtos descubrimientos, con los que se hicieron en el año de 77, le havian conducido al pensamiento, de que seria mas Ventajoso Variar la fundacion del Pueblo, que propuso sobre la marjen del Rio de la Porciuncula, por que quando formó eſte proyecto no eſtava inſtruido de aver aprovado VS. el de la Ocupacion del Canál; vajo cuio Supueſto le parecia más util, que se formasen los dos Pueblos, vno en el citado paraje diſtante cinco leguas de la primera Rancheria de la Asunta, y otro en el que ofreciese mas proporciones, entre las Misiones de Sn. Juan Capiſtrano y Sn. Gabriel; él primero para abaſtecer el Presidio y escoltas del Canál de Sa. Barvara; y el Segundo para proveer el de Sn. Diego; en la inteligencia de que antes qe. llegase Dn. Fernando Ribera, pasaria a reconocerlos personalmente, y há examinar si sus proporciones, correspondian álos informes que se le hauian echo, por el Teniente // D. Jph. de Ortega, y el Sargto, Juan Josef Robles, en cuio caso se Repartirian las Veinte y quatro familias en los dós eſtablecimientos, y no desconfiava podér aumentar algun otro Poblador, y que produjese eſta idea buenos efectos; pero que necesitando para su ejecusion la aprovacion de VS, esperava se sirviese Comunicarle su Resolucion, pa. tenér dispueſto todo lo Conducente, a que desde luego se Situasen las familias, que deuiesen poblar, y que hallasen en ellos los ganados y demas auxilios Necesarios, por que pensava eſtablecer aun tpo, los dos Pueblos, Mision de Sn. Buenaventura, y Presidio del Canál, y ebaquado eſto pasar á fundár la Mision de la Concepcion.

Y Supueſto que deuiendo pasar el Govor. a reconocer personalmente aquellos terrenos como lo ofrece en su Oficio, ninguno puede resolvér con mayores luces y acierto, los que sean mas aproposito, y de mejores proporciones para la fundacion de los dos Pueblos y facilitar sus progresos, me parece que por eſte motibo podrá VS, si fuere Servido, dejár a su Arvitrio la Eleccion ll de los parajes, en que deban situarse, encargandole que el Nuevo Presidio, que há de hubicarse en el Zentro del Canál, procure igualmente Colocarle, si fuere posible, en terreno aproposito y con tierras y Aguas pa. Siembras, a fin de que a su Abrigo pueda con el tpo fomentarse otra Poblacion, que es el Objeto, con que la piedad de S. M. eroga generosamente los gaſtos que Ocasionen Semejantes eſtablecimientos; y en Atencion a qe. los mandados hacer, en la Junta de los Rios Colorado y Gila, son de igual naturaleza que eſtos, y que para facilitar sus progresos se han dictado por VS. varias providencias mui Conducentes al asunto, qe. no pueden menos de sér adaptables a los de la Peninsula de Californias, me parece podrá VS. igualmte.; si fuere Servido mandar, se Remita Copia Certificada de todas al Govor. Dn. Phe. Neve, para que teniendolas presentes, y observando desde luego las que le pareciesen exequibles, informe sobre las demás, lo que hubiere y se le ofreciere; Sin embargo de lo // qual resolvera VS. Sobre todo lo que fuere de su agrado. Arispe 18 de Septre. de 1780.

GALINDO NAVARRO [Rúbrica]

Arispe 18 de Sepre. de 1780.

Me conformo con el parecer del Asesor, y en consecuencia hecha la contextazn. al oficio del Govr. de Californias No. 130 de 22 de Abril de eſte año sre el eſtablecimto. de las dos nuevas Polazes. dirijansele con separado las Orns corresptes. previniendo la obervancia interina del nuevo relamto. dese. el ia lo. de Eno del año proximo venture; Y pasandose las respueſtas al Govr. Intendte. de eſta Prova. y al Capital Dn. Ferndo. de Rivera y Moncada Comisionado para la recluta de tropa // y pobladores de aumto.; dese aviso de todo al Exmo Sr. Virrey, y cuenta á S. M. con copias del Expediente y documentos relativos.

fhode CROIX [Rúbrica]

Se dio cuenta en Carta No. 721 – de 28 de Febo. de 82.

Reglamento[1]

Para los Presidios de la Peninsula de Californias, ereccion de nuevas Misiones, y fomento del pueblo y extension de los Ebablecimientos de Monterey.

Haviendose dignado S. M. determinar por Real Cédula de 21 de Marzo de 1775 se varíe el Reglamento provisional que actualmente gobierna en la Peninsula de Californias, para dar el debido cumplimiento á esta Soberana Resolucion se ha advertido ser el medio mas oportuno y conforme adaptar en todo lo posible á las reglas establecidas por el Real Reglamento de Presidios, el gobierno economico de los de la Peninsula y su Tropa, variando el pie, paga y manejo de intereses de un modo que, proporcionando con ventajas la fuerza de las Guarniciones para las salidas y demas funciones del Servicio, se verifique ahorro á los presentes gastos que eroga la Real Hacienda en los Presidios de Loreto, San Diego, Monterey y San Francisco aumento de Oficiales, igualdad y proporcion en sus sueldos los de Sargentos, Cabos, Soldados, Ciruiano, Oficiales, mecánicos y Pobladores, de suerte que sean los precisos para la subsistencia, responsabilidad y atenciones de cada clase, comprehendidos los Dependientes del corto Departamento de Marina de Loreto; Sínodos que han de continuarse á los Religiosos Misioneros, y orden con que deben situarse nuevas Reducciones, estableciendo reglas que aseguren el fomento, pueble y extension de los antiguos y nuevos Establecimientos, con cuyo importante objeto, el de asegurar la comunicacion, y atraher al verdadero conocimiento de la Religion la numerosa Gentilidad que habíta el preciso estrecho y arriesgado paso del Canal de Santa Bárbara, está determinada su ocupacion, estableciendo en él un Presidio y tres Misiones con un Pueblo que, situado en su inmediacion, pueda abastecer de Viveres con la produccion de sus siembras dicho Presidio y el de San Diego: y respecto de

1. The English-language translation of this document can be found on pages 73–109.

no ser asequible que el Inspector de los Presidios de Frontera reviste los de esta Peninsula, por impedirlo la travesía de mar y enormes distancias á que están, se hace inescusable que el Gobernador exerza las funciones de Inspector (como lo ha practicado) atendido á ser el Gobierno puramente Militar, y no estár este Gefe comprehendido como Capitan de ninguno de los Presidios de su mando; y no siendo posible desempeñe por si este encargo, como, está ordenado, siendo de la Superior aprobacion se nombrará y creará un Ayudante que, bajo su direccion y órdenes, reviste los Presidios á que se le destine, cele la uniformidad, servicio, disciplina y subordinacion de la Tropa, como la mas puntual observancia de quanto está prevenido en el citado Real Reglamento, con la única variacion que advierten los Titulos siguientes.

TITULO PRIMERO.

1. No permitiendo el presente estado de la Península variar el orden establecido de transportar de Nueva España de cuenta y riesgo de la Real Hacienda las Ropas, Efectos, Víveres y Caballerias para la subsistencia y entretenimiento de la Tropa, Pobladores y demas Dependientes de los Presidios, deberá seguir esta practica remitiendose por el Factor de la Península y Comisario de San Blas lo correspondiente á las Memorias que han de pasarse anualmente por el Gobernador al Exmo Señor Virey, para que se digne determinar su compra y remision, exceptuado el Presidio de Loreto, cuya considerable distancia no permite la direccion de sus Memorias en tiempo oportuno, por lo que en derechura se pasan á S. E. por el Capitan.

2. Los Víveres, Vestuario, Armamento, Montura, Ropas, Caballerias y demas efectos que se remitan de México, San Blas ó Sonora, han de recibirse y distribuirse á la Tropa sobre precios en que resulten de primer compra, bajo cuya consideracion van reglados los sueldos; consiguientemente no han de tener otra intervencion que la del pago de los Individuos que la gozan y comprenderá este Reglamento.

3. Asi como al presente está al cuidado del Comisario de Loreto y Guarda Almacenes de los restantes Presidios el pago de la Tropa y Dependientes de ellos, como el recibo de las respectivas Memorias y su distribucion, correrá en lo sucesivo con inspeccion del Capitan en Loreto, y de el Comandante en los Presidios de los nuevos Establecimientos, á cargo del Habilitado que ha de nombrarse entre los Subalternos de la Compañia, bajo las reglas que se expresarán adelante.

4. El Pago de Situados ha de continuarse en la Real Caxa de México en el mismo orden que se practica, haciendose entrega al Factor de la Península,

en virtud de Superior Decreto del Exmo Señor Virey, de la cantidad que se regula suficiente á habilitar las Memorias de géneros y efectos, en que se incluirá el tanto que ha de remitirse en pesos á cada Presidio, acreditandose asimismo al Comisario del Departamento de San Blas el caudal necesario para la compra de Víveres y Efectos de Racion, como lo demas que por Factura de dicho Comisario le remita conforme á las Memorias; y respecto que la citada entrega y compras se executan en los últimos meses del año y se verifica el recibo en los Presidios en Mayo ó Junio del siguiente, no deberá variar el metodo establecido de aviar la Tropa, con arreglo al alcance que cada individuo se deduzca por su jauste del año anterior, subministrandose entre año las Raciones y demas gastos inescusables que ocurran al Soldado ó su familia, por cuya razon se escusa la asistencia con dos reales diarios á Cabos y Soldados, resultando satisfacer la Real Hacienda los Situados en fines del año en que se vencen, y pagarse la Tropa á mediados del subsecuente: con cuyo conocimiento y prudente regulacion al importe de los Víveres, Vestuario, Armamento, Montura, Ropas, Efectos y Caudal que necesiten las Compañias, contando con el total á que asciende el Situado, y que han de satisfacerse en pesos los Sueldos de Oficiales y Cirujano, verificado el descuento de lo que entre año reciban, como los alcances que aviada la Tropa le resulte, formarán los Habilitados las Memorias, teniendo presente para su deduccion los rezagos que existen; ya sea dimanados de la entrega que ha de hacerseles, ó por sobrantes de uno á otro año, é igualmente que el dinero que se pida no ha de exceder por ahora de la quarta parte del Situado, excluido el sueldo del Gobernador y Ayudante (si se cría este empleo) que han de percibirlo separadamente como les convenga.

5. Como los precios de Ropas y Efectos están sugetos á alteraciones, siempre que por esta razon, ó la de ascender la Memoria á mayor cantidad de la que corresponda á las dos quartas partes del Situado, no pueda verificarse el surtimiento, se suplirá la falta de la quarta parte que ha de remitirse en pesos; y respecto de que la restante quarta parte se regula para costear los Víveres y Efectos que comprehenda la Memoria de San Blas, en quanto no alcance, se suplirá en los terminos dichos.

6. Siempre que adelantadas las siembras, cosechas y esquilmos en los nuevos Establecimientos, puedan proveerse los Presidios en el todo ó parte de los Víveres que necesiten, en tal caso se pedirá por los Habilitados la cantidad que corresponda á su compra, á mas de la que queda señalada, baxará su equivalente en Semillas en la Memoria de San Blas, y proporcionalmente de la consignacion hecha en pesos para su surtimiento.

7. La suma dificultad y pérdidas que ofrece el transporte y conduccion de Caballerías desde Sonora á esta Peninsula, obliga á mantener con tres, ó quatro cada Soldado, y á que exista de cuenta de la Real Hacienda en cada Presidio una Recua de veinte y cuatro ó treinta mulas para la conduccion de la carga de las Embarcaciones, proveer de Víveres las Escoltas, y socorrer el Presidio que, por pérdida, arribada, ó considerable retardo de un Barco, falten las semillas y Efectos de primera necesidad; y substituiendo dichos motivos, el de la conduccion de Raciones á los Pobladores del nuevo Pueblo de S. Joseph Guadalupe, la que ha de hacerse á el Pueblo que está determinado fundar, y las demas faenas que han de ocurrir para el establecimiento del Presidio y Misiones en el Canal de Santa Bárbara, á que en el primer año ha de conducirse por tierra todo bastimento y demas preciso para su subsistencia, á que se agrega deberse acarrear en lo succesivo los frutos de los Pueblos para proveer los Presidios: no siendo verificable poner esta Tropa en el pie de Caballerías que está la de la Frontera, hasta tanto que aumentada la cria de caballada en la Península, se facilite, es conforme, que completandose las Recuas de Loreto y San Francisco al número de veinte y quatro mulas cada una con su correspondiente apero, y de treinta mulas la de S. Diego, se surta de otras treinta el Presidio que ha de situarse en el Canal, igualmente aviadas, todo de cuenta de la Real Hacienda, quedando su conservacion, y reemplazo de las que mueran ó se inutilicen, como el reparo y entretenimiento de aparegos y demas perteneciente, como el pago de un Arriero en cada Presidio, de cargo del fondo de gratificacion, como gasto general en lo succesivo; y en el caso de que por las otras atenciones á que está destinado, no alcance á cubrir este gasto, sea la falta de cuenta del Comun de las Compañias que en todo tiempo han de responder de la existencia de dichas Recuas, comprehendida la de Monterrey, que en el dia existe en quarenta mulas de carga.

8. Siendo inescusable mantener los oficios de Carpinteria y Herreria á estas recientes adquisiciones de Monterey, quedarán con los Sueldos que se les consignan los dos Maestros, el Carpintero, y tres Herreros que actualmente existen; y este gasto se comprenderá como parte del Situado de Monterrey y San Diego, en que están destinados, siendo éste el único que por esta razon ha de impender la Real Hacienda: pues quedando á beneficio de estos establecimientos todos los útiles y herramientas correspondientes á dichos oficios y el de Albañil, que sean existentes en la entrega que ha de formalizarse á los Habilitados, ha de costearse de su conservacion y reparo, y el producto de las composiciones y obras que se hagan á particulares, aplicandose el sobrante

que resulte á el pago ó racion de quatro Aprendices que han de solicitarse paradichos oficios, á cuyo efecto ha de llevarse la correspondiente cuenta; debiendose entender interina la conservacion de los referidos oficios, y respectivo gasto de la Real Hacienda.

TITULO SEGUNDO.

Pie, paga y gratificacion de las Compañias y Dependientes de Presidios y Departamento de Marina de Loreto; puestos que cubre la Tropa, y distancias á que estan situados.

1. La Compañia del Presidio de Loreto, Cabecera de la antigua California, consta y ha de permanecer en el pie de Capitan, Teniente, Alferez, y quarenta y quatro Plazas, inclusos dos Sargentos y tres Cabos, con que debe conservar el pequeño Destacamento de un Sargento y seis Soldados en el Real de Santa Anna del Sur, distante cien leguas del Presidio: cubre con un Oficial subalterno, dos Cabos y veinte y tres Soldados las tres Misiones de la Frontera del Norte, cuyo intervalo se regula de doscientas ochenta leguas de la última á Loreto, donde ha de continuar la existencia del Capitan, un Oficial subalterno, que ha de ser el Habilitado, un Sargento, un Cabo y diez Soldados: dista del siguiente trescientas cincuenta leguas.

2. El de San Diego constara de Teniente, Alferez y cincuenta y dos Plazas, inclusos un Sargento y cinco Cabos, aumentandose el pie actual el empleo de Alferez. Debe cubrir las tres Misiones de su distrito con un Cabo y cinco Soldados cada una, y verificada la fundacion del nuevo Pueblo, pondrá en él una Salvaguardia de quatro Soldados, que solo permanecerá los dos primeros años: con lo que queda reducida la Guarnicion á un Teniente, un Alferez, y treinta Plazas, inclusos un Sargento y dos Cabos, con que ha de atender á las salidas y demas funciones del Servicio: regulando al que sigue ciento setenta leguas.

3. El de San Carlos de Monterey constará de las mismas Plazas que el antecedente, proveyendose á la Compañia los empleos de Teniente y Alferez; quedarán suprimidas tres Plazas sencillas de su actual pie; debe continuar las Escoltas de un Cabo y cinco Soldados en cada una de las tres Misiones de su pertenecia; tiene empleados quatro Soldados en el pueblo de San Joseph; y quedarán existentes en la Guarnicion para las funciones del Servicio un Teniente, un Alferez, un Sargento, dos Cabos, y veinte y siete Soldados. Se halla quarenta y dos leguas del que sigue.

4. El de San Francisco constará de Teniente, Alferez treinta y una Plazas, in-

clusos un Sargento y quatro Cabos; se aumenta á su actual pie el empleo de Alferez, y se le suprimen tres Plazas sencillas; debe cubrir con dos Cabos y diez Soldados las dos Misiones de su término; y de resultarán para el servicio del Presidio y salidas un Teniente, Alferez, y diez y nueve Plazas, inclusos un Sargento y dos Cabos.

5. El Canal de Santa Bárbara se halla á setenta y quatro leguas del Presidio de San Diego, y setenta del de Monterrey; se dilata entre la Costa y Sierra de la Cieneguilla como veinte y seis leguas, siendo media á tres quartos su mayor anchura; es lleno de altas lomerias, barrancos y quiebras profundas, cuyo preciso paso, en que se regulan de ocho á diez mil Gentiles los que pueblan veinte y una Rancherias numerosas que á cortas distancias estan situadas en las alturas y puntas contiguas á la Playa, á cuya inmediacion, bien sea por ella, ó por la altura, dirige el camino real, lo que evidencia el riesgo á que pasan expuestas las pequeñas Partidas que le giran, y que si algun incidente pone de mala fé, ó declara enemiga aquella Gentilidad, quedaria cortada la comunicacion de los antiguos y nuevos Establecimientos, cuyo surgentes motivos han fundado la determinacion de ocupar este paso en la forma siguiente.

6. El Presidio que ha de situarse en el centro del Canal constará su Compañia de Teniente, Alferez, y veinte y nueve Plazas, inclusos un Sargento y dos Cabos; ha de establecerse á su abrigo una Reduccion, que en adelante variará su posicion á el parage inmediato que porporcione mas tierras y suficiente agua para el beneficio de labores, y entonces ha de darsele de la Guarnicion la Escolta de un Cabo y cinco Soldados; deben fundarse á los estremos de dicho Canal para su perfecta ocupacion otras dos Reducciones, y guarnecerse con un Sargento y catorce Soldados cada una; se considerarán dichas Plazas como supernumerarias á la Compañia del Presidio, interin se aseguran estos Establecimientos con la paz y buena admision de la Gentilidad: conseguido con los rápidos progresos que de ben esperarse en la espiritual conquista, se reducirán proporcionalmente hasta que queden en la regular Escolta de un Cabo y cinco Soldados cada una; los Sargentos se incorporarán de aumento á las Compañias de San Diego y Monterrey, y las diez y seis Plazas restantes se destinaran á guarnecer otras Reducciones que se determine fundar, en cuyo caso se agregarán á las Compañias mas inmediatas de los sitios en que se verifique.

7. El Situado anual del Presidio de Loreto será 12522 ps. 4 rs. á que agregados 1996 ps. a que asciende el correspondiente al Departamento de Marina, que por surplus han de acreditarse anualmente al Situado del Presidio, importa 14518 ps. 4 rs. distribuidos en esta forma.

Reglamento

	Pesos	Rs.
Sueldo anual del Capitan	1500	
Del Teniente	550	
Del Alferez	400	
De cada uno de los dos Sargentos 262 ps. 4 rs	525	
De cada uno de los tres Cabos 225 ps.	675	
De cada una de las treinta y nueve Plazas de Soldados á 217 ps. 4 rs.	8482	4
Por la Gratification de 10 ps. anuales por Plaza sencilla	390	
Total del Presidio	12522	4

Departamento de Marina
Del Referido Presidio.

	Pesos	Rs.
Sueldo de un Carpintero de Ribera al año	132	
De un Herrero	120	
De un Galafate	120	

Tripulacion de la Balandra el Pilar.

	Pesos	Rs.
Sueldo anual del Patron	120	
Del Guardian	84	
De ocho Marineros á 72 ps. cada uno	576	

Tripulacion de la Lancha Lauretana.

	Pesos	Rs.
Su Arraez al año	84	
De ocho Marineros á 60 ps. cada uno	360	
Por gasto, anual de carenas recorridas y arboladuras de una Balandra y dos Lanchas se regulan	400	
Total Situado del Presidio by Departamento	14518	4

Queda suprimida por este Reglamento la Tripulacion de la Lancha San Juan Nepomuceno, cuyo Buque ha de conservarse listo para armarle simpre que por grave motivo y por solo el término que la urgencia, sean precisas las tres Embarcaciones, y á este efecto quedará el actual arraez de Guardian de la Balandra.

El Situado Anual del Presidio de San Diego será de 13162 ps. 4 rs. distribuidos en el orden siguíente:

Sueldo anual del Teniente	550	
Del Alferez	400	
Del Sargento	262	4
De cada uno de los cinco Cabos 225 ps.	1125	
De Cada una de las 46 Plazas sencillas de Soldados 217 Ps. 4. rs.	10005	
Por la Gratificacion de 10 ps. anuales por Plaza sencilla	460	
	12802	4
Un Carpintero al año	180	
Un Herrero idem	180	
Total	13162	4

El Situado Anual del Presidio que ha de establecerse en el Canal de Santa Bárbara, será de 7577 ps. 4 rs. á que agregados 6895 ps. que importa el correspondiente á las dos Escoltas que han de proveerse interinamente asciende á 14472 ps. 4 rs. distribuidos asi:

Sueldo anual del Teniente	550	
Del Alferez	400	
Del Sargento	262	4
De Cada uno de los dos Cabos 225 ps.	450	
De cada una de las 26 Plazas de Soldados á 217 Ps. 4 rs.	5655	
Por la Gratificacion del fondo comun á 10 ps. por Plaza	260	
	7577	4

Escoltas.

De cado uno de los dos Sargentos 262 ps. 4 rs	525	
De cada una de las 28 Plazas de Soldados 217 ps. 4 rs.	6090	
Por la Gratificacion del fondo comun á 10 ps. por Plaza	280	
Total	14472	4

El Situado Anual del Presidio de S. Carlos de Monterey será de 17792 ps. 4 rs. diſtribuidos de eſte modo:

	Pesos	Rs.
Sueldo anual del Gobernador	4000	
Del Teniente	550	
Del Alferez	400	
Del Cirujano	450	
Preſt del Sargento	262	4
De cada uno de los cinco Cabos 225 ps.	1125	
De cada una de las 46 Plazas sencillas de Soldados 217 ps. 4 rs.	10005	
Por la Gratificacion del fondo comun á 10 ps. anuales por Plaza	460	
	17252	4
Un Carpintero al año	180	
Dos Herreros con 180 ps. cada uno	360	
Total	17792	4

El Situado Anual del Presidio de S. Francisco será de 8027 ps. 4 rs. distribuidos en eſta forma:

Sueldo anual del Teniente	550	
Del Alferez	400	
Preſt del Sargento	262	4
De cada uno de los quatro Cabos 225 ps.	900	
De cada una de las 26 Plazas de Soldados á 217 ps. 4 rs.	5655	
Por la Gratif. del fondo comun á 10 ps. anuales por Plaza	260	
Total	8027	4
Un Poblador en cada uno de los dos primeros años por sueldo y racion	116	3½
Por la racion en cada uno de los tres años siguientes que le eſtán concedidas	60	

TITULO TERCERO.

Vestuario.

1. A si como se han comprehendido en las Memorias anuales las Ropas y efectos correspondientes á uniformar la Tropa de estos Presidios, siguiendose al Soldado considerable atraso, ya por excedente lo que para vestuario se le ha subministrado, ó porque faltando Sastres para la construccion, permanecen tiempo con falta de las precisas prendas, ó inutilizan el género errando su corte, deberán los Habilitados pedir en lo succesivo 1 vestuario correspondiente á sus Compañias, hecho á proporcion de tallas, individuando las prendas ó vestidos pertenecientes á cada uno; y como quiera que el todo del vestuario he de ser conforme á lo prevenido por el Real Reglamento, asi como su distribucion, se tendrá presente, que no bastando para la continua fatiga de este servicio un par de Calzones, y algunos la Chupa, para la duracion de un año, ha de pedirse el aumento de estas prendas que se regule preciso é igualmente que siendo embarazosa la Cartuchera de madera y dobles Cañones, deben hacerse de una hilera y veinte y quatro cañones de oja de lata, que forrados en baqueta, fijen unidos en la correa que ha de ceñir el cuerpo, y á cuyo efecto ha de ser de vara y media de largo con el correspondiente ancho; la cañonera ha de cubrirla una cartera de baqueta suave, dará principio á seis dedos de la evilla, que será de laton, lisa, con dos clavillos y dos pequeñas bolsas en los extremos de dicha cañonera, la una con un pequeño polvorin de oja de lata.

TITULO QUARTO.

Armamento y Montura.

1. Ha de ser en todo igual á lo prevenido por el Real Reglamento; y no siendo asequible poner la tropa de esta Península en el pie de ocho caballerias cada Soldado por la dificultad de su transporte y conduccion, se mantendrán con las mas que se pueda, interin que fomentada la cria en los nuevos establecimientos, sea suficiente á la Remonta de todos los Presidios.

2. Respecto de mantenerse la cavallada á la inmediacion de los Presidios, á los que se trae diariamente mañana y tarde, no estando expuesta la tierra á rebatos de enemigos, y que una pronta salida no se demora por la union y cuidado con que conserva, no se variará la práctica establecida de tener quatro caballos de dia y ocho de noche atados en el Presidio, cuyo número se aumentará siempre que se advierta motivo que obligue á ello.

TITULO QUINTO.

Distribucion de Caudales, y orden con que han de llevarse las quentas generales y particulares por el Habilitado.

1. Supuesto que ha de asistirse entre año la Tropa por el Habilitado en los gastos particulares que ocurran á sus individuos y familias, que por no haber comercio en la Península, forzosamente han de impenderlos en los respectivos Almacenes, se excusa socorrer diariamente á Cabos y Soldados con dos reales diarios, como se practica en los Presidios de Frontera; bien que de ocurrir algun urgente motivo al que se halle con suficiente alcanze, y en el buen estado que corresponde, con conocimiento y orden del Capitan ó Comandante de la Compañia, podrán anticiparsele veinte ó treinta pesos; pero por ningun caso he hará á el que no esté en el estado y alcanze expresado, de que será responsable el Comandante.

2. Atendido que el cobro del Situado de estos Presidos se hace en fines del año, como queda expuesto, y que el avio y pago de la Tropa no se efectúa hasta mediados del siguiente, por cuyo medio, en qualquier tiempo que se verifique la salida del Saldado, supuesto el obierno economico que ha de seguirse, se hallará con suficiente alcanze, á mas del valor de armamento y caballerias, solo se retendrán á Cabos y Soldados cincuenta pesos de fondo, que han de descontarse en los quatro primeros años para los fines que expresa el Tit. 4. Art. 2. del Real Reglamento.

3. De dos descuentos que anualmente se verifican para el fondo de alcanzes de la Compañia, ha de hacerse por el Habilitado la correspondiente entrada en Caxa con lista que individúe los nombres de Cabos y Soldados, cantidad retenida á cada individuo, y total caudal á que á scienda; á quien para su resguardo se firmará un tanto de dicha Lista, con expresion de quedar depositada en Caxa la cantidad de su importe por el Depositario, que ha de reputarse como tal el Capitan en Loreto, y el segundo Oficial que no exerza la habilitacion en los restantes Presidios: el segundo y siguientes años se hará la introduccion del caudal perteneciente á este fondo con su respectivo ajuste, formandose el cargo de la existencia de fin del año anterior, y monto de los descuentos del presente, se manifestarián los pagos hechos en él, y el total en que queda dicho fondo.

4. El ajuste de la cuenta del año verificados los descuentos antecedentes, y el de dos por ciento que ha de percibir el Habilitado, ha de hacerse con intervencion del Capitan ó segundos Oficiales expresados en el antecedente Ar-

ticulo, y del Interesado ó Sugeto que nombre para que la examine, abonando en dinero de contado á cada uno lo que devengue, en el mismo orden que advierte el Real Reglamento.

5. El fondo de gratificacion del Presidio á razon de diez pesos por Plaza sencilla, tiene por objeto, á mas de los gastos generales, antícipar el coste de la racion con que ha de asistirse á los Indios Prisioneros, ó á los que se presenten á tratar de treguas, y anticipar la habilitacion de las Reclutas, bajo las precisas reglas prevenidas en el Art. 5. de este Titulo en el Real Reglamento el costo que ocasione el salario de un Arriero, reparo y entretenimiento de aparejos y demás avios, y el reemplazo de mulas de requa que mueran ó se inutilizen en cada Presidio, que dando responsables el comun de las Compañias (segun queda advertido) del tanto que no alcanze á cubrir el fondo, prorateandose el descubierto qué resulte proporcionalmente comprehendidos Oficiales, atendido á que quedan las requas destinadas á beneficio de las Compañias, y consiguientemente han de responder de su existencia en todo tiempo, y por ningun caso hacerse cargo á la Real Hacienda de lo que puedan exceder los gastos de ésta y demás atenciones á que está aplicado el fondo.

6. Su cuenta ha de llevarse por el Habilitado, intervenida por los demás Oficiales del Presidio, con la mayor exactitud y justificacion; anualmente se introducirá en Caxa con el Caudal correspondiente á este fondo su respectivo ajuste, con los documentos que comprueben la legitimidad de sus gastos, que ha de hacerse de acuerdo y determinacion de los Oficiales de la Compañia, los que sean inexcusables y no permitan la demora de consultar al Gobernador, y esperar su resolucion, lo que precisamente ha de observarse en todos los que no sean executivos, como dar cuenta de los que por serlo se hubiesen practicado, sin embargo de que ha de examinar en las Revistas su bueno y legal gobierno, para dar cuenta anualmente de las existencias y gastos juntamente con lo demás relativo al estado de cada Presidio y Compañia al Señor Comandante General.

7. Las cuentas generales han de llevarse en un Libro, que se intitulará de Caxa; su primer partida de cargo será la cantidad que resulte existente por la entrega ó cuenta anterior en ropas, efectos, víveres, reales ó caballerias; seguirán las del valor de las memorias que se reciban de México y San Blas, el total de alcanzes de la Compañia y dependientes del Presidio, y el importe producido de potros, reses y demás ganados que en el año se huvieren distribuido á la Tropa, cuyas partidas han de ser las últimas de cargo, asi en esta cuenta, como en las particulares. Los referidos cargos han de comprobarse con el Inventario

de entrega en el primer año, yen los siguientes con el Inventario de existencias, que ha de formalizarse en fin de cada año (con intervencion de los Oficiales del Presidio) y su respectiva cuenta: las Facturas originales de México y San Blas con copias de los correspondientes Recibos dados por el Habilitado, los particulares ajustes y cuentas de la Compañia y dependientes del Presidio, y los documentos que justifiquen las entradas pertenecientes á la Real Hacienda, que han de hacerse por lo respectivo á ganados en cuenta separada; las partidas de data son y han de calificarse el pago de prest y sueldos con los ajustes y cuentas particulares de Tropa y dependientes del Presidio; la introduccion en caxa del caudal correspondiente á la gratificacion comun, y retencion hecha á Cabos y Soldados, hasta verificar el fondo de alcanze prevenido en sus respectivos ajustes; las deudas de individuos de la Tropa y dependientes del Presidio por sus cuentas; y el monto de las existencias de fin del año se justificarán por su Inventario, con lo que, deduciendo del total de data el de cargo, se demostrará la igualdad, alcanze ó descubierto que resulte.

8. Los ajustes y cuentas particulares de Oficiales, Cirujano, Sargento, Cabos, Soldados y dependientes se llevarán en un Quaderno que anualmente ha de formarse á este efecto: dará principio con Indice que exprese los nombres y folio en que se halle la cuenta de cada uno, que encabezada con su empleo y nombre, se hará el asiento de la partida que le resultó el año anterior de alcanze ó débito, que se sacará al margen y rayará, para seguir las subministraciones que en el presente se le hagan. Las partidas han de instruirse con la cantidad, calidad, precio y total valor del efecto, notando al contramargen el mes y dia de su dacion, que ha de ser reglada en precios á los que consten de las originales Facturas, ó exprese el Arancel, que ha de formarse en fin de Diciembre; se cerrarán las cuentas, deduciendo del total de distribucion y débitos el de haber, se manifestará el alcanze que resulte, coya satisfaccion ha de notarse á presencia del interesado segun queda prevenido.

TITULO SEXTO.

Subministracion de las prendas de vestir y otras necesarias al avio de las familias de la Tropa.

1. No siendo combinable en estos Presidios sujetar el surtimiento de sus Memorias á las listas que previene el Real Reglamento dén los individuos de la Tropa de las ropas y efectos que necesiten para su avio y el de sus familias, asi por la intermision de un año ó mas en que ha de verificarse su arribo y reci-

bo, como porque no haviendo otro medio para surtirse el Soldado ó proveerle, que el de la remesa general, se seguiria falta de los renglones precisos, pues anciosos de percibir el sobrante de su haber en dinero, lo preferiria al forzoso entretenimiento de su muger, hijos y demás familia, por lo que es indispensable variar esta práctica en estos Presidios, y que solo dén dichas Listas los Oficiales, Cirujano y Sargentos, reglandose para la formacion de Memorias á lo prevenido en el Art. 4. Tit. 1. de este Reglamento.

2. Pudiendo verificarse que alguno de los géneros efectos que se remitan por el Factor no sean absolutamente de recibo justificado, y no siendo causado el deterioro por averia padecida en su transporte, se le hará cargo en primera ocasion, y de ser posible, con la misma embarcacion que lo haya conducido.

3. Siendo inevitables las mermas que padecen las semillas y efectos de racion despues de su recibo, principalmente el Maiz que comunmente se desembarca agorgojado, la Manteca y Panocha, que derrite y reviene el calor de las bodegas, y el segundo efecto permanece revenido, y aun llega á derritir las frecuentes nieblas y humedad de este temperamento, á que se agrega la diferencia y desperdicio que ofrece la distribucion por menor, y la que causa la conduccion de dichos efectos, víveres y menestras para la subsistencia de la Tropa empleada en escoltas, no debiendo el Habilitado reportar estas pérdidas, in menos las que ofrecen los géneros, cuyos aneages no corresponden con su respectivo vareo, siendo conforme sufra estas quiebras el Comun; para proceder con la justificacion que corresponde, no se le siga agravio, y quede indemnizado el Habilitado, se observará que, precediendo nombramiento, que harán los Cabos y Soldados de la Compañia, de dos Apoderados, en los mismos terminos que se prevendrá en el Cap. 9 del Tit. 13. á su presencia y de los Oficiales se haga tanteo de una, dos ó tres piezas de cada género, vareandolas por distintas manos; y descubierta la falta que resulte, y numero de varas que produzcan, se deducirá por el valor que senale la Factura á las piezas, cotejadas el precio de cada vara á el que ha de reglarse el dispendio de las restantes de su calidad, practicando lo mismo con todos los demás efectos que ofrezcan diferencia, se notarán todas las que se reconozcan en el mismo acto, y firmadas por los Oficiales y Apoderados, será el Arancel que fixe los precios de distribucion á los géneros y efectos que ofrezcan merma; y para cubrir las de semillas y éfectos de racion, se aumentará un real á el precio de cada fanega de Maiz, Frijol, Garvanzo y Lenteja; un real á cada arroba de Manteca y Arroz, y dos reales la arroba de Panocha, con lo que quedarán á cargo del Habilitado las mermas y diferencias prevenidas, como las que resulten por descuido en la colocacion y resguardo de quanto se fie á su cuidado.

TITULO SEPTIMO.

Pólvora.

1. Ha de observarse puntualmente lo prevenido en los Articulos 1, 2, 3 y 5 de este Tit. en el Real Reglamento, diferenciando el 4, en que el repuesto de Pólvora y Balas existente en cada Presidio, ha de ser correspondiente á diez y seis libras por Plaza, atendida la dificultad y riesgos que ofrece la conduccion desde México, donde ha de proveerse la falta que resultare, justificada en la cuenta particular que se ha de llevar de los consumos, que aprobada por el Gobernador, y á su pedimento, se suplirá por la Factoria de dicha Capital, dignandose determinarlo el Exmo. Señor Virrey.

TITULO OCAVO.

Provision de Empleos.

1. Bajo las reglas establecidas por el Real Reglamento en este Titulo, siempre que vacare la Compañia del Presidio de Loreto, Tenencia, ó Subtenencia de los restantes de la Peninsula, propondrá el Gobernador los referidos empleos, dirigiendo las Propuestas al Senór Comandante General.

2. Para la provision de Teniente y Alferez de la Compañia de Loreto, propondrá el Capitan tres Sugetos en quien concurran las calidades que corresponden, y estén en actual servicio, pasando la Propuesta al Gobernador, y éste al Señor Comandante General con su aprobacion ó notas.

3. Para el reemplazo de Plazas vacantes de Sargentos, hará el Capitan igual propuesta, como los Tenientes de los restantes Presidios en que no hay Capitan (y han de exercer sus funciones en esta parte y demás relativo á las obligaciones de dicho empleo como Comandantes de la Compañia) entre los que se hayan distinguido mas por su conducta y valor, cuidando en cuanto sea posible de que sepan leer y escribir, y el Gobernador aprobará el que le parezca conveniente. Las Plazas de Cabos las nombrará por se el Capitan y Tenientes Comandantes de Presidio, con la diferencia, que éstos han de pasar el nombramiento para su aprobacion al Gobernador.

TITULO NOVENO.

Revistas Mensuales.

1. El Comandante de cada Presidio pasará mensualmente revista á la Com-

pañia, y formará un extracto con los nombres de Oficiales, Sargentos, Cabos, Soldados, Cirujano y demás dependientes: á los que se hallasen presentes pondrá al margen una P: á los empleados el destino, y los empleos ó plazas vacantes una V. Los reemplazos de las vacantes del mes anterior se justificarán por nota en dicho extracto: si fuesen de empleo de Oficial, con expresion de la fecha del cúmplase del Señor Comandante General, y Certificacion firmada de todos los Oficiales, del dia en que se le dió posesion; si de Capellan, Sargento, ó Cabo, con este último documento, y si de Soldado, copiando la partida de asiento, que ha de ponerse en el Libro maestro, y el papel de tiempo de diez años, que ha de darse á todos á su entrada.

2. Para justificar las salidas solo variará de lo prevenido por el Real Reglamento en este Titulo, en las que se verifiquen por retiro de Soldados, respecto á que no permitiendo la suma distancia de esta Peninsula lo verifiquen los mas hasta el regreso de las Embarcaciones que arriban á los Puertos con el Situado, y de cuya tripulacion se solicitan los reemplazos, por ser el medio que se proporciona en estos Presidios; consiguientemente ha de obligar dicho motivo á las Revistas las Licencias de cumplidos, ó que por otra razon convenga separar de las Compañias: por lo que se observará que, precediendo la licencia del Gobernador, se exprese en el extracto su fecha, y certifiquen los Oficiales el die en que se verifique el retiro, exceptuadas las ocasiones en que se halle presente el Gobernador.

3. Debiendo acreditarse como Surplus á el Situado del Presidio de Loreto el correspondiente á su pequeno Departamento de Marina, se incluirán sus individuos en los extractos de revista mensualmente con distincion, y á continuacion de la Compañia, observando con ellos respectivamente las formalidades que quedan prevenidas para el asiento de sus Plazas en el Libro maestro, y justificar las vacantes y reemplazos de Soldados; á diferencia, que el Capitan podrá por si licenciar á los Marineros segun convenga al servicio.

4. Las Revistas han de pasarse en todos los Presidios del primero al quarto dia de cada mes; y quedando en cada uno el extracto original, se sacarán dos copias con las mismas formalidades, las que han de remitirse en primera ocasion de Loreto y San Diego, y mensualmente de los demás Presidios.

TITULO DECIMO.

Trito con los Indios enemigos ó indiferentes.

1. Hallandose en paz y tranquilidad esta Península y su numerosa Gentilidad, mediante los moderados castigos practicados con los que en distintas

partes se inquietaron, causando hostilidades y muertes, junto con el buen trato, humanidad y dulzura que experimentaron los Prisioneros, permanecen amigos, conservandose libre la comunicacion de los Presidios y demás establecimientos, no deberán alterarse las reglas que anteriormente se ordenaron, conforme á las que prefine el Real Reglamento en este Titulo, que ha de cumplirse exactamente en todas sus partes, segun lo dicte la variacion y casos que puedan ocurrir.

TITULO ONCE.

Funciones del Gobernador como Inspector de los Presidios de la Peninsula.

1. Han de ser en todo conformes por lo respectivo á los Presidios del Gobierno á las que exerce el Inspector Comandante de los Presidios de Frontera, segun y como está órdenado en el Tit. 12. del Real Reglamento, con la única variacion de deber revistarse el de Loreto cada segundo año, por la enorme ditancia y áspero comino que intermedia: para cuyo efecto y el de que ha de desempeñar juntamente las demás atenciones del Gobierno, se le destinará un Ayudante, que ha de tener el grado de Capitan; y atendidos los gastos y continuous viages que ha de hacer para las Revistas y demás á que se le comisione, siendo aprobada su creacion, le regulo acreedor á el sueldo anual de dos mil pesos.

TITULO DOCE.

Funciones y facultades del Capitan y demás Oficiales, Sargentos, Cabos y Soldados.

1. Han de ser en todo iguales á las que á cada clase prefine el tit. 13. del Real Reglamento, con la variacion que queda provenida por lo respectivo á Tenientes Comandantes de las Compañias y Presidios en los nuevos establecimientos.

TITULO TRECE.

Obligaciones, Nombramiento é Instruccion de Habilitados.

1. La primera obligacion del Oficial Habilitado es la de acreditar el acierto de la eleccion y confianza que de él hace su Compañia, fiandole el manejo, custodia y distribucion de sus intereses, procediendo en todo con la limpieza y honor que es inseparable de su profesion.

2. Llevará las cuentas generales de cargo y data con la mayor claridad, justificacion y orden que queda prevenido, para que al cabo del año examinadas y aprobadas por el Capitan en el Presidio de Loreto, é intervenidas por los Oficiales que no exerzan la Habilitacion en los demás Presidios que no tienen Capitan, se eprueben igualmente por el Gobernador.

3. Tambien llevará con las mismas circunstancias y ordenacion advertida la cuenta particular de cada individuo, enterandose con frecuencia de las de Soldados, para sujetar las distribuciones que en el avio general y entre año se les haga á el alcanze de cada uno, de modo, que exceptuados los Reclutas ninguno ha de percibir cantidad que no tenga devengada, prefiriendo en su dacion las prendas de vestuario, armamento y montura, y caballerias que necesite, y han de constar por las Revistas semanarias que han de pasarse.

4. Siempre que muera ó se licencíe algun Soldado, supuesta la urgencia de comprar sus caballerias y armamento para aviar al Recluta que lo reemplaze, ó completar las faltas que tengan otros, precediendo su justa tasacion, que han de intervenir los herederos si se hallasen presentes, las tomará el Habilitado, y las distribuirá (conforme á la orden que la comunique el Comandante de la Compañia) sobre los mismos precios en que las reciba, practicando lo mismo en caso de tomarlas por el fondo, para reintegrarle por deuda al difunto, cumplido ó icenciado.

5. Bajo la prohibicion y pena que previene el Art. 7 Tit. 14. del Real Reglamento, no podrán los Habilitados cargar al Soldado en las subministraciones de víveres, vestuario y demás efectos, mas de lo que resulte en las respectivas Facturas por primer costo, con el único aumento que expresa el Arancel, y se deduzca por la operacion prevenida en el Art. 4. Tit. 6. de este Reglamento, quedando igualmente comprehendido en la pena señalada en dicho Titulo, si incurriese en quiebra culpable, ó extravio de caudales.

6. Seguirán correspondencia con el Factor de la Peninsula y Comisario de San Blas, por quienes se les dirigirán en derechura las correspondientes remesas, facturas y conocimientos; y será al cuidado del Factor solicitar los ajustes que anualmente han de formalizarse por Oficiales Reales de la Caxa de México, con arreglo á los extractos de Revista á da Presidio, los que dirigirá á los Habilitados, que han de archivarlos con los extractos generales, y servirles de gobierno de lo que á buena cuenta pueda resultar percibido de uno á otro año, alcanze que quedó.

7. Siendo por ahora inexcusable se transporten de Sonora Caballos y Mulas para mantener en estado de servicio las Compañias de estos Presidios, prece-

diendo la correspondiente superior orden, deberá anticiparse el caudal preciso para su compra, y verificado el arribo, y distribucion de caballerias, segun las que á cada Compañia se destinen, con arreglo á su numero, calidad y precio de primer compra, formarán los Habilitados sus recibos, que han de pasarse al Gobernador, para que por su mano se dirijan á Oficiales Reales de la Caxa de México para que se formalice el debido cargo; en inteligencia, que las bestias que mueran, se pierdan ó inutilicen despues de la entrega en la Península, ha de cargarse prorateado su importe en las restantes, y sobre los precios que resulten han de distribuirse.

8. Sin embargo que estos Habilitados no han de hacer salidas para surtir la provision de víveres, ropas y demás efectos, siendo ligados á los gastos, responsabilidad y cuidado de los repuestos y su distribucion por menor, llevar las cuentas generales y particulares de Tropa y dependientes del Presidio, deberán descontar al Capitan, Oficiales, Cirujano, Sargento, Cabos, Soldados y dependientes dos por ciento las agencias y gastos que le ocasiona su comision.

9. Quando se huviere de nombrar Habilitado en el Presidio de Loreto, respecto de no haver en él Capellan (ni en los restantes de la Peninsula) suplirá la falta de este voto un segundo Apoderado de la Compañia, que, en consideracion de tener empleadas 32 Plazas de las 44 de su dotacion en los Destacamentos del Real de Santa Anna del Sur y frontera del Norte, prevendrá el Capital con la anticipacion que convenga, que los Sargentos, Cabos y Soldados juntos en sus respectivos destinos nombren dos Apoderados por la Compañia entre ellos mismos, lo que executado, se dirigirán los votos por escrito de los Individuos de cada puesto en derechura al Capitan, que hará practicar lo mismo á la Tropa existente en el Presidio, con asistencia del Patron de la Balandra y Oficiales de Maestranza del Departamento de Marina, que han de votar por Sugeto de la Compañia; y vistos los que resulten nombrados por pluralidad de votos, y de hallarse empleados en los Destacamentos, se releverán para que se trasladen al Presidio, mandando el Capitan al Oficial destinado en la Frontera remita su voto cerrado, é inmediatamente que se verifique convocará á su casa al Oficial subalterno, y á los Apoderados de la Compañia; abierto y visto en el Lugar que corresponda el voto del Oficial ausente, quedará nombrado uno de los Oficiales subalternos, y no otro por Habilitado.

10. Si de los cinco votos huviése dos por uno y tres por otro, havarán de conformarse los dos que fueron de contrario dictamen, y constituirse responsables, como si huviesen votado á su favor.

11. En los Presidios de los nuevos establecimientos en que solo hay dos Ofi-

ciales subalternos, se procederá al nombramiento de dos Apoderados en cada Compañia en los mismos términos y anticipacion que queda prevenida, lo que executado, convocará el Comandante al Alferez y Apoderados para nombrar uno de dichos Oficiales y no otro por Habilitado; en caso de que los quatro votos huviese tres por uno, quedará executada la eleccion, debiendo conformarse el que fuese de contrario distamen, y constituirse responsable, como si huviere votado á su favor; en el caso de resultar dos votos á favor de cada uno, decidirá el Gobernador.

12. Luego que esté formalizada la eleccion se extenderá el Nombramiento y Poder, de que ha de sacarse copia para dar cuenta con ella al Gobernador, debiendo cada tres años proceder de nuevo á la nominacion de Oficial Habilitado, bien para reelegir el actual, ó para nombrar otro.

13. Consiguiente á los referidos primeros nombramientos deberá hacerse entrega á los respectivos Habilitados por le Comisario del Presidio de Loreto, y Guarda Almacenes de los de San Diego, Monterrey y San Francisco, por formulas Inventarias de todos los géneros, víveres y efectos que existen en los Almacenes, con la debida distincion de calidades, medida, peso y valores sobre precios de primer compra, y gruesa que forme su total, en que no han de incluirse los efectos que no se han distribuido á la Tropa y Dependientes, inclusos Pobladores, pues de estos ha de formalizarse separado Inventario, señalando con claridad su estado y valor en quanto sea posible, lo que asi practicado, quedará en deposito en poder del Habilitado, hasta tanto que dando cuenta con dicho Inventario al Superior Gobierno, se determine la salida que deba darse á lo que de esta clase resulte.

14. Debiendo quedar las Mulas de Requa con todo lo correspondiente á sus aperos, herramientas de Carpinteria, Herreria y obras materiales á beneficio de los Presidios y Compañias, que han de responder de su existencia, segun queda precenido para la debida constancia, se procederá á la entrega de dichos útiles, Mulas de carga, aperos, costaleria, aparejos, y demás avios, precediendo valuacion, que con la debida expresion del estado, calidad y valor de cada pieza, ha de hacerse por los Peritos que á este efecto se nombren por el Comandante del Presidio que ha de intervenir la entrega y valúo firmando con los Peritos y Habilitados, Comisario ó Guarda Almacen las diligencias, que ha de acumularse al Inventario.

15. Existiendo en el Presidio de Monterrey un pie de Ganado Bacuno, que en el dia excede de quinientas cabezas de todas edades, otro de Yeguada, que igualmente pasa de ciento y setenta cabezas, y como doscientos y cincuenta de

Ganado menor de pelo y lana, con algunas Burrales y de Ganado de zerda, y en el Presidio de S. Francisco hay ciento veinte y quatro cabezas de Ganado Bacuno, perteneciente todo á la Real Hacienda, deberán comprehenderse en el primer Inventario de entrega con distincion deespecies y edades en Ganado mayor y Yeguada, quedando á cargo de los Habilitados que, baxo las órdenes del Gobernador celarán el pastorio y cuidado de dichos Ganados, su aumento, distribucion á Pobladores con calidad de pago ó reintegro, y conservando el vientre dará salida de Potros, Toros, Novillos, Carneros, Castrados de Pelo, Zerdos y demás que por viejo ó infecundo deba expenderse en pie, llevará la cuenta de estos Ganados, para dar la cuenta de sus productos y aumento á la Real Hacienda anualmente, como se expresará adelante.

16. El Comisario de Loreto y Guarda Almacenes de los restantes Presidios han de formalizar sus cuentas de modo que no queden los Habilitados sujetos á responder en lo succesivo al Real Tribunal y Audiencia de Cuentas de resultas de las anteriores: conseqüentemente ningun otro Documento debe quedar en su poder que en tanto del último ajuste ó cuenta, y los Inventarios de entrega, y ha de ser solo el cargo de cada Habilitado, y parte de pago de sus respectivos Situados la cantidad en que excedan el valor de los enseres distribuidos y cargables á la Tropa, Dependientes y Pobladores, y el de sus débitos al total de alcanzes (vencidos desde el añode de 1774, inclusive hasta el dia de la entrega) que han de satisfacerse enteramnte á los Interesados; pero si por el contrario excede la partida de alcanzes á la de los débitos y enseres, su residuo será á favor del Habilitado en quien se verifique, y ha de acreditarsele por la Real Caxa de México con el primer ajuste que se le formalice deducido el aumento respectivo.

17. Como en el transporte de las remesas anuales ocurren y causa el calor de las Bodegas de la embarcacion y otros incidentes, pérdidas, averias y mermas principalmente en la Manteca, Panocha, Caldos y Semillas, debe verificarse la entrega con entera satisfaccion del Habilitado, precediendo peso, medida, y desatará de los citados renglones y demás que convenga, y en el caso de resultar averiado, roto ó mal condicionado algun fardo, tercio ó caxon, para calificar su deterioro en el todo ó parte, se procederá á su formal reconocimiento á bordo con intervencion del Comandante de la Embarcacion y de él del Presidio, confrontando por la Factura los géneros ó efectos que contenga, y efectuado, se certificará por dichos Oficiales el menoscabo ó pérdida que haya causado la averia, ó algun otro incidente, que deberá expresarse, y asi practicado, se desembarcará y recogerá el Habilitado dicha Certificacion, que ha deponerse por

cabeza de las diligencias de tasacion, que ha de hacerse en el Presidio con intervencion del Capitan y Oficiales subalternos, antecediendo nombramiento de los Peritos (que hará el Comandante) que con presencia de los precios y Factura, y del daño causado, con citacion de él, y de los generos ó efectos que le tengan, se señalara el justo valor á que queden reducidos, y al que sin alteracion han de distribuirse y cargarse á la Tropa; el Habilitado se formará cargo del líquido valor en que queden los géneros y efectos averiados, como de los que no lo sean, segun resulte de las diligencias, de que dexando Copia certificada por los Oficiales en el Presidio, se remitirán las originales por el Habilitado al Factor, para que por ellas compruebe y se acredite la pérdida.

18. Para evitar la confusion con que se hace la entrega y medida del Maiz y Frijol en las Bodegas ó Pañoles de la Embarcacion, en las que forzosamente ha de seguirse menoscabo al que entrega midiendose bien, por recalar los valances la Semilla en la medida, ó al que recibe, por medires mal, ó derramarse al tiempo de vaciar la medida én los costales, por la prisa é incomodidad con que se executa, y á que atribuyen los Guarda Almacenes mucha parte de mermas; para excusar en lo succesivo dichos inconvenientes, se hará la medicion de granos en tierra, bien sea en la Playa, ó en los Presidios inmediatos al desembarcadero, como siempre se executo en Loreto, y algun año en Monterrey, con corta ó ninguna falta, habiendose experimentado crecidas en la contraria práctica.

19. Los Habilitados otorgarán asi de los Fardos, Tercios y Caxones remitidos de México, como de los víveres y efectos que lleguen de San Blas, á continuacion de los Conocimientos, con expresion de las faltas, pérdidas ó mermas que resultaron en la entrega, y el tanto recibido en cada Semilla, Arina y efectos de racion, cuyor documentos firmados por el Habilitado se entregarán al Sugeto que cenga hecho cargo de la remesa, por quien ha de firmarse en los Conocimientos que por duplicado se remiten de la Comisaría de S. Blas la declaracion de la entrega que haya verificado cada ramo ó efecto de los contenidos en los mismos Conocimientos, que han de quedar en poder del Habilitado para calificar su recibo, á cuyo efecto deberá remitirlos (quedando una Copia certificada por los Oficiales de la Compañia) al Factor de la Península para que lo presente en donde corresponda, y por ellos se haga el debido abono, respecto de que conforme al total importe de las Facturas, se habrá formado el cargo al Situado, por el atrazo con que forzosamente han de llegar estos comprobantes.

20. Habiendose establecido do pocos años á esta parte hacer entrega de la

remesa general á los Contramaestres de las Embarcaciones, los que por falta de inteligencia y precisa asistencia en ellas, ocasionan atrazo para puntualizar su entrega, debiendo ser en lo succesivo un Oficial el que reciba, es conveniente se varíe esta práctica, y que de no ser el encargado el Comandante de la Embarcacion, lo sea el Piloto, en quien hay mas proporcion y responsabilidad para dicha comísion.

21. Estando establecido que el Capitan del Presido de Loreto, como Teniente de Gobernador, dé las Licencias á los Armadores que entren al busco de Perlas en su Costa é Islas contiguas, regulando el tanto que ha de pagar por quinto cada Canoa, que actualmente está reglada en cien pesos, atiendida la escazes á que han venido los Placeres, por cuya razon pasaron años en que no entró Armador alguno, no excediendo el presente de dos ó tres Canoas las que lo verifican, cuyo producto con orden de dicho Capitan lo ha cobrado el Comisario que ha dado su correspondiente entrada á la Real Hacienda con el producido de la venta de Sal, y algunos Toros del Ganado orejano que compra la Tropa y Vecinos del Real de Santa Anna: debiendo seguirse esta práctica en lo succesivo por los Habilitados, darán éstos anualmente la correspondiente entrada del producto de estos ramos y demás que pertenezcan á la Real Hacienda en cuenta separada, é intervenida por el Capitan, en la que se datarán los gastos que ocasionen lascarenas, recorridas y arboladuras de la Balandra y Lanchas del Departamento, la que con los correspondientes justificantes de cargo y data, se dirigirá al Factor de la Península, para que la presente en el Real Tribunal de Cuentas, y se hagan los cargos ó abonos que correspondan al Situado.

22. Respectivamente deberán los Habilitados de Monterrey y S. Francisco formar anualmente cuenta de cargo y data de los Ganados que sean de su cargo, con distincion de especies, expresion del aumento de cabezas, y producto en pesos de las que en el año se huviese expendido, para cuyo efecto se arreglarán al Formulario que irá al fin de esta Instruccion.

23. Asimismo ha de ser el cargo del Habilitado de Presidio en cuya inmediacion ó termino se sitúe nuevo Pueblo de Gente de razon, formar asiento y abrir cuenta á los Pobladores, hacerse cargo y dar los correspondientes resguardos de las cantidades que para su habilitacion se les haya suplido en Sonora, como de los granados ó herramientas que para el mismo efecto se remitan de otros Presidios, acreditarles su respectivo haber desde el dia de su entrada, y verificar el cobro de la subministracion que á cada Poblador resulte y deba descontarsele, formando anualmente cuenta, en que con la debida claridad y comprobacion se den los gastos y entradas que correspondan á la Real Hacienda.

24. Los asientos que á todo Poblador ha de formar el Habilitado, han de instruirse con su nombre, calidad, edad, patria, y Pueblo en que queda avecindado, y con igual distincion se expresará el nombre, calidad y edad de su muger, hijos y hijas, dia, mes y año en que se le dió entrada á el goce de sueldo y racion que está consignada á cada uno, reglandose en esta parte á lo que irá prevenido en la Instruccion de Poblacion, de no oponerse á ello las condiciones con que se hayan registrado los que de Sonora vengan á poblar estos establecimientos.

25. La entrada de nuevo Poblador y data de su haber en la cuenta particular que queda prevenida, se justificará con la orden que ha de anteceder del Gobernador, y copia de la partida de asiento. Las salidas por muerte se comprobarán con copia de la partida de entierro y cese de sueldo ó racion que en cada año resulte, se distinguirá en la partida en que con separacion ha de datarse el residuoque de uno á otro perciba en el año el individuo á que termine, pues su comprobacion se deducirá del respectivo asiento, respecto á que de todas se ha de acompañar copia á la primer cuenta.

26. En los dos primeros años ha de descontarse á los Pobladores el importe de las herramientas que huvieren recibido, y en los siguientes tres años se verificará el pago de todo lo demás que se les huviere suplido para la habilitacion de sus labores, conforme á lo que se prevendrá en su correspondiente Instruccion.

27. El Maiz, Frixol, Garvanzo y Lentejas que produzcan las cosechas del Pueblo, reservando los vecinos lo preciso para su subsistencia y siembras, no tiene ni pueda darsele por ahora otro destino que el de proveer los Presidios. Consecuentemente los Habilitados comprarán estas semillas sobre los precios que están establecidos, ó en adelante se establezcan, con consideracion á que han de conducirse con las Requas de los Presidios.

28. Si en el Presidio á que se agregue Pueblo existe algun pie de ganado perteneciente á la Real Hacienda, se acumulará su cuenta á la de Poblacion, en la que se formará el correspondiente cargo el Habilitado del producto de las cabezas que se huvieren distribuido, é igualmente ha de comprehender en ella con la correspondiente aprobacion lo producido por qualquier otro efecto perteneciente á dicha Real Hacienda, teniendo presente, que toda la costaleria de Esmiquilpa que se remita de San Blas (exceptuada la de empaque de Arina que viene comprehendida en el valor de cada tercio, y las cargas de costales que se distribuyan á su cuenta á la Tropa) como los cascos de Barril, han de volverse de un año á otro, para por este medio excusar su repetido gasto; á los abrigos y petates de fardos que vienen de México, como á los caxones,

se les procurará dar salida á los que lleguen buenos, y los que por podridos ó rotos no la tengan, como los cabezeados de cuero, deberán considerarse como gasto legítimo de la Real Hacienda, calificando lo que asi resulte, con certificacion firmada por los Oficiales que intervengan el Inventario de existencias de fin de año, la que ha de acompañarse á la expresada cuenta particular, que ha de dirigirse anualmente al Gobernador, por quien reconocida, aprobada y visada, se remitirá á los Oficiales Reales de las Caxas de México, para que por ella se acrediten los gastos que correspondan al Habilitado.

FORMULARIO.

Cuenta de Cargo y Data de los Ganados que quedan existentes en el Presidio de San Carlos de Monterrey pertenecientes á la Real Hacienda, que por comision están á mi cargo como Habilitado de la Compañia, en que con distincion de especies, manifiesto en sus respectivas cuentas el cargo que se dedujo por el Inventario de entrega, la nacencia del presente año, la distribucion de cabezas que en él se hizo, su producto en pesos, la existencia y aumento que resulta en fin de Diciembre de 1780.

	Cabezas.	Pesos
Cuenta de Yeguas y Potros.		
Primeramente: son data ciento noventa cabezas, que con la distincion de clases que consta del Inventario de entrega quedaron existentes en	190	
Son cargo treinta y dos Potrillos producidos de la nacencia del presente año	32	
Son cargo treinta y ocho Potrancas de la misma nacencia	38	
	260	
Data en su especie, y producto en pesos.		
Son data veinte Potros demaderos que se distribuyeron á seis pesos cada uno en la Compañia	20	120
Son data diez Potros de tres años que se vendieron al Habilitado del Presidio de San Francisco al mismo precio	10	60

Son data dos Yeguas que murieron, cuyos fierros se manifestaron y quemaron	2	
Data	32	
Cargo	260	
Quedan existentes en fin de Diciembre	228	
La existencia del año anterior fué de	190	
Su aumento y producto en el presente año es	38	180

Cuenta de Ganado Bacuno.

Son cargo quinientas setenta cabezas, que en las clases que expresa el Inventario quedaron existentes en	570	
Son cargo ochenta y tres Terneros producidos en la nacencia del presente año	83	
Son cargo ciento y seis Terneras de dicha nacencia.	106	
	759	

Data en especies y producto en pesos.

Son data quarenta y seis Novillos de quatro años que se remitieron á D..... N.... Habilitado de..... para distribuir á Pobladores, de cuyo cargo queda dar entrada de su importe al respecto de seis pesos cabeza á la Real Hacienda	46	276
Son data diez Toros que se distribuyeron á la Tropa á cinco pesos	10	50
Son data quatro Vacas, que por viejas se vendieron á seis pesos cada una	4	24
Son data dos Toros que se lastimaron, y fué distribuida la carne de cada uno en veinte raciones a dos reales	2	10
Son data tres Terneros y dos Terneras que mataron los Lobos	5	
Data	67	
Cargo	759	
Quedan existentes en fin de Diciembre	692	
La existencia del año anterior fué de	570	
Su aumento y producto en el presente es	122	360

Con este orden seguiran las cuentas de los demás Ganados poniendo á continuacion resumen de las cantidades que produxeron en pesos para manifestar su total, contra el que se datarán las partidas producidas por Ganados que hayan salido para Pobladores, cuya satisfaccion deba hacerse por otro Habilitado, y las únicas de gasto que han de ofrecer por el salario del Pastor de Ganado menor, y dos ó tres arrobas de Yerba de Puebla que ha de pedirse uno ú otro año, con lo que deduciendose la data del cargo, quedará demostrado el que resulte contra el que dá la cuenta, y relacionando al pie el total cargo y distribucion de pesos, pondrá la fecha y firmará.

TITULO CATORCE.

Gobierno Politico, é Instruccion para Poblacion.

1. Siendo el objeto de mayor importancia para dar cumplimiento á las piadosas intenciones del Rey nuestro Señor, y perpetuar á S. M. el dominio del dilatado terreno que en la extension de mas de doscientas leguas comprehenden los nuevos Establecimientos de los Presidios y respectivos Puertos de San Diego, Monterrey, y S. Francisco, adelantar la Reduccion y hacer util al estado en lo posible tan vasto Pais, habitado de innumerable Gentiladad, exceptuados mil setecientos quarenta y nueve Christianos de ambos sexos que tienen las ocho Misiones que se hallan sobre el comino que direge del primero al último Presidio, erigiendo Pueblos de gente de razon, que congregada fomente la labranza, plantío, y cria de ganado y succesivamente los demás ramos de industria, de modo que á discurso de algunos años basten sus producciones á abastecer de víveres y caballerias las Guarniciones de Presidios, excusando por este medio el dilatado transporte, riesgos y pérdidas con que de cuenta de la Real Hacienda se conduce, con cuya justa idea se halla poblado y fundado el Pueblo de San Joseph, y está determinada la ereccion de otro, para el que han de dirigirse Pobladores con sus familias de la Provincia de Sonora y Sinaloa, cuyo progresivo aumento y el de las familias de la Tropa, proporcionara el establecimiento de otras Poblaciones y Reclutas para las Compañias Presidiales, libertandose el Real Erario de los forzosos gastos que actualmente impende para el logro de uno y otro; y conviniendo establecer reglas que lo aseguren, se observará la Instruccion signiente.

2. Asi como hasta ahora fueron consignados á cada Poblador, á mas de la racion, 120 ps. en cada uno de los dos primeros años, y solo la racion en los tres siguientes, regulada en real y medio diario, francos, gozarán por lo equi-

valente en lo succesivo ciento diez y seis pesos tres y medio reales en cada uno de los dos primeros años, entendiendose comprehendida en dicha cantidad la racion, y por ella en los años siguientes sesenta pesos en cada uno, con lo que queda compensado con ventaja el antecedente goce; deducido el aumento con que se pagaba, y baxa con que se les subministró la Racion, cuyos efectos y demás han de recibir al coste desde que aprobado, se declare la práctica de este Reglamento; siendo prevencion, que el referido tiempo de cinco años ha de contarse para sus goces desde el dia que se verifique la posesion de Solares y Suertes de tierras que han de repartirse á cada Poblador, como se expresará adelante, debiendo correr el tiempo que anteceda desde sus registros baxo las condiciones de Contratas; y para que se evite este gasto, se providenciará de modo, que luego que lleguen nuevos Pobladores sin intermision se sitúen y dé la referida Posesion.

3. A cada Poblador y al Comun de Pueblo han de darse con calidad de reintegro en Mulas y Caballos, que sean de dar y recibir, y pago de los demás, genado mayor y menor, baxo los justos precios que han de arancelarse, y las herramientas al coste, como está ordenado, dos Yeguas, dos Bacas con una cria, dos Ovejas, y dos Cabras, todo de vientre, y una yunta de Bueyes ó Novillos, una reja ó punta de Arado, un Azadon, una Coa, una Hacha y una Hoz, un Cuchillo de monte, una Lanza, una Escopeta, y una Adarga, dos Caballos y una Mula de carga; igualmente y á cargo del Comun se darán los padres que correspondan al número de cabezas de ganado en sus especies del todo del vecindario, un Burro maestro, otro comun y tres Burras, un Barraco y tres Puercas, una fragua aviada de yunque y demás herramientas que le corresponda, seis barras, seis palas de fierro, y la herramienta necesaria de Carpinteria y Carreteria.

4. Los Solares que se concedan á los nuevos Pobladores se han de señalar por el Gobierno en los sitios y con la extension correspondiente á la que tuviere el terreno donde se establezcan los nuevos Pueblos, de modo que quede formada plaza y calles, conforme á lo prevenido por Leyes del Reyno, y con su arreglo se señalará Exido competente para el Pueblo y Dehesas con las tierras de labor que convenga para Propios.

5. Cada Suerte de tierra, asi de riego como de temporal, ha de ser de doscientas varas de largo, y doscientas de ancho, por ser este el ámbito que regularmente ocupa una fanega de Maiz en sembradura; el repartimiento que de dichas Suertes, como de los Solares ha de hacerse á nombre del Rey nuestro Señor á los nuevos Pobladores, se hará por el Gobierno con igualdad y proporcion al terreno que logre el beneficio de riego, de forma, que precedi-

endo la correspondiente demarcacion, y reservando baldíos la quarta parte del número que resulte contando con el número de Pobladores, si alcanzansen, se repartirán á dos Suertes á cada uno de regadio, y otras dos de secadal, y de las realengas se separaran las que parecieren convenientes para propios del Pueblo, y de las restantes se hará merced á nombre de S. M. á los que de nuevo entrasen á poblar por el Gobernador, igualmente que de los respectivos Solares, y señaladamente á los Soldados, que por haber cumplido el tiempo de su empeño, ó abanzada edad, se retiren del Servicio, como á las familias de los que mueran, los que habilitarán sus labores con el fondo que cada uno debe tener, sin que á estos se asista de cuenta de la Real Hacienda con sueldo, racion ni ganados, por ser limitada esta gracia á los que con aquel destino se extrañan de su pais para poblar éste.

6. Las casas fabricadas en los Solares concedidos y señalados á los nuevos Pobladores, y las Suertes de tierra comprehendidas en sus respectivas mercedes, serán hereditarias con perpetuidad en sus hijos y desciendientes, ó hijas que casen con Pobladores útiles, y que no tengan repartimiento de Suertes por si mismos, cumpliendo todos ellos con las condiciones que irán expresadas en esta Instruccion; y para que los hijos de los poseedores de estas mercedes tengan la obediencia y respeto que deben á sus padres, ha de ser libre y facultativo en éstos, si tuvieren dos ó mas hijos, elegír el que quisieren de ellos, siendo secular y lego, por heredero de la Casa y Suertes de Poblacion, y tambien podrán disponer que se repartan entre éllos, pero no que una sola Suerte se divida, porque han de ser todas y cada una de por sí indivisibles é inagenables perpetuamente.

7. Tampoco podrán los Pobladores ni sus herederos imponer censo, vinculo, fianza, hipoteca ni otro gravamen alguno, aunque sea por causa piadosa sobre Casa y Suerte de tierra que se les conceden, y si alguno lo hiciere contraviniendo á esta justa prohibicion, quedará privado de la propriedad irremisiblemente, y por el mismo hecho se dará su dotacion á otro Poblador que sea util y obediente.

8. Gozarán los nuevos Pobladores para mantener sus ganados del aprovechamiento comun de aguas y pastos, leña y madera del Exido, Monte y Dehesa que ha de señalarse con arreglo á las Leyes á cada nuevo Pueblo, y además disfrutar á privativamente cada uno el pasto de sus tierras propias, pero con condicion, que debiendo tener y criar toda clase de ganado mayor y menor, no siendo posible cuide por sí cada uno el corto número de cabezas que para pié les quedan consignadas, pues de ello se siguiria desatender las labores y

obras públicas, deberá por ahora paſtorearse unido el ganado menor de la Comunidad, de cuyo cargo ha de ser el pago del Paſtor, y por lo respeƈtivo á rodear el ganado mayor y traerle al corral, como Yeguas y Burras, segun convenga, han de serlo dos Pobladores, que diariamente, ó como les parezca, nombrarán entre sí de caballada con lo que eſtará cuidado el ganado en sus especies, evitado el riesgo de alzarse, y atendidas las labores y demás faenas del comun, cuidando cada individuo señalar sus respeƈtivas cabezas de ganado menor, y marcar el mayor, para el que se darán los regiſtros de fierros correspondientes sin derecho alguno; con prevencion, que cada Poblador en lo succesivo no ha de exceder de cincuenta cabezas de cada especie el que posea, para que de eſte modo se diſtribuya entre todos la utilidad que producen los ganados, y que no se eſtangue en pocos Vecinos la verdadera riqueza de los Pueblos.

9. Serán esentos y libres por término de cinco años los nuevos Pobladores de pagar diezmos ni otro derecho alguno de los frutos y esquilmos que les produzcan las tierras de su dotacion y ganados, con tal que en el primer año contado desde el dia que se les señalen los Solares y Suertes conſtruyan en la forma posible sus casas y las habiten, abran las zanjas correspondientes al riego de sus tierras, poniendo á las lindes divisorias en lugar de mojones árboles frutales ó silveſtres que sean útiles, á razon de diez en cada Suerte, é igualmente se abra la azequia ó zanja madre, formen presa, y demás obras públicas y precisas para el beneficio de las labores á que con preferencia ha de atenderse por el Comun, de cuyo cargo ha de ser dar conſtruidas las Casas Reales en los quatro años, y en el tercero una troxe capaz y suficiente para Pósito, en que han de cuſtodiarse las producciones de la siembra de Comunidad, que al respeƈto de un almud de Maiz por Vecino, ha de hacerse desde dicho tercer año, haſta el quinto inclusive en las tierras que se señalen por propios del Pueblo, debiendo hacerse todas las faenas que ofrezea haſta poner sus cosechas dentro del Pósito por el Comun, á cuyo beneficio han de servir únicamente; y para su gobierno y aumento se formarán oportunamente las Ordenanzas que han de observarse.

10. Despues de los cinco años satisfarán los Diezmos á S. M. para que los aplique segun fuere de su Real agrado, como que enteramente le pertenecen, no solo por el Patronato Real absoluto que tiene en eſtos Dominios suyos, sino tambien por ser novales, pues han de producirse en terrenos haſta ahora inclutos y abandonados, y que van á hacerse fruƈtíferos á coſta de los grandes dispendios y gaſtos que eroga la Real Hacienda.

Pasado el referido término de los cinco años, én recono cimiento del directo y supremo dominio, que pertenece al Soberano, pagarán los nuevos Pobladores y sus descendientes media fanega de Maiz por cada Suerte de tierra de regadío, y en beneficio de ellos mismos será obligacion indispensable y comun de todos concurrir á reparar la azequia, presa, tageas, y las demás obras públicas de su Pueblo inclusa la Iglesia.

11. Multiplicado el ganado de zerda y burrada, ahijados los Burros que convenga para garañones de las Yeguas, siendo asequible la reparticion de cada una de las dos especies, se executará de comun consentimiento de los Pobladores entre sí con toda la igualdad posible, de modo que del primer ganado que dé cada Vecino con dos Cabezas, macho y hembra, y con una del segundo, lo que verificado, se señalarán y marcarán por sus dueños.

12. En los cinco años prevenidos estarán obligados los nuevos Pobladores á tener dos yuntas de Bueyes, dos arados, dos rejas ó puntas para labrar la tierra, dos hazadones, con la demás herramienta precisa de labranza, y finalizadas en los tres primeros años enteramente sus casas, y pobladas en ella seis Gallinas y un Gallo, prohibiendose absolutamente que en el término señalado de cinco años puedan enagenarse por venta, cambio ú otro pretexo, ni matar ninguana cabeza de ganado de las que se les subministran, ni de las de su respectivo procreo, exceptuado el ganado menor de lana y pelo, que á los quatro años es preciso darle salida, pues de lo contrario muere, y en su conseqüencia podrán disponer á su arbitrio de las cabezas que sean de dicho tiempo, pero no de las que no lo sean, baxo la pena al que contraviniese á esta providencia, dirigida á su propio beneficio y aumento de sus bienes, de quedar por el mismo hecho privado del goce de racion que se le concede por un año, y el que en qualquier modo reciba una ó mas cabezas de dicho ganado en el referido tiempo, de qualquier estado ó condicion que sea, será obligado á devolverlas.

13. Cumplido el término de cinco años conservando el vientre de todas especies, exceptuado el de zerda y burras, que solo será obligado á tener cada Poblador una Puerca, y un Burro ó Burra, teniendo habilitadas sus labranzas con las yuntas de Bueyes y Novillos señaladas, hallandose aviados de Mula de carga y Caballos precisos, serán libres para vender los Toros, Novillos, Potros ó Caballos, Burros, Carneros, Castrados de pelo, Zerda y Puercas, quedando prohibido se mate Baca, no siendo vieja ó machorra, y por consiguiente infecunda, Ovejas ó Cabras que no sean de tres años arriba, ni vender Yeguas ni vientres útiles hasta tanto que se verifique por cada Poblador la posesion de quince Yeguas con un Caballo padre, quince Bacas con un Toro, doce Ove-

jas y un Carnero entero y diez Cabras y un Macho.

14. Será prohibido á todo Poblador y Vecino vender Potro, Caballo, Mula ó Macho, ni cambiar dichas bestias no siendo entre sí mismos, estando aviados de las que les sean necesarias, pues á las restantes no ha de darseles otro destino que el de la Remonta de la Tropa de los Presidios, y han de pagarse á los justos precios que se establezcan, exceptuando todo Caballo ó Mula especial en los mis mismos Pueblos, baxo la pena de veinte pesos, que han de exigirse á el que contraviniere á esta providencia por cada cabeza á que diese otra salida que la que queda expresada, lo que se aplica por mitad al denunciador, y gastos de República.

15. El Maix, Frixol, Garvanzo y Lenteja que produzcan las cosechas de los Pueblos, reservando los Vecinos lo preciso para su subsistencia y siembras, ha de comprarse y satistacerse de contado sobre los precios que estén establecidos, ó en adelante se establezcan para la provision de los Presidios, y de su importe se harán á cada Poblador los prudentes descuentos que convengan, para reintegrar á la Real Hacienda de las cantidades que para su habilitacion se les hayan suplido en reales, caballerias, ganados, herramientas, semillas y demás efectos, de modo que en los cinco primeros años ha de quedar verificado el pago.

16. Todo Poblador y Vecino, Cabeza de familia á que se hayan repartido ó en adelante se repartan Solares y Suertes de tierras, y los que los succedan, serán obligados á mantenerse equipados con dos Caballos, silla aviada, escopeta y demás armas que quedan expresadas, y han de subministrarseles al coste para defender sus respectivos distritos, y acudir sin abandonar aquella primera obligacion donde con grave urgencia se ordene por el Gobernador.

17. De las mercedes de Solares, Tierras y Aguas concedidas á los nuevos Pobladores, ó Vecinos á que se concedan en lo succesivo, se librarán por el Gobernador ó Comisario que nombre á este efecto los correspondientes despachos, de que ha de tomarse razon y de los regístros de fierros en el Libro general de Poblacion que se ha de formar y guardar en el Archivo del Gobierno, en el que se pondrá por cabeza copia de esta Instruccion.

18. Y conviniendo para el buen gobierno y policia de los Pueblos, administracion de Justica, dirigir las obras públicas, repartimiento de las tandas de agua, y celar el cumplimiento de quanto queda prevenido en esta Instruccion, se les dé á proporcion de sus vecindarios Alcaldes, Ordinarios y otros Oficiales de consejo anuales, se pondrán por el Gobernador en los dos primeros años, y en los siguientes nombrarán por sí y entre sí los oficios de República que se

hayan eſtablecido, cuyas elecciones han de pasarse para su confirmacion al Gobernador, por quien se continuará dicho nombramiento en los tres años siguientes si advirtiese convenir así.

TITULO QUINCE.

Ereccion de nuevas Reducciones.

1. Respeƈto de que situadas en el Canal de Santa Bárbara las tres Reducciones que eſtán determinadas, quedará cubierta la Demarcacion que ha gobernado de Sur á Norte el eſtablecimiento de las ocho anteriormente fundadas sobre el comino que dirige del Presidio de San Diego al de Monterrey, y de éſte al de San Francisco, y consiguientemente queda facilitada la comunicacion de los nuevos Eſtablecimientos, pues quedan las once Misiones y Presidios diſtantes entre sí de trece á veinte leguas, exceptuado el intervalo que media de la de S. Antonio á S. Luis, y de S. Juan Capiſtrano á S. Gabriel, que se regulan de veinte y cinco leguas: es de suma importancia para adelantar la reduccion de la numerosa Gentilidad que puebla eſta parte de la Península, variar el eſtablecimiento de nuevas Reducciones á los rumbos opueſtos, proporcionando en quanto lo permitan los sitios, que han de solicitarse de las calidades que conviene para la eſtabilidad, de forma que cada una de las que en lo succesivo se sitúen (que á excepcion de una ó dos serán las reſtantes al Eſte) queden en la diſtancia de catorce á veinte leguas de dos de las antiguas, por cuyo medio se ocuparán los intervalos que eſtas tienen entre sí, se irán ciñendo las Rancherias de Gentiles, se aumentará considerablemente las Christiandad y descubrirá la Tierra.

2. Supueſto que es mas de doscientas leguas la extencion en que se hallan situados los referidos Eſtablecimientos de Monterrey, no eſtando descubierto el ancho de la tierra, se infiere ha de corresponder con exceso, atendido se cuenta por miles lo mas que se dilata, y conseqüentemente se hace inexcusable verificar el aumento de Reducciones con proporcion á el vaſto Pais ocupado; y aunque debe executarse succesivamente en el orden que queda expresado, segun se aseguren las anteriores fundaciones minorando sus Escoltas, para que la Tropa sobrante guarnezca las que se aumenten, siendo forzoso sean muchas, en consiguiente han de gravar considerablemente el Erario, o caminar con morosidad la ereccion, y para facilitarla conviene que exceptuadas las tres Reducciones que han de situarse en el Canal de Santa Bárbara con dos Religiosos cada una, por las juſtas causas que allí concurren y quedan

expuestas, las demás que subsigan se establezcan conforme á la antigua práctica de esta y demás Provincias internas con un Ministro, pero sin variacion de la limosna de quatrocientos pesos que á el año estan consignados á cada uno, en cuya candidad han de entenderse comprehendidas todas las necesidades religiosas, asi como el avió temporal de Mision y labranza, en los un mil pesos concedidos para cada fundacion, permitiendose para el mas pronto incremento de las nuevas, que las antiguas las socorran con las cebezas de ganado y semillas, que sin falta en sus especies, regúle el R. P. Presidente puedan dar, y con un Ministro en el primer año de la fundacion.

3. Las ocho Misiones actualmente establecidas quedarán con los dos Ministros que cada una tiene; pero no han de reemplazarse los que por muerte ó retiro vayan faltando, hasta tanto que queden reducidas á un solo Ministro, á excepcion de las inmediatas á los Presidios, en que han de subsistir dos Religiosos, y uno con la precisa asistencia al Presidio como Capellan de él, interin no se determine proveerlos de Capellanes seculares: conseqüentemente si resultase la falta en estas Misiones, ó en las del Canal, pasará á ocupar su lugar uno de las de San Juan Capistrano, San Gabriel, San Luis, San Antonio, ó Santa Clara, ó concurrir como queda dicho, á nuevas fundaciones.

4. En el mismo orden que explica el Artículo segundo deberán reducirse á un solo Ministro las Doctrinas que administran los Religiosos del Orden de Santo Domingo en la antigua California, exceptuada la de Loreto, en que han de existir dos Ministros, uno como Capellan del Presidio, y las dos últimas del Norte que al presente ó en adelante sean fronterizas, y en un y otras se reemplazarán las faltas que ocurran con los segundos Ministros de las restantes, interin subsistan, quedando todas con el sinodo de trescientos cincuenta pesos que á cada uno están señalalados; pero sin arbitrio los Prelados de remover con este ni otro motivo alguno á los Religiosos de una á otra Doctrina, para lo que precisa y cumplidamente ha de guardarse la forma del Real Patronazgo, en todas sus partes, y casos que puedan ocurrir.

5. Supuesto estar solo fundadas la Reduccion de Nrâ. Srâ. del Rosario de Viñadaco y la de Santo Domingo de las cinco que deben situarse conforme á la demarcacion anteriormente acordada por la Real Junto de Guerra y Real Hacienda, para cubrir el camino que intermedia de la Frontera al Presidio de San Diego, siendo de la mayor importancia verificar la ereccion de las tres restantes, con lo que quedará facilitada la comunicacion de los antiguos y nuevos Establecimientos, deberá executarse con la posible brevedad.

Es cuanto dexo expuesto lo que la experiencia y conocimiento adquirido, mi zelo y amor al Real Servicio, y cumplimiento de las Superiores Ordenes me han dictado por mas conveniente para desempeñar la Real Resolucion y piadosas intenciones del Rey.

FELIPE DE NEVE.

Real Presidio de S. Carlos de Monterrey
1. de junio de 1779.

Es copia de su original, que queda en la Secretaria de la Comandancia General de mi cargo, de que certifico.

ANTONIO BONILLA.

Arispe, de Febrero de 1780.

Ha visto el Rey el Reglamento para el gobierno de la Provincia de Californias, formado por el Gobernador de ella D. Felipe Neve en virtud de lo dispuesto en Real Orden de 21 de Marzo de 1775. del qual remite V. E. Testimonio con Carta de 19 de Enero de este año número 856. Se ha dignado S. M. aprobarlo, y de su orden lo prevengo á V. E. para su inteligencia y gobierno. Dios guarde á V. E. muchos años.

JOSEF DE GALVEZ,
Senor Virrey de Nueva Espana

San Lorenzo, 24 de Octubre de 1781.

Mexico 26 de Marzo de 1782.

Sáquese copia certificada de esta Real Orden. y agregada al Reglamento que se expresa para constancia de la aprobacion que ha merecido á S. M., imprimanse los exemplares correspondientes, y diriganse con los respectivos Oficios los necesarios al Señor Comandante General de Provincias internas, á los Oficiales Reales de estas Caxas, al Real Tribunal de Cuentas, al Factor Don Manuel Ramon de Goya, al Comisario del Departamento de San Blas, y al Gobernador de Californias, para su constancia y cumplimiento en la parte que á cada uno toca: de cuya providencia se avisará en respuesta de dicha Real Orden.

MOYORGA.

Es copia de su original, de que certifico. Mexico tres de Abril de mil setecientos ochenta y dos.

PEDRO ANTONIO DE COSIO.

Para el Archivo del Gobierno. Monterrey 18 de Septiembre de 1784.

PEDRO FAGES.

Correspondencia Tocante a la Instrucción[1]

Con los justos fines de defensa conservacion y fomento de le Provincia de Californias, en que particularmente se interesan el servicio de Dios y del Rey, hé resuelto la Ocupacion del Canál de Sta. Barbara con vn Presidio de este nombre, y tres Misiones, la ereccion de vn Pueblo con el titulo de la Reyna de los Angeles sobre el Rio de la Porcinncula, y S. M. há aprovado el que mande fundár a las margenes del de Guadalupe Titulado Sn. Joseph.

Para proporcionár el feliz logro de estos nuevos inportantes establecimo. halló por conveniente y me pidio el Sr. Govor. de aquella Prova. Dn. Phelipe Neve en varias representazes. la venida de Vm. á esta vanda, y haviendo Yo condescendido gustosamte. es llegado el caso de exercitar el zeloso desenpeño de Vm en los encargos que previene // la adjunta Instruccion.

Ellos se reducen á la ventajosa Recluta de Familias y Soldados pa. Californias, de modo que no padesca notable perjuicio esta Provincia en su corta Poblazn y á la vtil crecida y necesaria remonta de Mulas, Cavallos, Yeguas y demás que necesitan los antiguos y nuevos establecimtos. de la Peninsula.

Vm deve con reflexion y preferencia á todo imponerse de mis prevenciones, y representarme antes de su salida de esta Capital, y despues en el tiempo que enplée en su Comision las dudas y dificultades que se le ofrescan para que Yo pueda aclararlas y vencerlas.

En el Articulo 14 de la Instruccion digo á Vm que á los Reclutas no se les há de engañar ofreciendoles mas de lo que haya de cumplirseles, y conprehendiendo que este Punto delicado necesita de mayor claridad advierto á Vm qe. al Recluta Poblador se le há de asistir con // el sueldo mensal de diez pesos y razn. diaria de estilo por el perentorio termino de tres años que hán de contarse desde el dia de su admision: Que á cada vno se le darán dos Bacas, dos

1. Provincias Internas Tom. 122, Archivo General de Mexico. The English-language translation of these documents can be found on pages 111–15.

Bueyes, dos Yeguas, dos Cavallos, vna Mula, dos obejas dos Cabras, y las precisas erramientas y vtensilios para las Lavores del Canpo: Y que todos estos auxilios, y los de vestuario y Montura que aora reciven lo irán reintegrando á la Real Hacienda, (a ecepcion del inporte del Sueldo mensál y raciones) con parte de los frutos semillas, y procreacion del Ganado de manera que no les falte para su precisa asistencia y se verifique el justo indicado reintegro.

Los Reclutas Soldados como que gozan de Fixo y mayor sueldo y se goviernan por distintas reglas, satisfarán de sus haveres por medio de prudentes descuentos los gastos que causen en su actual avilitazn. y de sus familias de vestuarios, Monturas, Armams. viveres y remonta. //

La mala inteligencia que há dado el vulgo al Reglamto. de Californias persuadiendose los mayores perjuicios en los recargos ó descuentos que alli se hazen á los Sueldos de Oficiales tropa y Pobladores, podrá retraér á muchos de aprovechár la oportuna ocacion que aora se les presenta de conseguir vn honrrado y feliz establecimto. y de hazér vn leal servo al Rey que merecerá en todos tiempos su soberano agrado y justa remunerazn.

Para desvanecer aquellas dañosas impreciones és menester que Vm procure valerse de prudencia y maña sin faltar en lo mas minimo á la verdad y pureza que son el Norte de mis disposiciones bajo el concepto de que estoy tratando seria y eficazmente en ocurrir al remedio de los imaginados perjuicios que me persuado tengan mas la apariencia que de realidad, pues todos los qe. se experimentan asi en estas fronteras como en la de Californias no provienen verdaderamte. de las providencias de Ordenanza sino del vicioso modo con qe. suelen observarse, cuio perjuicio és de más facil remedio metodizando las reglas, aclarando las que pr. el tiempo y // las experiencias obliguen á alguna variacion, y zelando sobre su exacto y devido cumplimto.

Estoy cierto en qe. lo dará Vm puntual á las inportantes Comisiones qe. le confio como Vm deve estarlo de que recomendaré a S. M. este nuevo particular servicio para qe. se digne dispensarle las gracias que sean de su Real agrado, y en esta inteliga. advirtiendo á Vm que yo dispondre la avilitazon de vestuars. Monturas y demas pa. las reclutas y familias de que trata el Arto. 22 de la Ynstrucon. y dever rendir su primera marcha á los Alamos, acompaño el adjunto Pasaporte á fin de qe. Vm no demore la Suya.

Dios &a. Arispe 27. de Dizre. de 1779.

[COMANDANTE-GENERAL TEODORO DE CROIX]

Sr. Dn. Ferndo. de Rivera y Moncada.

// 26

Exmo Sr.

Mui Sor. mio: La Provincia de Californias es vna de las que particularmente me encarga S. M. en las Reales Instrucs. y el Govor. Dn. Phelipe Neve, á consecuencia de las ordenes del Exmo. Sr. Virrey antecesor de V. E. y de las mias me há propuesto varios puntos relativos á la mejor defensa, conservacion y fomento de aquel importante Pais.

Examinados con proligidad los Informes repetidos del Governor. y mereciendome el mismo buen concepto qe. al difunto Sr. Virrey hé dispuesto la Ocupacion del Canál de Sta. Barbara con vn Presidio de este nombre y tres Misiones, la erecion de vn Pueblo con el titulo de la Reyna de los Angeles sobre el Rio de la Porciuncula, y S. M. se dignó aprovár el que se fundó á las margenes del inmediato de Guadalupe titulado Sn. Joseph.

Estas providencias exigen el aumto. de Tropas qe. manifiesta el Estado // adjunto No. 1 para distribuirlas con arreglo al Documto. no. 2 y á fin de que tengan efecto son necesarios los auxilios de recluta de familias Pobladoras y Soldados acopio de remontas y otros varios que expondre á V. E. en distintos oficios.

Para facilitar los que en este refiero forme la Instruccion de que incluyo Copia encargué la practica de sus reglas al Capitan Dn. Fernando de Rivera y Moncada, y yá este oficial há dado principio á sus Comisiones, pero necesitando para su desenpeño que V. E. se sirva auxiliarlas acompaño á este fin la adjunta nota No. 3. que indica las necesarias disposiciones de V. E. y pues por mi parte hé dado las conducentes á la Cuenta y Razn. de gastos que deve presen- // tar el Comisionado Rivera luego que concluya la Recluta de tropa y familias Pobladoras, y el acopio de remontas, quedan hasta este caso pendientes mis sucecivos avisos y remision de Documtos. á V. E. para los cargos y abonos que resulten á los Presidios de Californias y á las familias, y para el reintegro de los Suplementos que hicieren las Reales Caxas de Guadalaxara y Alamos.

SR. MAYORGA.

Servr. &. Arispe 9 de febo. de 1780.

// 29

[Adjunto] No. 2
Diſtribuzn. de las Tropas de Californias
segun los Detalls de Govor. Dn. Phelipe Neve

	Ca-pits.	Te-nientes	Alfe-ress	Sar-genes.	Ca-vos	Sol-dads	To-tal
Presidio del Loreto	1		1	1	1	10	14
Rl. de Sta. Ana del Sur				1		6	7
Misiones dela frontera del Norte		1			2	23	26
Presidio de Sn. Diego		1	1	1	2	27	32
Misiones de su diſtrito					3	15	18
Pueblo nuevo de la Reyna de los Angeles						4	4
Presidio de Monterrey		1	1	1	2	27	32
Misiones de su diſtrito					3	15	18
Pueblo nuevo de Sn. Joseph						4	4
Presidio de Sn. Franco		1	1	1	2	16	21
Misiones de su diſtrito					2	10	12
Presidio nuevo de Sta. Barbara y Misn. del Centro		1	1	1	2	26	31
Mision de Sn. Buenaventura				1		14	15
Ydem de la Purisima Concepcion				1		14	15
Totales	1	5	5	8	18[1]	211	249

Arispe 9. de Febrero de 1780.

1. The mistaken figure of 18 was used in the original. It should read 19.

Instrucción[1]

Teodoro de Croix á Fernando de Rivera y Moncada.

// 4[2]

Instruccion que deve observar el Capitan Dn. Fernando de Rivera y Moncada para la Recluta y avilitacion de familias pobladores y tropa, acopio de remontas, transporte de todo, y demás auxilios que há solicitado y se conceden al Coronel Dn. Phelipe Neve Governador de Californias para el resguardo, beneficio y conservacion de los nuevos y antiguos establecimientos de aquella Peninsula.

1.

Resuelto el aumento de dos Oficiales Subalternos en el Presidio de Monterrey, el de vn Alferez en el de Sn. Franco, lo mismo en el de Sn. Diego, y la Creacion de vn Tente. vn Alferez y tres Sargtos. en el nuevo Presidio de Sta. Barbara que há de erigirse en el centro de la Canál de este nombre hé expedido los corresptes. interinos despachos de Tentes. á los Alferezes Dn. Alonso Villaverde, y Dn. Diego Gonzalez, y de Alferezes al Sargo. Dn. Mariano Carrillo, y á los Cadetes Dn. // Manuel Garcia Rovi y Dn. Ramon Laso de la Vega reservando el despacho del Oficial qe. falta de esta clase pa. proveerlo á consulta del Govor. de la Prova, de Californias, y asimismo se hán sacado tres Sargentos, dos Cabos y 20 Soldados voluntarios de las Compañias Presidiales de esta Prova. para qe. continuen sus servicios en la citada de Californias.

2.

De los Citados Individuos existen dos en la Peninsula, y los demás deverán

1. Provincias Internas Tom. 122, Archivo General de Mexico. This document was transcribed for the Historical Society of Southern California by Vernon D. Tate. The English-language translation of this document can be found on pages 117–29.

2. Numerals refer to page numbers in the original manuscript.

reunirse el dia 1. de febrero proximo en Sn. Miguel de Orcasitas disfrutando desde el proprio dia los Sueldos y haveres corresptes. á sus nuevos empleos conforme al Reglamto. que govierna en Californias.

3.

Determino eſta Reunion para que // Sugetos los Oficiales, Sargtos. y Cavos á las inmediatas Orns del Capitan Dn. Fernando de Rivera elija los que concidere mas aproposito para que le ayuden al desenpeño de sus Comisiones.

4.

Como es regulár que para eſte desenpeño necesiten asi al pral. comisionado como los qe. hán de ayudarle algunos auxilios de Dinero para su asiſtencia y marchas, me pedirá el primero las cantidades que considere precisas y juſtas para cada vno á fin de que Yo disponga las anticipaciones por la Rl. Caxa de los Alamos á buena cuenta De los respeƈtivos Sueldos y Haveres.

5.

Evacuadas eſtas previas diligencias diſtribuirá el Capitan Rivera su gente en los deſtinos oportunos, y pidiendome los Corresptes. Pasaportes partirá sin demora á hazer la recluta de // Tropa y familias, y el acopio de Mulas y Cavallos en el numero que previenen las dos adjuntas relazes. ns. 1 y 2.

6.

*Prevenciones para la Recluta.*Para la proporcion y logro de la insinuada recluta y remonta no limito territorios pero señalo al Comisionado los que comprehenden las Provincias de Oſtimuri, Sinaloa y demás que median haſta Guadalaxara inclusive, pues en los que no recocen la Comanda. genl. de mi cargo procedera, en virtud de superior permiso que hé pedido al Exmo Señor Virrey bajo cuio concepto siendo diſtintas las atenciones de recluta y las de remonta prevendré vnas y otras con separacion.

7.

Veinte y quatro familias y 59 Hombres son los que por aora se // necesitan en Californias para erigir vn nuevo Presidio y Poblazn. pero si eſte numero de Gente se saca de los territorios de mi mando hará falta con el que yá se ha extraido, y con el que sucesivamente podrá extraerse para el necesario repueble de la Sonora en que igualmte. és interesada la California, como que vna y otra

Provincia deven vnirse y comunicarse por los eſtablecims. de los Rios Colorado y Gila, y si bien es mas aproposito para ellos y para los de la Peninsula la Recluta de Gente de eſtos Paises internos, és asimismo cierto que no hay la suficiente para ambas atenciones y que será siempre preciso ocurrir á las Provincias inmediatas que vulgarmte. llaman de tierra afuera, bajo culos presupueſtos há de dedicar su esmero el Comisionado á llenár la idea de hazer vna ventajosa Recluta para la California, sin que sea mui sensible á la Poblazn. de Sonora arreglandose en lo // posible á los puntos que previenen los Articulos siguientes.

8.

Para dirijirse el Capitan Dn. Fernando de Rivera á la Ciudad de Guadalaxara há de trancitar forsozamte. por todas las Provincias sujetas á la Governazn. de Sonora en las que tiene libre arvitrio para reclutar asi las familias como los Soldados, pero conciderando que no podrá conseguir el todo de la Recluta voluntaria sera indispensable que la complete en Guadalaxara y de eſta manera se minorará la extracion de Gente de Sonora.

9.

Yá se hán sacado tres Sargentos, dos Cabos y 20 Soldados de los Presidios de eſta frontera, y deviendo mantenerse vacantes sus Plazas para ocuparlas con igual numero de Reclutas de las calidades que se prevendra en su lugar y há de traer de Guadalaxara el Capitan Comisionado, es consiguiente // que para los Presidios de Californias solamte. tendrá que reclutar 34 Hombres, y si logra el completo de eſtos Vltimos en las Provincias. del Govierno de Sonora, no repetira eſta Recluta en Guadalaxra. entendiendose lo mismo por lo que corresponde á las familias pobladoras; pero, dudandose de eſtos logros tendrá presente el Comisionado el numo. de Gente que reclute en los territorios internos para completar en los de afuera, el que se necesita y se le há prevenido pa. la California.

10.

*Recluta de las 24 familias Pobladoras.*La Caveza ó Padre de cada familia há de ser. Hombre de Campo, Labrador de exercicio, Sano, robuſto, y sin conocido vicio ó defeɑo que pueda conſtituirle perjudicial en vnos Pueblos que ván á cituarse en medio de numerosa Gentilidad docil, y sin malicia pero facil como toda clase de Indios á las primeras // inpreciones del buen ó mal exemplo de los Españoles que se radican en sus Paises para civilizarlos con el buen trato y para atraerlos gustosos con la practica de la verdad Justicia y buenas costumbres al conocimto. de nra Sagrada Religion, y al suave Dominio de nro Catholico Monarca.

11.

En el numero de las expresadas familias hán de incluirse vn Albañil, vn Carpintero que entienda de hazer Yugos, arados, Rodadas y Carretas, y vn Herrero que bastará con que sepa calzar rejas, azadones, hachas y Barras.

12.

*Reclutas para los Presidios de California.*Los Reclutas Soldados para la California hán de sér Casados, y de las mismas Calidades y circunstancias qe. los vecinos Pobladores, añadiendo las de mayor robustéz y aptitud para las fatigas del servicio de frontera.

13.

Reclutas para los Presidios de Sonora. Todos los que se recluten para los Presidios de Sonora hán de sér Solteros, Mozos que no pasen de 25 á 30 años, y que no vajen de 18 de dos varas lo menos de estatura, de buen color, robustéz, presencia y sin defecto en el cuerpo y rostro.

14.

Ningun Recluta há de entrár forzado sino voluntario, y no se le há de engañar ofreciendole más de lo que se há de cumplir, y explicará esta Instruccion.

15.

Desde el dia en que sea admitido el Recluta hán de disfrutar los *qe. se destinen á Californias y Sonora* los Haveres que les corresponden respectivamte. por los Reglamentos de aquella Provincia y *de estas fronteras*, y el vecino Poblador su sueldo de diez pesos mensales y la racion de estilo, pero á cada Recluta *sin distincion* se le asistirá con el socorro diario de dos Rs. en dinero // donde tuvieren comodidad para invertir en mantenerse, y en viveres quando transiten por parajes despoblados ó de frontera donde de nada les sirve la moneda, reservando el resto de sus haveres para cubrir los enpeños que hán de causar su marcha y avilitazn.

16.

Todos los Reclutas sin distincion se empeñaran por diez años que enpezarán á correr desde el dia de la fecha de sus filiaciones.

17.

Las que se formalizen á los Soldados serán con arreglo al formulario de las ordenanzas geners. del exercito, pero con la expresion genl. de que sientan la Plaza en vno de los Presidios de Californias ó *Sonora*, deviendo entregar el comisionado las correspondtes. filiaciones *al Govr. militar de esta* Dn. Jacobo *Vgarte y Loyola* y al de aquella Dn. Phelipe Neve para que estos Jefes distribuyan como les // paresca los Reclutas en las Compañias presidiales.

18.

A los vecinos Pobladores se les filiará del proprio modo y con el mismo empeño de diez años para qualquiera de los Pueblos de Sn. Joseph de Guadalupe ó de la Reyna de los Angeles de la Porciuncula, añadiendose á continuazn. de sus filiaciones las de sus Mugeres, hijos, hijas, y Hermanas ó Parientas Solteras que voluntariamte. quieran aconpañarlas, pues á estas se les posibilita tomár estado con los Individuos de tropa qe. se mantienen Celibatos en la California por falta de Mugeres Españolas, segun las noticias comunicadas á este Superior govierno.

19.

Convendrá que el Comisionado lleve desde Sn. Miguel de Orcasitas en su compañia para // solo las atenciones de Reclutas tres Oficiales ó dos oficiales y vn Sargo. y ademas pequeña partida de tropa.

20.

En su marcha hasta los confines de la Jurisdiccion del Virreynato de Nueva España és regular la proporcion de hazer algunos Reclutas de Soldados y vecinos para Californias, y como á vnos y otros se les há de asistir con sus socorros diarios, se les há de avilitár, y conducir nombrará el Comisionado á vno de los oficiales que le acompañen con parte de su pequeña Partida para que desde el Lugar de Prova. interna donde se hiciere el vltimo Recluta retroceda recogiendo á este y á los demas y los transporte al Rl. de los Alamos.

21.

En el interin que se verifica el retroceso // del Oficial comisionado cuidarán los Justicias de asistir al Recluta ó Reclutas con el socorro diario de dos Rs. dexando en podér de aquellos el Capitan Dn. Ferndo. de Rivera la cantidad corta qe. considere suficiente segun los dias qe. pueda tardar el regreso del Subalterno encargado. de recogér los Reclutas.

22.

Con ellos no há de hazer otros gastos el Oficial Subalterno qe. el de los Socorros diarios, vagajes, y demas mui preciso para la marcha hasta el Rl. de los Alamos, pues alli, donde hay mejor proporcion, se avilitaran los reclutas Soldados, Pobladores y familias de todo lo pertenezte. á Vestuarios, Armas, Montura y Remonta.

23.

Para los incinuados gastos de asistencia diaria y transporte de Reclutas Nececita el Capitan Dn. Ferndo. Rivera la anticipazn. de algun dinero, pero no pudiendo Yo regularla, me expondrá dho Capitan la qe. // estime suficiente para disponer su libramiento por el Govr. Intendte. de esta Prova. Dn. Pedro Corvalan, pues en el caso de que sean mayores los gastos qe. la Cantidad que aora se entregue, se admitirán y pagarán los Libramtos. del Capitan Rivera en la Caxa de los Alamos dandoles aquel con distincion y claridad que exprese los fines en que se haya invertido la cantidad librada, y los ofics. Rs. de aquella Caxa me pasarán sus avisos por conducto del Govr. Intendte.

24.

Desde la Raya de estas Provincias hasta Guadalaxara continuará el Capitan Dn. Fernando de Rivera la Recluta de Pobladors. y Soldados pa. Californias llevandolos en su Compa. á aquella ciudad, ó encargando su transporte á otro oficial Subalterno, y el cuidado de socorrer á los Reclutas con el diario de dos Rs., Bagajes y demas auxilios nesesarios de marcha.

25.

// Luego que llegue á Guadalaxara se presentará al Sr. Regente, y entregandole el Pliego adjunto pedirá alojamiento para los Reclutas de que trata el antecedente Articulo (1), para los oficiales y tropa de su Partida, *y para la Gente que há de reclutar en dha Cindad y deve deſtinarse a los Presidios de Sonora.*

26.

Si el Capitan no huviere podido conpletár en la marcha las Reclutas pa. Californias hará las que falten en Guadalaxara, y ocurrirá con el Pliego qe. acompaña á oficiales Rs. de aquella Caxa para que en virtud de las ordenes que oportunamte. les comunicará el Exmo Sr. Virrey entreguen las cantidades necesarias para avilitar á los Reclutas de Veſtuario y menages de Montura con arreglo á la relazn. no. 3.

27.

// Por Sn. Blas hán de transportarse á la California los Reclutas Soldados y Pobladores que hiziere el Comisionado para la Peninsula desde los Confines de eſtas Provincias haſta Guadalaxara, bajo cuia inteliga. avilitados los Reclutas y sus familias de lo qe. necesiten de Veſtuarios y demas que expresa la Relazn. no. 3. marcharán á su deſtino, quando lo disponga el Sr. Regente, bajo la direccion y orns de otro de los oficiales Subalternos á quien dará el Capitan Dn. Ferndo. de Rivera las Inſtrucciones por escrito de lo que deva executar, entendiendose que haſta el dia del enbarco de Reclutas en Sn. Blas se les há de asiſtir con el socorro diario en dinero ó viveres segun lo permita la posibilidad.

28.

Para los socorros de eſtos Reclutas // gaſtos de marcha haſta Guadalaxara me dirá el Capitan Comicionado la prudente cantidad que podrá anticiparsele por la Caxa de Alamos, y para los Mismos fines haſta Sn. Blas ocurrirá a pedir la qe. se necesite á oficiales Rs. de Guadalaxara.

29.

Hé dicho en el Arto. 26 que eſtos Sres. Minros. entregarán al Capitan Dn. Ferndo. de Rivera los Caudales para avilitar á los referidos reclutas de Californias de Veſtuarios y demas que se indica, pero tendrá entendido que eſta avilitacion há de hazerse con intervencion y anuencia de los citados Minros. y que há de conſtar en las cuentas que sobre eſte punto deve rendir y pasarme el Capitan Comisionado.

30.

Recivirá por via de suplemto. de la Rl. Caxa de Guadalaxara y con calidad de reintegro por la de Alamos el dinero qe. necesite // para socorrer á los Soldados Reclutas de Sonora, costear sus Bagajes, y suministrarles las prendas de Vestuario y montura que previene la Relazn. no. 4.

31.

Hecha y havilitada esta recluta, y despachada por Sn. Blas la de California encargará la marcha de la primera al otro oficial Subalterno con parte de la Gente de la partida de tropa, y tomando el Capitan la restante se adelantará para evacuar la Comision de Remonta.

32.

El todo de ella lo expresa la Relazn. no. 2. pero si se posterga su solicitud no podra combinarse las providencias para que los auxilios lleguen de vna vez con poca diferencia á Californias, y se perderán muchos dias.

33.

Para aprovecharlos al mismo tiempo // que el Capitan Comisionado desenpeña sobre su marcha á Guadalaxara *el encargo* de Reclutas, puede tambien ocurrir al de remonta, teniendo quien le ayude á su solicitud y acopio, y para esto echará mano de los demas oficiales y Sargtos. provistos pa. Californias, y de los Cayos y Soldados que se reunirán en Orcasitas.

34.

Es escusado prevenir al Capitan Dn. Ferndo. de Rivera los Parajes donde puede facilitarse la remonta, y el de su reunion oportuna pues tiene sobrada inteliga. del territorio, tambien lo es la prevencion sobre la calidad de las Mulas y Cavallos pues yá save que para qe. este Ganado sea vtil en la California há de tener además de las circunstancias de sano fuerte, de Rollo, hueso y regular alzada, la de *nuevo* pues las Bestias Viejas se inutilizan en // marchas dilatadas, y no es posible su renplazo en qualquier tiempo, y por vltimo conprehendo inecesario encargar al Comicionado el cuidado al tiempo de celebrar las compras las condiciones ventajosas de ellas, y la economia en el ajuste de precios, pues estos son puntos que acreditarán su zelo inteliga. y cumplimto. de sus obligaciones; pero si le prevengo que en el supuesto de que las remontas no hán de reunirse (si fuere posible) en paraje determinado *hasta* la llegada de las Reclutas, procure estipular con los vendedores de Remonta que los Cavallos

Mulas Yeguas y demás han de mantenerse de su cuenta y riesgo en sus Agostaderos hasta qe. los Oficiales y tropa que elija el Capitan Comisionado los vayan recogiendo y trasportando al Paraje de Reunion que se señalará oportunamte. pues esto no quita pa. qe. el Hacendero // ó Ranchero vendedor perciva sin demora el importe de las Bestias que vendiere con tal que haga obligacion formál de entregárlas en su completo y de las Calidads. y circunstancias que se estipulen, siendo de su cuenta y riesgo las qe. se mueran pierdan o inutilizen ó se lleven los Indios Enemigos hasta el dia de la entrega á los Comisionados pa. recoger las remontas.

35.

Para acopiarlas me informará el Capitan Dn. Fernando de Rivera el Caudal que necesite. y si será mejor que por sus Libramtos. se paguen á los Hacenderos en la Rl. Caxa de los Alamos el importe de las Bestias que faciliten.

36.

Segun lo prevenido hasta el precedte. Articulo deven venir los Reclutas Soldados y Pobladores que se huvieren para Californs. // en el Pais interno al Rl. de los Alamos y al cargo de vn Oficial Subalterno: los que se recluten para la misma Prova. en territorios de afuera hán de transportarse á Guadalaxara, y de alli á Sn. Blas para su oportuno enbarco bajo las ordenes de otro oficial Subalterno, y los Reclutas destinados á los Presidios de Sonora que hán de hacerse en Guadalaxara deven conducirse por otro Oficial en derechura á Sn. Miguel de Orcasitas, dedicandose el Capitan Comisionado en su marcha con el auxilio delos demas Oficiales Sargentos Cabos y Soldados inteligentes á la solicitud, ajuste y compra de la remonta, y en su regreso á la recolleccion y transporte de ella al paraje oportuno de su reunion.

37.

Este Paraje há de proponermelo la practica del Comisionado en inteliga. de que toda la // Remonta há de transportarse por los Rios Gila y Colorado, y de que facilitaré los auxilios precisos para su custodia hasta el dia en que salga la Expedicion, y quando llegue este caso los que se necesiten para su feliz logro.

38.

Podrá ser convente. para desenbarazar la marcha por tierra, el transporte por Mar de las familias Pobladoras y de la Tropa pa. Californias que deve reunirse en los Alamos. El Comisionado me informara lo qe. se le ofresca y paresca sobre eſte punto á fin de diƈtar mis resoluzes.

39.

Todos los Individuos que exerzan Comision delegada por el Capitan Dn. Ferndo. de Rivera deven llevar cuenta y razn. clara y formál de los Caudales que recivan, y atenciones en qe. los inviertan, // tanto para satisfacer á los Interesados, quanto para rendirlas á su Comandte. quien deve aprovarlas silo merecieren y juſtificar con ellas sus cuentas gens.

40.

Quatro há de rendir el Capitan Dn. Ferndo. de Rivera la la. de la remonta, 2a. de las familias Pobladoras, 3a. de los Soldados reclutas para Californias, y 4a. de los qe. vengan pa. los Presidios de eſta Prova. arreglandose á los formularios que le pasará el Govr. Intendte. a quien entregará las cuentas para qe. disponga su glosa ó reconocimto. les ponga su aprovazn. y me dé cuenta.

41.

Como no todo puede tenerse presente ni es dable advertir todas las ocurrencias nuevas que regularmte. ofrezen eſtas Comisiones menudas y prolijas, procurará el Comisionado vencer con su zelo praƈtica y experiencias las dificultades.

42.

Finalmte. de qualquiera paraje donde haya proporcion de Correos me avisará el eſtado de sus Comisiones, y si ocurriere algun punto grave ó novedad que pida vrgente Superior auxilio ó resoluzn. me despachará sus Cartas por cordillera, pues asi se superarán las dificultads. y Yo podré convinar mis sucesivas providencias.
Arispe 27 de Dizre. de 1779.

[Adjunto] No. 1 // 17

Relazion del Numero de Familias para el nuevo Pueblo de la Reina de los Angeles, y del de Soldados para Californias que deve reclutar el Capitan Dn.

Fernando de Rivera y Moncada en los Parages, y de las Calidades y Circunstancias que previene la Ynstrucn. que se le acompaña con esta fha.

Reclutas	Su Numero.
Famas. Pobladoras	24
Soldados pa. Californias	59
Total	83

Nota: Que en las veinte y quatro familias Pobladoras hán de incluirse vn Albañil, vn Carpintero, y vn Herrero.

EL CAVRO. DE CROIX [Rúbrica]

Arispe 27 de Diziembre de 1779 (4 Copias).

// 18

[Adjunto] No. 2

Relacion de la remonta que deve hazer el Capitan Dn. Fernando de Rivera y Moncada para la Provincia de Californias con arreglo á lo que se le previene en la Instrucn. que acompaña.

		Mulas	Cavallos.
Para los Quatro actuales Presidios del Loreto, Sn. Diego, Monterrey y Sn. Franco.		350	130
Para el nuevo de Sta. Barbara		153	102
Para los 24 Pobladores de la Porciuncula		48	24
Para los Pueblos de Sn. Joseph, y del expdo. de la Porciuncula	Mulas	551	256
	Cavallos	256	
	Yeguas de vientre	60	
	Ydem aburradas	80	
	Burros Garañones	6	
	Cavallos Padres	4	
	Ydem desperillados	4	
	Totál de todo	961	

Arispe 27 de Dizre. de 1779 (Dos Copias).

Correspondencia Tocante a los Pobladores[1]

1781 Mayo 16 S. Gabl.
Neve al Corn. Gl. Salida de familias sobre envio de soldo.

Que el 12 de Mzo salieron de Loreto 17 familias a cargo del alfz. Ramon Laso para la bahía de S. Luis a donde llegó el 24 de Abl. y que continúa su marcha por tierra á este destino y que José Zúñiga le sigue con las restantes familias. Que saldrá el Sargto. Juan José Robles con 12 soldados para el Colorado a encontrar al Capn. Ferndo. Rivera a quien pide, que asegurado de la cómoda conduccion del todo de su espedicion, los devuelva. pp. 286–88.

1781 S. Gabl.
Neve al Com. Gl.
Julio 13.
Da cuenta la viruela cundió en Loreto. p. 310.

Jul. 14.
Que llegaron a esta Misn. en este dia el Ten. Diego Gonzalez y los alféreces J. Argüello y Cayto. Limon con 35 reclutas y 30 familias de ellos. Que en el corto tiempo que intermediara de estar restablecida la mulada a la entrada de aguas que en este terreno empiezan en Novre. no es posible trasportar con 62 mulas de carga que trae la espedicion las familias, 750 fanegas de granos y Memorias de la tropa en 7 meses o mas, pues contando con que cesen las lluvias en Febro. son intransitables para recuas los caminos en mas que un mes despues y no es asequible formar almacenes para resguardo de todo donde por escasez de palisada es forzoso se hagan de adobe, por lo que no emprende la fundacion

1. Bancroft Library transcripts. The English-language translation of these documents can be found on pages 131–33.

del Preso. del Canal hasta el inmediato año luego que terminen las aguas. Que la resolucion de Ferndo. Rivera de haber quedadose en el Colorado le impide poder revisar las cuentas de reclutas y pobladores. pp. 311–14.

Envia de doctos. p. 314.

Agto. 29 (2 doc.) Cta. milr. Envio de doctos. pp. 314–15.

Sep. 10

Que regresó a esta Mision de vuelta del Colorado adonde iba a incorporarse con Ferndo. Riva. el alfz. Cayetano Limon quien noticia que aquella Gentilidad dió muerte al capitan Ferndo. Rivera y Moncada con su tropa e igualmte. a los religiosos tropa y vecinos de aquellos Establecimtos. y a corta distancia de ellos al cabo Pascual Bailon, nueve solds, un poblador y un arriero que llevaban víveres y ganados para dhos establecimtos. Que Limon reconoció los cadáveres así en el pueblo como en su inmediacion a la márgen del río y segun lo destrozado y enjuto de ellos infiere que el hecho sucedió como 40 dias antes de su llegada el 21 preste. al Colorado, y que le atacó considerable Indiada haciéndole fuego y disparando mas de 4 leguas matándole dos solds. y el (Limon) atravesado de bala bajo del brazo izquierdo.

Que ha tomado las providencias convenientes a fin de que no trascienda esta noticia a los naturales de estos establecimientos. pp. 315–17.

Octbre. 28 (6 doc) pp. 318–28.

Que remite 52 cuentas que por pérdida de las originales ha formado a 52 reclutas hechas por Ferndo. Riva. con arreglo a sus declaraciones y estrajudiciales informes, y que comprende algunos por malicia a olvido no confiesan algunas prendas de ropa oreales que recibieron, y no siendo fácil la indagacion delos últimos, por lo respectivo a ropas podrá aclararse si conservan los mercaderes de Los Alamos los apuntes de las que respectivamte. dieron.

Envio de doctos. p. 318

Id. (2 doc) p. 319

Id. (2 doc) pp. 319–20.

Oct. 29

Que para pié de la Compa. de Sta. Barba. ha sacado un cabo y siete solds. de cada una de las Comps. de Monterey y S. Diego, pues quedandole diez lo considera sufte. numo. pa qe. desde luego queda la Compa. en estado de hacer el servo. Que ha sido forzoso construir 40 pequeñas casas de palisada y terrado para que cómodamte. pase esta tropa y sus familias la temporada de aguas. pp. 320–22.

Que habiendo llegado a esta Misn. el 18 del pas. Agto. el Tente. José Zúñiga providenció que los reclutas, pobladores y familias que traia a su cargo campasen a una legua de distancia a causa de venir algs. criaturas recientemte. salidas de la viruelas de donde pasaron a situarse al terreno en que queda fundándose el pueblo de Los Angeles y ya concluida la zanja madre continuan fabricando sus casas y lo estan los corrales para el ganado el que no se las ha repartido para que solo atiendan a la conclusion del pueblo y verificado entren a barbechar las tierras para la siembra de trigo. Que a este pueblo solo llegaron 11 pobladores y solo son utiles ocho. pp. 322–23.

Que no habiendo llegado los Situados de estos Presidios los podrá abastecer hast Abl. prox. Que las Comps. Sta. Barba. y S. Franco. tendrán libre todo el Situado del inmediato año y aun alcances Sta. Barba. en fin de Dic. pres. Monterey y S. Diego alcanzarán como 17.000 pv. en dho mes y mas de 21.000 pr. Loreto sin contar con los antiguos alcances de estos tres últimos Pres. S. que son mas de 20.000 pv. pp. 323–25.

Se da cuenta que Loreto no recibió provision de S. Blas y que se socorrió la frontera con 98 fans. maiz. p. 325.

Que el 5 de Jun. ult. fué nombrado Habilito. en Loreto el alfz. José M. Estrada y procedió a la entrega el comisario Franco. Alvarez Osorio que formó con desarreglo los doctos. y que ordenó se formen de nuevo. pp. 326–27.

Vestuario y Montura de los Pobladores[1]

Relacion de las pundas de vestuario y montura con qe. han de habilitarse los soldados y pobladores y sus familias qe. se recluten desde el Real del Rosario, hta. Guadalajara.

HABILITACION DE UN SOLDADO – Una chupa de tripe a paño azul de Querétaro con forros de manta, vuelta, solapa y collarin de paño de segunda, tinte en grana; botón amarillo con asa. – Un par de calzones de tripe azul, forros de manta, charreteras del mismo tripe y botón amarillo. – Un sombrero negro de Fezcuco. Una capa de paño azul de Querétaro, con las vueltas a forro de bayeta encarnada – Una mascada negra de Barcelona – Una camisa de pontiví – Otra idem de manta. – Dos pares de calzoncillos de manta de puebla Dos pares de medias de lana de dos hilos finas de la tierra – Un par de botas de gamuza – Dos pares de zapatos abotinados – Dos pañitos de polvos poblanos – Cinta pa. el sombrero y pelo. – Una silla baquera con los aperos correspondtes. todo de buena calidad, pero con estribos de palo y sin anquera ni colgadura – Un freno caballar y otro mular – Un par de espuelas vaqueras, pero pequeñas, segun está prevenido y se observa en estas fronteras. – Un sudadero o carona de jerga – Una funda grande de escopeta – Unos cojinillos de media mochila – Una cartuchera de 21 a 24 tiros, de cañones y demás, como lo pidió el Gob. de la Provincia.

HABILÍTACION DE UN POBLADOR – Una chupa de paño azul de Querétaro forrada de manta, con boton blanco o amarillo y sin divisas. – Un par de calzones de tripe como los del soldado – Un pañito o corbata de lienzo pa. el cuello – Dos camisas de manta – Dos pares de calzoncillos idem – Medias de lana, botas de gamuza, zapatos abotinados, pañitos de polvos, y cinta pa. el pelo y sombrero como el soldado –

HABILITACION DE FAMILIA – *Para una mujer* – Tres camisas – Tres pares de enaguas; unas de sarga, otras de bayeta y faldellin – Dos varas de crea

1. The English-language translation of these documents can be found on pages 135–36.

pa. armadores – Dos pares de medias de Bruselas – Dos idem de calcetas – Dos pares de zapatos – Dos rebozos – Un sombrero – Seis varas de cinta.

Para muchacho – Una chupa de paño de Querétaro – Un par de calzones idem – Dos camisas de manta – Dos pares de calzoncillos idem – Un par de medias de lana – Dos pares de zapatos – Un sombrero – Una fresada –

Para muchacha – Dos camisas de crea – Dos pares de naguas de manta – Un paño de rebozo – Unas naguas de bayeta – Un faldellin de paño – Dos pares de medias o calcetas – Dos pares de zapatos – Una fresada

Nota: Ademas de las prendas referidas en la precedente relacion, podrá el Cap. Comido, proveer a los reclutas de algunas otras qe. considere de precisa necesidad, interviniendo en las compras y diſtribucion, como en las cuentas de eſtas suminiſtraciones, los Señores oficiales reales de las cajas de Guadalajara – (La misma fecha).

Son cópias de sus originales de que certifico – Arispe 10 de Febrero de 1780 – antonio bonilla [Firmado] pp. 393–422.

Cuentas de Habilitacion de los Pobladores[1]

No. 71

ANTONIA MESA, negro de edad de 38 años, natural del Real de Los Alamos, casado su muger Anna Gertrudis Lopez de dicho Real, mulata de edad de 27 años, 2 hijos, Antonio Maria, y Maria Pasquala, el primero de 8 años, y el segundo de 10. Se regiſtro de Poblador para los Nuevos Eſtablecimientos de Monterrey, en la Villa de Sinaloa en 4 de Junio de 1780, y queda avecindado en el Pueblo de la Reina de los Angeles.

Primeramente tomo por principio de cuentas de mano del Capitan Don Fernando de Rivera lo siguiente –

		Deve.	
	Ps.	Rs.	Grs.
1 Silla con su fuſte de Casa de Don Prudencio, en 13 ps. 4 rs.	013	4	0
1 par de Armas de montar en 20 rs.	002	4	0
1 terno de fierros de silla, en 12 rs.	001	4	0
2 frenos y un par de espuelas a 9 rs. pieza	003	3	0
2 pares de Riendas y un Cabreſto, en 10 rs.	001	2	0
2 guruperas, a 3 rs.	000	6	0
1 Bota para agua	001	0	0
3 ps. para un par de Botas de pone	003	0	0
2 Sombreros, a 18 rs.	004	4	0
1¼ varas de Cotense para maleta, a 6 rs.	000	7	6
1¼ dichas de Ruan para paño, a 6 rs.	000	7	6
2 pares de Zapatos para la muger, y un par (de) dichos para hombr	001	7	0
1 fresada camera en Casa de Cornes, en 4 ps. 4 rs.	004	4	0
1 real de hilo para el paño	000	1	0

1. Provincias Internas Tom. 199, Archivo General de Mexico. The English-language translation of these documents can be found on pages 139–54.

Por 94 diarios a 2 rs. cada uno desde el 10 de Noviembre de '80 hasta (hta) el 2 de Febrero de [17]81, que salio socorrido del R[ea]l de Los Alamos	023	4	0

Copia de su Libreta que principio desde el dia – 4 de Junio de [17]80, de letra del Alferes [Alfs. D.] Don Man[ue]l Ruiz–

En dicho dia 4 de Junio, 2 ps. de diario, y 6 grs. valor dela libreta	002	0	6
En 5 de dicho, 3 ps. para una mascada	003	0	0
En 13 del mismo de diario, 2 ps.	002	0	0
En 14 para Bastimento y diario para marchar a los Alamos	003	6	0
En 29 cargo para bastimento, 3 ps. (vastimto)	003	0	0
Item 10 rs. de Flete, o bagaje hasta el Fuerte	001	2	0
En 8 de Julio para carne fresca, 12 rs.	001	4	0
En 9 de dicho 1½ Almudes de maiz, a 6 rs.	001	1	0
Item ½ [Almud] de frijol, en 3 rs.	000	3	0
En 15 de dicho, ½ Almud de maiz	000	3	0
Item 2 dichos de lo mismo	001	4	0
Item 2 reales para Cigarros	000	2	0
En 22 de dicho, un Almud de maiz en 6 rs.	000	6	0
Item un dicho de frijol, en item	000	6	0
Item 2 reales de Jabon	000	2	0
En 24 para curarse, 4 rs.	000	4	0
En 28 del mismo, ½ Almud de maiz	000	3	0
En 29 de dicho, 2 Almudes de maiz	001	4	0
Item, 2 reales para Jabon	000	2	0
En 5 de Agosto 2 Almudes de maiz y frijol a 6 rs.	001	4	0
Item 1 par de Zapatos de muger, en 6 rs. y 2 rs. de jabon	001	0	0
En 5 de Agosto 12 reales para bastimento	001	4	0
En 9 de dicho ½ almud de frijol en 3 rs.	000	3	0
En 12 de dicho 1 almud de dicho y 2 rs. en plata	001	0	0
Item 6 rs. en rs. para maiz	000	6	0
En 17 de dicho, 1 almud de maiz y frijol	000	6	0
En 19, 2 almudes de maiz y 2 rs. para jabon	001	6	0
En 22, ½ almud de maiz	000	3	0
Item un almud de dicho en 6 rs.	000	6	0
En 27 de dicho 2 almudes de maiz y frijol	000	6	0
Item 2 reales en dinero	000	2	0
En 2 de Setiembre, 2 almudes de maiz y frijol, en 6 rs.	001	4	0

Item 2 reales en dinero	000	2	0
En 9 de dicho 2 almudes de maiz y frijol, y 2 rs. en rs.	001	6	0
En 16 de dicho, en rs. de su Racion, 14 rs.	001	6	0
En 23 de dicho de su diario en rs. 14 rs.	001	6	0
En 30 del mismo de su Racion en rs. 14 rs.	001	6	0
En 7 de Octubre, 14 rs. de su racion	001	6	0
En 14 de dicho, 14 rs. de racion	001	6	0
En 18 de dicho, Cargo 42 ps. que importaron los efectos ministrados para su vestuario como const por menoren la *Minuta*	042	0	0
Idem cargo 48 ps. 4 rs. 8 grs. importe (impte.) de lo subministrado a su muger, como consta por la misma	048	4	8
Idem (yt) cargo 26 ps. 1 grano, imp[or]te de lo subministrado a sus hijos como consta de la dicha	026	0	1
En 21 de dicho mes, cargo [co], 20 reales de diario hasta ultimo de este	002	4	0
En 24 un par de zapatos de Cordovan, en 6 rs.	000	6	0

Haviendo leido el todo de su cuenta combiene serlas partidas q[u]e señala, las mismas que recibio y puso una cruz, firmando Don Josef Arguello.

Son a favor del Capitan Dn. Fernando Rivera	231	3	3
Suma del Frente	231	3	3
Se le habona al contenido en esta cuenta los Diarios que le corresponden desde el 4 de Junio que se registro de Poblador, hasta el 2 de Febrero que salio socorridode los Alamos	061	0	0
Idem se le habona 10 rs. importe de un bagaje en que se condujo de la Villa del Fuerte a el Real de los Alamos	001	2	0
	062	2	0
Resulta liquido en contra del Poblador	169	1	3

Conquerda con la cuenta que se ha formado a este Individuo, conforme a su Declaracion, e informes que se han tomado a causa de haverse perdido las originales que existian en poder del Capitan Don Fernando Rivera y Moncada en su muerte hacaesida en el Rio Colorado. Mission de San Gabriel y Setiembre 18 de 1781.

V. B. [Visto Bueno] JOSÉ DE ZÚÑIGA. [Rúbrica]

NEVE [Rúbrica]

No. 72

ANTONIO VILLAVICENCIO, Español de 38 años, natural de la Villa de Chihuahua, casado, su muger Maria de los Santos Severina, natural del Real del Rosario, india de edad de 26 años, una hija Maria Antonia Josefa, mestiza de 8 años. Se registro de Poblador para los Nuevos Establecimientos de Monterrey en la Villa de Sinaloa, en 6 de Junio de 1780, – y queda avesindado en el Pueblo de la Reyna de los Angeles.

	Deve		
	Ps.	Rs.	Grs.
Primeramte. declara haber tomado 20 ps. que le parese se pagaria al difunto Dn. Migl. Aviles minero de Sivirifoa	020	0	0
Item tomo en la sitada Villa 4 varas de Bretaña a 7 rs. Para camisas a su muger	003	4	0
6½ varas de sarga a 12 rs. para Naguas	009	6	0
1½ de dichas (a 2½ rs.) de Mitan pa. forro	000	3	9
1¼ de seda y 4 varas de liston de a un real	000	6	6
7 vs. de Revecillo a 1 rl. y 12 rls. de echura al Sastre	002	3	0
8 vs. de Manta Lanquina a 4 rls.	000	4	0
13 rls. de la Arras quando fue padrino	001	5	0
1 par de Medias de seda en 3 ps. 4 rs.	003	4	0
2 Bagajes desde Sinaloa a los Alamos a ½ rl. por legua	005	0	0
1½ vars. de paño Querétaro para Chupa	003	0	0
4 dhas. de Manta de ⅔ para forro a 3 rs.	001	4	0
¼ de seda y 14 rls. de echura	002	0	6
1½ de Botones a 3 rs.	000	4	6
2½ varas de tripe a 2 ps. para Calzons.	005	0	0
¼ de seda y una dozena de botons. en 5½ rs. todo	000	5	6
1 Peso y 2 rs. de echura, y 3 vars. de manta a 3 rs. pa. forro	002	3	0
6½ vs. de paño de Queréto. a 2 pesos para Capa	013	0	0
¼ de seda y la echura al sastre	001	2	6
1½ vrs. de Bayeta de Castilla para forro a 20 rs.	003	6	0
Un sombro. negro de Tarea en 18 rs.	002	2	0
16 vs. de manta de ⅞ para 2 mudas de Ropa a 4 rs.	008	0	0
½ de seda en 5 rls.	000	5	0
1 vara de Bretaña para Pañuelos en 6 rs.	000	6	0
2 pañitos poblanos en 5 rs.	000	5	0
2 Pars. de Zapatos en 5 rs.	001	2	0

2 dhos de Calzetas a 4 rls.	001	0	0
3 ps. para un par de Botas	003	0	0
1½ varas de liston a 2 rs.	000	3	0
1 paño de Bretaña en 6 ps. para camisas a la mugr.	006	0	0
1 par de Naguas de Bayeta azl de las que dio el Alf. Ruiz, *en el Rl. de los Alamos*, en 3 ps. 2½ rs.	003	2	6
1 faldellin de Paño de Queretaro de los qe dio el diho	007	2	6
2 armadores de Crea de los que dio el diho	002	7	0
2 pars de calzetas a 4 rs.	001	0	0
3 pares de naguas blancas poblanas, a 15½ rs.	005	6	0
2 pares de medias de Nimes a 14 rs.	003	4	0
2 pares de zapatos pa. mugr. a 6 rs.	001	4	0
2 rebozos a 11½ rs.	002	7	0
1 sombo. Negro de Tarea en 18 rs.	002	2	0
6 varas de liston a un rl.	000	6	0
1 fresada y ½ camera en 4 ps. 4 rs.	004	4	0
5 varas de Crea pa. Camisa a 5 rs.	003	1	0
6 varas manta lanquina a 4 rs.	003	0	0
1 pañito de Rebozo chico, en un peso	001	0	0
1 onza de seda en 10 rs.	001	2	0
1½ vars. de Bayeta *azl*. a 6 rs.	001	1	0
1 diha. de Mitan en 2½ rs.	000	2	5
2 vars. de Liston	000	2	0
2 vs. de seda y 6 rs. al sastre de la echura	001	0	0
1¼ vars. de Paño *azl*. Queretaro a 2 ps. pa. faldellin	002	4	0
2 vars. de Liston, 2 rs. de seda y 6 rs. echura al sastre	001	2	0
1 fresada Pastora, en 9½ rs.	001	1	6
2 Pars. de Zapatos de muchachita a 4 rs.	001	0	0
1 Silla de Casa de Dn. Prudo., en 13 ps. 4 rs	013	4	0
1 par de Armas de Montar, en 20 rs.	002	4	0
1 terno de fierros de silla, en 12 rs.	001	4	0
1 Cabresto en 3 rs.	000	3	0
2 pars. de Riendas a 3 rs.	000	6	0
2 frenos, y un par de Espuelas a 9 rs. pza.	003	3	0
3 pesos para un fuste y estribos	003	0	0
2 votas para Agua	002	0	0
1¼ vars. de Cotense para Maleta	000	7	6

3 pares de zapatos a 5 rs.	001	7	0
Un par dhos. a su Muger, en 6 rs.	000	6	0
Por 231 diarios a 2 rs. desde el 6 de Junio inclusive tomo partido, hta. el 2 de Febrero de 1781 que salio socorrido del Rl. de Los Alamos	060	2	0
	251	5	3

Y habiendole leido las partidas de su cuenta a eſte yndividuo, dijo eſtar conforme, y ser las mismas qe. tiene recibidas, las señalo con una Cruz, y firmo a su ruego el Alfz. Dn. Ramon Laso.

Sumas del Frente al favor del Cap. Moncada	251	5	3
Se le habonan al contenido 5 pesos que tiene cargados del importe de 2 bagages en que se trasporto con su muger del Rl. de Sinaloa a el de Los Alamos	005	0	0
Ydem 241 a 2 rs. conque se le socorrio, desde el 6 de Junio de [17]80, haſta el dos de Febrero de [17]81, por racion	060	2	0
	065	2	0
Resulta liquido en contra del Poblador	186	3	3

Conquerda con la cuenta, que se le ha formado al contenido, conforme a su declaracion e informs que se han tomado ha causa de haberse perdido las originales que exiſtian en poder del Capitan Don Fernando Moncada, en su muerte hacaesida en el Rio Colorado, Mision de San Gabriel, y Septiembre 13 de 1781.

V. B.

JOSÉ DE ZÚÑIGA.

NEVE.

Cuentas de Habilitacion de los Pobladores

No. 73

JOSEF BANEGAS, indio de edad de 28 años, Natural del Rl. de Bolaños, casado su muger, Maria Maxima Aguilar, natural del [Rosario] yndia de edad de 20 años, un hijo Cosme Damien, de un año y dos meses. Se registro de poblador para los Nuevos Establecimientos de Monterrey, en el Rl. del Rosario, el 11 de Agosto de 1780, y queda avesindado en el Pueblo de la Reina de Los Angeles.

	Deve		
	Ps.	Rs.	Grs.
Primeramente declara haber tomado en el Rl. del Roso.			
Por el Capitan Dn. Fernando Moncada, 6½ vs. de sarga en la tienda de Josef Maria Farro, a 12 rs. vara	009	6	0
1½ dhas. de Mitan a 2½ rs.	000	3	9
4 vars. de Liston a 1 rl. y ½ de seda	000	6	6
7 varas de Revecillo a un real	000	7	0
1 de Bretaña corriente, *Pza.*	006	0	0
1 onza deseda en 10 rs.	001	2	0
1 Silla Rosareña en 10 ps. 4 rs.	010	4	0
1 par de Coxinillos nuevos, en 3 ps. 4 rs.	003	4	0
1 Terno de fierros de silla en 12 rs.	001	4	0
2 frenos y un par de espuelas, a 9 rs. pza.	003	3	0
2½ vars. de tripe azl, a 20 rs.	007	4	0
3 vs. de Manta de ⅔ a 3 rs. pa. forro	001	1	0
¼ de seda y 10 rs. de hechura	001	4	6
1 doza. de Botons. de Metal, en 3 rs.	000	3	0
6 vars. Paño Queretano a 2 ps. pa. *Capa*	012	0	0
¼ de seda y la echura al sastre	001	2	6
1½ vars. Paño de Quereto. a 2 ps.	003	0	0
2 varas de manta de ⅔ a 3 rs. pa. forro	001	4	0
1½ dozenas de Botons pa. la chupa a 3 rs.	000	4	6
¼ de seda y 14 rs. de echura al sastre	002	0	6
1 sombo. en 18 rs.	002	2	0
3 pares de Calzetas a 4 rs.	001	4	0
16 varas de Manta Lanquina a 4 rs. para 2 mudas de ropa	008	0	0
½ onza de seda en 5 rs.	000	5	0
1 vara de Bretaña para pañuelos en un peso	001	0	0
2 Pañitos Poblanos a 2½ rs.	000	5	0
2 Pars. de zapatos de hombe. a 5 rs.	001	2	0

1¼ vars. de Liston pa. barbiquejo en 3 rs.	000	3	0
4 reales para unas botas en San Sebastian [Obispado de Durango]	001	6	0
1 pieza de Bretaña en 6 ps.	006	0	0
2½ varas de Bayeta a 6 rs.	001	7	0
1 vara de Mitan en 2½ rs.	000	2	6
3 varas de liston a un rl., y ¼ [vara] de seda	000	5	6
6 rs., hechura de las Naguas	000	6	0
1 onza de seda blanca	001	2	0
9 varas de Ruan flonte. a 6 rs.	006	6	0
1 par de medias de Mugr. en 3 ps. 4 rs.	003	4	0
2 vars. de Crea para Armadores, a 5 rs.	001	2	0
2 pars. Calzetas a 4 rs.	001	0	0
2 revozos al 1½ rs.	002	7	0
1 sombo. en 18 rs.	002	2	0
6 varas de liston de a un rl.	000	6	0
2 pars. de Zapatos de Mugr. en 12 rs.	001	4	0
1 fresada mo. camera en 4 pesos 4 rs.	004	4	0
1 dha. pastora para su hijo, en 9 reales	001	1	0
1¼ vs. Cotense para maleta, a 6 reales	000	7	6
6 rs. pa. unos estribos	000	6	0
3 vars. de Ruan para dos paños de manos a 6 rs.	002	2	0
3 varas de Crea pa. la muchachita a 5 rs.	001	7	0
1 par de Riendas de Casa de Dn. Prudo., en 3 rs.	000	3	0
2 Jaquimas, y 2 Cabrestos, las Ias. a 3½ rs. y las otras a 3 rs.	001	5	0
1 Bota para Agua en un peso	001	0	0
1 Quarteron de Baqueta en 5½ reales, ¼ po.	000	5	6
1 real para Zudadero	000	1	0
3 Guruperas a 3 rs.	001	1	0
1 mascada en 18 rs.	002	2	0
Por 2 bagages del Real de Roso. a los Alamos, que regulan 120 leguas, 15 ps.	015	0	0
Por 176 diarios a 2 rs. desde el 11 de Agosto de [17]80, hta. el 2 de Febrero de '81, qe. salio socorrido del Rl. de los Alamos, 44 ps.	044	0	0

Habiendosele leido el todo de su cuenta a este individuo expuso. ser conforme las partidas de Generos, y efectos qe. contiene con las qe. ha recivido, y las señalo con una Cruz, firmañdo a su ruego el Alfs. Don Rarnon Laso a Sn. Gab.

Son a favor del Capitan Don Femo. Ribera y Moncada	194	6	3
Suma del Frente	194	6	3
Se le habonan 2 bagages con que se condujo el y su muger del Rl. del Rosario a el de los Alamos, a medio rl. por legua	015	0	0
Idem se le habonan 176 diarios a 2 reales que persivio y tiene cargados desde el 11 de Agosto de '80 hasta el 2 de Febrero de 1781, por racion	044	0	0
Resulta liquido en contra del Poblador	059	0	0
	135	6	3

Conquerda con la cuenta que se le ha formado al contenido conforme a su declaracion é informs. que se han tomado, a causa de haberse perdido las originales que existian en poder del Capitan Don Ferno. Rivera y Moncada en su muerte hacaesida en el Rio Colorado. Mision de San Gabriel, y Septiembre 20 de 1781.

V. B. JOSÉ DE ZÚÑIGA.

NEVE.

No. 74

ALEJANDRO ROSAS, Yndio de Edad de 19 Años, natural del Rl. del Rosario casado, su muger Juana Rodriguez, natural de San Blas, coyota de edad de 20 años. Se registro de Poblador para los Nuevos Establecimtos de Monterrey, en la Villa de Sinaloa, el 7. de Noviembre de 1780, y queda avesindado en el Pueblo de la Reina de los Angeles.

	Debe.		
	Ps.	Rs.	Grs.
Primeramte. declaró haber tomado por primera partida en la Villa de Sinaloa, por los Dres. de suasamiento, 25 ps.	025	0	0
1 la. de zera en 5 rs.	000	5	0
1 par de medias de seda en 4 ps.	004	0	0
6½ varas de sarga pa. Naguas de la Mugr.	009	6	0
1½ dhas. de Mitan a 2½ rs.	000	3	3
¼ de seda en 2½ rs. y 7 vars. de Revesillo a 1 rl.	001	1	6
4 vars. de liston a un rl.	000	4	0

2 pesos de la hechura al Sastre	002	0	0
1 pieza de Bretaña corrte. en	006	0	0
1 de seda en onza	001	2	0
2 pars. de Calzetas a 4 rs.	001	0	0
2 dhos. de zapatos a 6 rs.	001	4	0
2 rebozos a 11½ rs.	002	7	0
1 va. de Crea para Armador en 5 rs.	000	5	0
1 sombrero en 18 rs.	002	2	0
1½ vs. de liston pa. barbiquejo a 2 rs.	000	3	0
2½ vs. de Tripe azl. a 20 rs. para calzones	007	4	0
3 dhas. de manta de ⅔ para forro a 3 rs.	001	1	0
¼ de seda en 2½ rs.	000	2	6
1 doza. de Botons. y la hechura todo en 11 rs.	001	3	0
16 vars. Manta Lanquina a 4 rs.	008	0	0
1 de seda en 10 rs.	001	2	0
1 Gurupera en 3 rs.	000	3	0
3 vars. de liston de a un real	000	3	0
1 pza. de Bretaña que saco *en* Los Al*amo*s en 6 ps.	006	0	0
6 vars. Paño de Queretaro a 2 ps. para Capa	012	0	0
¼ de seda y un peso de la hechura	001	2	6
2 pares de calzetas a 4 rs.	001	0	0
2 pares Zapatos de hombre a 5 rs.	001	0	2
1¼ varas de Cotense para Maleta	000	7	6
¼ dhas. de Ruan para Paño de manos	000	7	6
1 real de seda pa. coserlo	000	1	0
1 vara de Bretaña para Paños	000	6	0
1 fresada Camera en 4 ps. 4 rs.	004	4	0
1 sombrero Negro de Tarea, en 18 rs.	002	2	0
1 silla aviada con fuste en *el Rosario*	010	4	0
1 terno de fierros de silla en 12 rs.	001	4	0
2 frenos y un par de Espuelas a 9 rs.	003	3	0
1 par de Riendas en 3½ reales	000	3	6
1 Bota para agua en 1 peso	001	0	0
1 silla Rosareña pa. muger en	010	4	0
2 Bagages a un real pr. legua desde el Roso. hta. el Rl. de los Alamos	015	0	0
1 par de zapatos a su muger para salir de Los Alamos	000	6	0

Por 88 diarios a 2 reales cada uno desde el 7 de Novre. que tomo partido, hasta el 2 de Febrero que salio socorrido	022	0	0
1 par de cojinillos en 3 pesos	003	0	0
Leida la cuenta del Ynteresado contesto sus partidas, y as señalo con una Cruz, y la firmo el Alferez Dn. Josef Arguello.			
Son a favor del Capitan Don Fernando Rivera y Moncada	178	6	9
Se le habonaron al contenido en esta cuenta 15 ps. Importe de los bagages en que se condujo el y su muger del Rl. del Rosario a los Alamos	015	0	0
Item se le habonan 88 diarios a 2 reales que tomo y tiene cargados desde el 7 de Nbre. de [17]80 hasta el 2 de Febrero de [17]81	022	0	0
	037	0	0
Resulta liquido en contra del Poblador	141	6	9

Concuerda con la cuenta que se le ha formado al contenido, conforme a su declaracion é informes que se han tomado a causa de haberse perdido las originales que existian en poder del Capitan Don Fernando Moncada, en su muerte acaesida en el Rio Colorado. Mision de San Gabriel y Setiembre 18 de 1781.

V. B. JOSÉ DE ZÚÑIGA.

NEVE.

No. 75

PABLO RODRIGUEZ Yndio de edad de 25 años, natural del Rl. de Santa Rosa, jurisdicion de Bolaños, casado, su muger Maria Rosalia Noriega natural del Real de Panuco, jurisdicion del Rosario, india de edad de 26 años, una hija Maria Antonia, de un año. Se registro de Poblador para los Nuevos Establecimientos de Monterrey en el Rl. del Rosario en 13 de Agosto de 1780, y queda avesindado en el Pueblo de la Reyna de los Angeles.

	Debe.		
	Ps.	Rs.	Grs.
Primeramente declara haver tomado por primer partida, un peso en reales de mano del Capitan Dn. Fernando, pa. curarse en el Real del Rosario	001	0	0
3 vars. de Bretaña ancha comprada en Casa de Don Lorenzo Moro a 10 rs. vara	003	6	0

1 sombrero negro de Tarea en 18 rs.	002	2	0
1 par zapatos de muger	000	6	0
1 par dhos. de hombe.	000	5	0
1 par espuelas en 9 rs.	001	1	0
1 silla Rosareña aviada	010	4	0
2 frenos a 9 rs.	002	2	0
1½ vars. de Paño de Quereto. a 2 ps. para Chupa	003	0	0
4 dichas de manta de ⅔ a 3 vs. para forros	001	4	0
1½ dozenas de Botons a 3 rs.	000	4	6
¼ de seda y 14 reales de hechuras	002	6	0
2½ varas de Tripe para Calzons, a 2 ps.	005	0	0
3 dhas. de manta para forro a 3 rs.	001	1	0
¼ de seda y una dozena de botones	000	5	6
Un peso echura al sastre	001	0	0
16 varas manta Lanquina a 4 rs.	008	0	0
1 de seda en 10 rs., onza	001	2	0
2 pars. de calzetas a 4 rs.	001	0	0
2 pares de zapatos de hombe a 5 rs.	001	2	0
2 pañitos Poblanos a 2½ rs.	000	5	0
1 vara de Bretaña en 6 rs.	000	6	0
6½ vars. de paño para Capa, a 2 pesos	013	0	0
¼ de seda y un peso al sastre	001	2	6
3 ps. 4 rs., pa. un par de botas	003	4	0
1 pzs. de Bretaña par Camisas	006	0	0
1 par de medias de seda en 3 ps. 4 rs.	003	4	0
1 mascada de Marca	002	2	0
6½ vs. de sarga a 12 rs.	009	6	0
1½ dhas. de Mitan para forro a 2½ rs.	000	3	9
¼ de seda en 2½ reales	000	2	6
4 varas de liston a un rl. y 7 de revecillo	001	3	0
2 pesos de la hechura al sastre	002	0	0
2 varas de crea para armadores	001	3	0
1 onza de seda en 10 rs.	001	2	0
3 varas de Bayeta azl. para Naguas a 6 rs.	002	2	0
1 dha. de mitan en 2½ reales	000	2	6
¼ de seda y 3 varas de liston a un real	000	5	6
2 pares de zapatos a 6 rs.	001	4	0

1 fresada camera en 4 ps. 4 rs.	004	4	0
1 cabresto en 3 reales y una Jaquima en 3½ rs.	000	6	6
1 Bota de Agua en 1 peso	001	0	0
1 terno de fierros de silla en 12 rs.	001	4	0
1¼ varas de cotense pa. Maleta a 6 rs.	000	7	6
1¼ varas de Ruan bramante pa. paño de manos	001	1	6
4 varas de manta para pañales a su hija, a 3 rs.	001	4	0
2 dhas. de bayeta azl. para *mantillas* a 6 rs.	001	4	0
Por 2 bagages del Rosario a los Alamos a mo. real po. legua	010	0	0
Por 173 diarios a 2 reales cada uno desde el 13 Agosto de [17]80 hta. el 2 de Febrero de [17]81	043	2	0
Item 1 reboso que recibio en el Rl. de los Alamos	001	3	6
	168	4	3

Nota: Que este individuo aunque trajo dos bagages le dieron uno sin pago desde 20 leguas del Rosario hta. Sinaloa qe. se regulan 80 leguas, y se le vajan los correspondientes cuarenta reales, y habiendose le leido el todo de su cuenta, dijo ser las partidas en ellas constantes, las mismas que tiene recibidas, y son a sucargo, y la señalo con una Cruz, firmando a su *ruego* el Alfs. Dn. Josef Argüello.

Sumas del frente a favor del Capitan D. Ferno. Rivera y Moncada	168	4	3
Se le habonan a el contenido 10 pesos que tiene cargados del importe de los bagages en que se condujo con su muger del Rl. del Rosario a el de los Alamos	010	0	0
Item se le habonan 173 diarios a 2 reales que persivio y tiene cargados desde el 13 de Agosto de [17]80 hasta el 2 de Febrero de 1781	043	2	0
	053	2	0
Resulta liquido en contra del Poblador	115	2	3

Conquerda con la cuenta que se le ha formado al contenido conforme a su declaracion e informes que se han tomado ha causa de haberse perdido las originales que existian, en poder del Capitan Don Fernando Rivera y Moncada en su muerte hacaecida en el Rio Colorado. Mision de San Gabriel y Setiembre 18 de 1781.

V. B. JOSÉ DE ZÚÑIGA. [Rúbrica]

NEVE [Rúbrica]

El Padrón de los Angeles[1]

Peninsula de California

Padron del vecindario, el qe. tiene el pueblo de la Reyna de los Angeles fundado el 4 de Ste. del 1781, al margen del Río de Porciúncula, y a distancia de 45 Leguas del Presidio de San Diego, 27 del parage designado pa. fundar el Presidio de Santa Barbara, y como a Legua y media de la Mision de San Gabriel. en expresion de nombres, y edad de los vecinos, sus mugeres, hijos y hijas, e igualmente se señalan las cabezas de Ganado, y sus especies, qe. se les han repartido, y pr. nota las qe. quedan de cargo del comun, como Padres de todas especies, herramientos, de Labranza; carpintería; y demás qe. han recibido a saber.

Nombres	Hombres	Mugeres	Niños	Niñas	Edades
Josef de Lara Español	*				50
Ma. Anta Campos Inda. Sabina		*			23
Josef Julian			*		4
Juana de Jesus				*	6
Ma. Faustina				*	2
Josef Anto. Navarro Mestiso	*				42
Ma. Regina Dorotea, Mulata		*			47
Josef Maria			*		10
Josef Clemente			*		2
Maria Josefa				*	4
Bacilio Rosas Indio	*				67
Ma. Manuela Calistra, Mulata		*			43
Josef Maximo			*		15
Carlos			*		12

1. Archives of California, Provisional State Papers, Missions and Colonization, Tom. 1, Bancroft Library, pp. 101–02. The English-language translation of these documents can be found on pages 161–163.

Nombres	Hombres	Mugeres	Niños	Niñas	Edades
Anto. Rosalino			*		7
Josef Marcelino			*		4
Juan Eſtevan			*		2
Ma. Josefa				*	8
Anto. Mesa Negro	*				38
Ana Gertrudis Lopez, Mulata		*			27
Antonio Maria			*		8
Ma. Paula				*	10
Anto. Villavicencio Español	*				30
Ma. de los Stos Soberina India		*			26
Ma. Anta Josefa				*	8
Josef Banegas Indio	*				28
Ma. Maxima Aguilar India		*			20
Cosmé Damien			*		1
Alejo. Rosas Indio	*				19
Juana Rodriguez Coyota		*			20
Pablo Rodriguez Indio	*				25
Ma. Rosala. Noriega India		*			26
Maria Antonia				*	1
Manl. Camero Mulato	*				30
Ma. Tomasa Mulata		*			24
Luis Quintero Negro	*				55
Ma. Petra Ruvio Mulata		*			40
Josef Clemente			*		3
Maria Gertrudes				*	16
Maria Concepcion				*	9
Tomasa				*	7
Rafaela				*	6
Josef Moreno Mulato	*				22
Ma. Guade. Gertrudis Mulata		*			19
Anto. Miranda Rodrigz. chino viudo	*				50
Juana Maria				*	11
Totales	12	11	11	12	

Nota: Que a los 11 prims. pobladores, se repartieron, amas de los Ganados qe. quedan demoſtrados soles. en qe. han conſtruido sus casas, qe. pr. ahora son de Palisada embarrada y terrado y 2 suertes de tierra de regadio pa. siembra de 2 fanegas de Maiz, a cada uno, con mas una Reja, un Azadón, y una Acha, y al comun del Pueblo la precisa Herramienta de carreteria qe. como los Ganados qe. quedan demoſtrados, han de satisfacer a la Rl. Hacda, sobre los pre-

cios eſtablecidos, de qe. les queda hecho el correspte. cargo, a continuacn. de sus asientos, en el libo. mero. de Poblacn, siendo prevencn. quedan señalados, solar, suertes de tierra, Herramientos y Ganados corresptes, al Poblador Anto. Miranda Rodriguez, qe. se halla en el Preso. de Loreto, y se lo entregaran luego qe. se preſte. al referido Pueblo: San Gabl. y Nove. 19 de 1781. pp. 420–21.
103

Plano de el Pueblo de la Reyna de los Angeles, y tierras de Labor qe. se han medido en numo. de 30 suertes de 200 varas de largo, y las mismas de ancho cabida de una fanega de sembradura de Maiz, en cada una, las cuatro primeras son de tres cientas varas de Largo y ciento de ancho, los Marjenes Divisorios son de tres varas de ancho.

PUEBLO DE LA REYNA DE LOS ANGELES

Extracto de la Reviſta qe. pr. relacion pase yo Don José Franco. de Ortega, Tente. y Comte. de la Compa. qe. ha de Guardecer el Preso. de Sta. Barba, a los Pobladores, qe. gasan sueldo y racion en el referido Pueblo en 2 de Dice. de 1781.

Nombres		
Felix Villavicencio	P. en	el citado Pueblo
Antonio Mesa	P. "	Im.
Jose Lara	P. "	Im.
Jose Vanega	P. "	Im.
Pablo Rodriguez	P. "	Im.
Anto. Navarro	P. "	Im.
Jose Moreno	p. "	Im.
Basilio Rosas	P. "	Im.
Alejandro Rosas	P. "	Im.
Antonio Rodriguez	CP. "	Im. en Loreto
Luis Quintero	P. "	en el dho. Pueblo
Resumen		
Con sueldo y racion	P. "	11
Im.	CP. "	1
Total	"	12

Nota: Que habiéndose comprehendido en la Fa. 105

Nota del Antr. Extracto, al desertor Rafl. Mesa, como soldado se demuestra en su filiacion original, qe. ultimamente llegó, qe. su asiento fue de Poblador; pr. lo qe. queda excluido de la compania, correspondiéndole su haber de Poblador desde 12 de Junio de 1780, hta. el 10 de Octe. del mismo en qe. deserto – Ortega.

Es conforme a la revista, y como dho. es, he pasado a los Pobladores qe. estan en actual gose, en el referido Pueblo, en el dia, mes, y año expresados de que certifico.

JOSEPH. FRANCO. DE ORTEGA. p. 423

Reparticion de Solares y Suertes de Tierra de Regadio y Secadal[1]

1786 – Agosto 14, Monterey.

PEDRO FAGES: REPARTICION DE SOLARES Y SUERTES DE TIERRA DE RAGADJO Y SECADAL

Por cuanto en el Tit. 14 del Rl. Reglamto. qe. gobierna en esta Peninsula se previene el arreglo, metodo, y ordenacn. conqe. deben repartirse las solares y suertes de tierra de regadio y secadal, con todo lo demás anexo al cultivo de labores, cria de Ganados, y fomento de los Pueblos de Gente de razn. qe. se situen en los territorios adjactes. á los Presos. de estos nuevos establecimientos, y conviniendo verificar las formalidades requisitas pa. dar posesn. á los vecinos del Pueblo de la Reyna de los Angeles pa. qe. subsistan en quieta y pacifica uniformidad; Pr. tanto Comisiono al Afs. del Preso. de Sta. Bárba. Dn. José Argüello, pa. qe. pase á dcho. Pueblo y con arreglo á la instruccion de sitado Rl. Reglamto. dé posesn. á nombre de S.M. (Q.D.G.) á cada uno de los Pobladores de las suertes de tierras, y solares qe. les están consignados, practicándolo pr. autos formales, qe. seguirá á continuacn. de esta mandamto. y formando pa. cada interesado un despacho con insercion de copia de este Expedte. y de las Diligs. respectivas á cada uno, los remitira pa. su revalidacn. (y qe. sirvan de Titulos) á este Gobo. pa. en su vista determinar lo qe. sea mas convente. siendo prevension qe. debe hacerse constar qe. quedan los vecinos entendidos de lo qe. es realengo, y lo qe. del comun, como son los Ejidos, agua, pastos, leña, etc., qe. deben expresarse en cada despacho, ó diliga. de Posesn. qe. la admiten bajo las condiciones y penas qe. previene la insinuada

1. Archives of California, Provisional State Papers, Missions and Colonization, Tom. 1, Bancroft Library. The English-language translation of these documents can be found on pages 165–69.

Inſtruccn., como los privilegios, ecsepciones, y gracias con qe. el soberano les hace eſta merced, qe. firmaran ellos, ú otro á su ruego, con el comisionado, y teſtigos; Y pr. últmo. qe. en el libo Mtro. se tome razn. de cada una de eſtas Posesiones, como de los fierros qe. se les dan pa. marcar sus Ganados; y qe. de todo se saqe. teſtimonio qe. se archivará en el expresado Preso. de Sta. Bárbara.

AUTO DE OBEDECIMIENTO

En el Pueblo de la Reyna de los Angs. á 4 dias del mes de Sete. de 1786, Yo Dn. José Argüello Alfs. de la Compa. del Rl. Preso. de Sta. Bárbara, en conseca. del mandamto. qe. antecede del Sr. Tente. Corl. Dn. Pedro Fages, Gober. de la Peninsula; Dije se proceda á su puntual cumplimto. de posesionar á los vecinos del citado Pueblo de la Reyna de los Angeles á nombre de S.M. (Q.D.G.) de los solares y suertes de tierras qe. les eſtan consignado, con arreglo á lo dispto. en la inſtron. qe. inserta el Rl. Reglamto. de eſta Prova. pa. los Pueblos de Gente de razn.; y enterado de sus articulos, con lo demás anexo al literal conteſte del citado expedte.: mandé qe. concluidas qe. sean eſtas diligs. con las formalidades y requisitos necesarios, actuadas y con dos teſtigos de asiſta. se remitan (conforme y como se manda) á dcho. Sr. Gobr. pa. su revalidacn., ó lo qe. sea de su Supr. agrado; y se saque teſtimo. de ellas qe. se archivará, en el Rl. Preso. de Sta Bárba. así lo proveé, mandé, y firmé de qe. doy fé –

JOSEF ARGUELLO.

NOMBRAMIENTO Y ACEPTACION DE DOS TEBIGOS DE ASIBENCIA

En dho. Pueblo, y en el día mes y año expresados, Yo elref do. Alfs. Comiso.; en viſta delanto qe. antecede; siendo preciso nombrar 2 teſtigos pa. qe. asiſtan a las subsecuentes diligs. pa. cuyo efecto mande comparecer ante m. al cabo Victe. Felix, y al soldo. Roque de Cota (ambos del Preso. de Sn. Diego) á quienes haciendo saber dcho. nombramto.; respondieron le aceptaban, prometiendo su asiſta. con puntualidad á cuanto se ofreciera durante eſtas diligs.; y lo firmaron conmigo de qe. doy fé –

JOSÉ ARGÜELLO–VICE. FELIZ–ROQUE DE COTA.

AUTO DE POSESION AL PRIMER POBLADOR FELIX VILLAVICENCIO DE SU RESPECIVO SOLAR –

En el refdo. Pueblo, y en el día, mes, y año citados; Yo el nominado Alfs.

comiso., en continuacn. de eſtas diligs., mande comparacer ante mí y teſtigos de asiſta. á los 2 Pobladores incluso el hijo de Anto. Navarro, qe. pr. eſtar ausente eſte hace las veces de su Padre; y eſtando todos presentes, dí posesn., en nombre de S. M. de su respeƈtivo solar de 20 vs. de ancho, y 40 de largo, al Poblador Felix Anto. Villavicencio, á qn. le hice saber; y respondío queda entendido de los Privilegios, escepciones y gracias con el soberano le concede eſta merced bajo las penas impueſtas á los desobedientes: y preguntado si admite su efeƈtuada posesn? responde la admite, se obliga y ofrece cumplir las obligaciones conſtituidas en su eſtablecimto., y pr. no saber escribir hizo la señal de la Cruz, firmandolo yo con los de mi asiſtencia de qe. doy fé – entre rengls.–Excepciones: vale –

JOSÉ ARGÜELLO–X–VICE. FELIX–ROQUE DE COTA.

DILIGENCIA DE POSESION DE 4 SUERTES DE TIERRA PERTENECIENTES A DICHO VILLAVICENCIO

En dho. Puebo. y en el día, mes y año citados: Yo el referido Alfs., acompañado de los de asiſta. y Pobladores, pasé a las tierras de labor, donde precedida la correspte. medida de 200 varas en cuadro pr. cada suerte de tierra dí posesion á dho. Felix Anto. Villavicencio de sus 4 suertes de tierra qe. le corrrespden. todas de regadio, respto. de haber las suficites. de eſta especie, y habiendose efeƈtuado dicha Posesion con las mismas formalidades y requisitos qe. expresa la antecedte. diliga. y satisfecho y enterado de todo pr. no saber escribir hizo la señal de la Sta. Cruz, firmandolo yo con los de mi asiſta. de que doy fé

JOSÉ ARGÜELLO–X–VICE. FELIX–ROQUE DE COTA.

DILIGENCIA DEL FIERRO DE HERRAR DEL CITADO VILLAVICENCIO

En dho. Pueblo, y en los dias, mes y año, Yo el refdo. Alfs. teniendo presentes á los Pobladores ante mi y los de asiſta., he entreguí al nominado Villavicencio su correspte. fierro de herrar (cuya forma se demueſtra al margen) quedando inteligenciado ser el mismo con qe. debe herrar sus Ganados mayores, y dho. fierro se ha regiſtrado sin dro. algo. segn. previene el Arto. 8 de la citada Inſtruccion: y pr. no saber firmar hizo la señal de la Sta. Cruz, firmandolo y con los de mi asiſta. de qe. doy fé –

JOSÉ ARGÜELLO–X–VICE. FELIX–ROQUE DE COTA.

AUTO PARA SEÑALAR LAS TIERRAS DE PROPIOS Y REALENGO COMO EJIDO Y DEHESAS –

En el Pueblo de la Reyna de los Angeles a 5 dias del mes de Sete. de 1786. Yo Dn. José Argüello Alfs. de la Compa. del Rl. Preso. de Sta. Bárba., y comisiondo. pa. estas diligs. dije qe. hallandose concluidas las posesiones de solares, y suertes de tierra qe. a cada un poblador correspondió: Pasé con ellos, y los testigos de mi asista. á las tierras existes. sin sortear y efectuada la correspte. medida desde cerca de la Presa., hta. el lindero ó termino diviso. de las tierras repartidas, en cuya medicion resultaron 2200 varas de largo de norte á Sur, las qe. se han señalado pa. propios del Pueblo; quedando realengas todas las tierras de la parte opuesta de este rio y pueblo qe. pasan de 2000 vars. de largo, como así mismo las qe. no son comprendidas en las referidas suertes de Posesion ni de propios, señalando les, y igualmte. suficiente ejido pa. pueblo y dehesas, pa. pastar sus ganados, todo lo cual le hice saber y entender, como tambn. el goze de mantener sus ganados del aprovechamto. comun de aguas, y Pastos, leña y Madera con todo lo demás anexo al Espiritu de la citada Instruccion de Pueblos de Gente de razon; a todo lo cual respondieron acordes, quedan entendidos; y pr. no saber escribir hicieron la señal de la Santa Cruz, firmándolo yo con los de mis asista. de que doy fé –

JOSÉ ARGÜELLO–X–VICE. FELIX–ROQUE DE COTA.

En el Rl. Preso. de Sta. Bárba. a 18 dias mes de Sete. de 1786. Yo Dn. José Argüello Alfs. de la compa. de dicho Preso. y comiso. en las prestes. diligs., en vista de su conclusn., y habiendose tomado razon de cada una de los respectivs. posesnes. y sus tierrs. en el libro de Poblacn. del cargo del Tente. y Comte. de dho. Preso. Dn. Felipe de Goycoechea pr. qn. se sacó testimo. de todo qe. quedó archivado; dije se remitan estos originales al Supr. Gobr. de esta prova, como previene su encabezamto., asi lo provei, mandé, y firmé de qe. doy fé –

JOSÉ ARGÜELLO.

Seria Roman was the typeface selected for the text. Designed by Martin Majoor beginning in 1996, the impetus for Seria grew out of his "dissatisfaction with the use of Scala [a previous typeface design of his] in a more literary way," as he describes it. He lengthened the ascenders and descenders and made the capitals shorter than the lowercase ascenders. Seria's generous vertical proportions are one of the dominant features that make it a particularly legible face. Seria's italic is remarkable for its reduced angle of inclination and upright capitals, echoing early sixteenth-century Venetian italic faces. Requiem Text and Display have been used for initials, title page, and stamping on the cover. Requiem was designed by Jonathon Hoefler of The Hoefler Type Foundery, New York City. The text paper is Finch Vanilla Opaque, natural color, vellum finish. ∞ The book has been bound in two editions. The Historical Society of Southern California edition is a one-piece binding in Arrestox cloth with Passport Text endpapers. The jacket, designed by Hortensia Chu, is plastic laminated for durability. A three-piece cover was selected for the Zamorano Club limited edition of 250 copies. Front and back cover panels are stamped in matte, black-pigmented foil on Classic Laid Text, camel hair color; the same paper is used for the endpapers. The book's spine and slipcase are Brillianta cloth. ∞ Designed by Dana Church Cordrey, the book was manufactured under his supervision at Dual Graphics, Inc., Brea, California. The binding is by Roswell Bookbinding, Phoenix, Arizona.